NARCISSUS

NARCISSUS

MICHAEL JEFFERSON-BROWN

B. T. Batsford Ltd
London

First published 1991
© Michael Jefferson-Brown
All rights reserved. No part of this publication may be
reproduced in any form or by any means without permission
from the Publisher.

ISBN 0 7134 6102 0

Typeset by J&L Composition Ltd, Filey, North Yorkshire
And printed in Hong Kong

For the Publisher
B.T. Batsford Limited
4 Fitzhardinge Street
London W1H 0AH

Contents

v

Contents

By the same author:

1

Daffodils today

In all temperate parts of the world, where the seasons are defined by weather and changing vegetation, the daffodil reigns supreme of all spring flowers. It is a unique creation, a flower of unusual design specifications and of astonishing diversity within these limitations. Viewed objectively the specifications are not promising. An upright stem bends more or less at right-angles and produces six petals pointing outwards behind a pipe-shaped protuberance at the centre. The shape of a tulip, a lily, or a daisy makes sense; the daffodil almost courts disaster. It is, however, this very quality which helps to engender its unique magic.

The flowers fade and the leaves later falter. The daffodil is not a leading foliage plant, but any untidiness in dying can be masked by neighbouring herbaceous and shrubby endeavour. Given their favoured environment the bulbs flourish. They are left for two or maybe three seasons and then lifted to preclude any overcrowding and excessive competition for food and sunlight. How satisfying to ease up the harvest: where a single bulb was interred there are now two, three, four or more.

Of all bulbs this is the most easy to handle. Daffodil scales completely envelop the central growing parts in a fairly secure package. Of course, they may be bruised and damaged, but they are less fragile than most, certainly than lilies, whose scales are separate and more vulnerable, and tulips. They may be stored for several months if need be, and so have a long commercial 'shelf life'. Distribution could not be easier. After packing, they may go across the world with no trouble. No horticultural product, bar seeds, could be easier to market and distribute.

Growing centres

Britain is the major grower of daffodils for both flowers and bulbs, with approximately 4,000 hectares. Holland has 1,600 hectares. There are no relevant statistics for the USA. Other commercial areas are Canada, New Zealand, and Australia. One or two types are grown as specific crops, like 'Soleil d'Or' in the Isles of Scilly and 'Paperwhite' in Israel and Japan. Amateur and small-scale growing is world-wide where the climate allows. Enthusiasts are found all over Europe, in the east as well as the west; there are very dedicated Japanese fanciers; growers and breeders in Australasia are well organized; and the American Daffodil Society founded in 1954 is hugely successful, giving the flower great publicity and educating the general public. With well over 1,600 members it is the largest organization devoted to the interests of the daffodil in the world. Its nine regional societies organize shows where trained judges maintain the highest standards, lectures, garden visits and newsletters. The shared interests and enthusiasm of the members foster lively social activity, and an annual convention is held in a different area each year.

The daffodil is one of the most important of ornamental crops.

In Britain the two largest organizations split the bulk of the trade in bulbs and flowers. Lingarden is a growers' co-operative. Angloflora is a private business.

Based outside Spalding, the most concentrated centre of bulb culture, Lingarden was set up in 1964 when 31 growers banded together. It started in a shared office. Now with over 130 grower–members it handles some 10,000 tonnes annually. From dealing initially only in bulk deals it is now a leading prepacker. Big extensions have recently been built to allow further rapid expansion of the contract packing done for large retailers.

Lingarden exported 20 tonnes of bulbs to Holland in 1969. This was the beginning of their export trade. The following year Dutch customers took over 100 tonnes; they liked Lingarden's carefully graded quality bulbs. American orders have risen steadily and now account for more bulbs than all the exports to Europe together. Each day in the autumn period 300 tonnes may be coming in and going out, and a total of 2,500 tonnes now go abroad each year.

Maurice Crouch is one of the main forces behind British daffodil production. Originally he and his family farmed many acres in East Anglia. Greenhouses were built to force huge quantities of daffodils for British markets. He purchased a further five acres of glass ten years ago and christened the project Angloflora. The nursery foreman, Frank Rusman, remained and is now managing director in charge of marketing of bulbs and flowers at home and abroad, while Maurice Crouch bought up the well-known Cornish farm of the Secrett family at Truro. He now has some 900 acres under his control there. Another grower, Mr Tom Parker, also moved down into Cornwall where he now farms some 800 acres. Bulbs and flowers from all these holdings are handled by Angloflora and are sold worldwide.

In 1987 Angloflora exported some 3,500 tonnes of bulbs, and 125,000,000 flowers. In two days in February 1988 just under 5,000,000 flowers were exported. By any measure such operations are big business.

Daffodils have been grown commercially for many decades in the USA and British Columbia, Canada, and fanciers have been well served by specialist firms. The Daffodil Mart run by the Heath family has for many years offered a very wide range of cultivars from all parts of the world. A number of bulb-growing enterprises were started by immigrant Dutchmen for bulb and flower production. More specialized businesses have grown from the enthusiasm of breeders. Grant Mitsch led the way and his work is now carried forward by his daughter and son-in-law, the Havens. Their novelties have received world-wide recognition; Murray Evans has been breeding top-line flowers for decades, his seedlings being much appreciated by fanciers; Charles H. Mueller has an established business growing a wide range of daffodils as well as other bulbs; and recently Dr John Reed, trading as Oakwood Daffodils, has produced catalogues listing an international selection of some of the finest new kinds as well as sought-after older cultivars.

The public seems to have an insatiable appetite for flowers. One sign of this in the USA, Europe and Australasia is the ever-growing number of bulbs sold in garden centres and chain stores, with an emphasis on attractive packaging. Loose bulbs in showcases catch the eye with bright illustrations. Others are offered as individual lots, a few bulbs in a net or aerated plastic carton with colourful portrait. Substantial stocks of a cultivar are needed before it makes sense to prepack it, and this places some limit on the types offered. Moreover, although a wide choice is needed, too wide may bewilder. Competitive trading means that firms make their packs as attractive as possible. Whether this leads to improving the illustration or the bulbs is a moot point, but possibly it does both. This marketing helps small garden owners who want a few bulbs of several kinds.

Large quantities of a few cultivars are sold in nets of 25 kilos. These may be offered loose at garden centres with paper bags placed handily by a pile of bulbs. Self-service is invited.

The visual characteristics of bulbs are important in point-of-sale marketing. Not all are equally good-looking. *N. poeticus* kinds are small and do not like being out of the ground. Some types, notably older trumpets, may be subject to basal rot attacks in store. Some good flowers have miserable bulbs. Bulb appearance is not the least of the features in growers' minds when contemplating new types.

Efficient world-wide marketing has laid the bogey of overproduction that threatened some years ago in Britain. Demand is increasing steadily, especially in the USA. Lots are forced and the bulbs then discarded; many are used on a temporary basis on amenity sites; new dwellings need bulbs; and few gardeners ever think they have too many – they want more and greater variety each season.

Marketing flowers

Cut flowers are welcome for the same reasons as those in the garden. Years ago they were rushed to market after opening, and the purchasers saw what was being bought. They were not easy to bunch and pack, and market and weather conditions could play havoc with the trade. Carlo Naef in Covent Garden helped to revolutionize attitudes almost overnight. Flowers were picked and sold at the 'goose neck' stage, after upright-pointing buds had bent over. They were sold with buds swelling and colour discernible. The tendency then became to offer them at earlier and earlier stages. Now many are sold as 'pencils', the buds still at an early upward-pointing stage and green. Buds are of course easier to market.

Whilst 'goose necks' may give the florist's customer pleasure as the flowers open, and may last longer than the former fully opened specimens, many would agree that some pencils sold are unlikely to develop properly and, if they open, collapse quickly. A sensible compromise is needed. Double flowers, so promising as fat bulbs, must not be cut too early. They need to be showing colour, when there is a good chance of the petals unfurling and not staying glued together like an unhappy miniature cabbage.

Narcissi are on the cut-flower market for over half the year.

Breeding activity

Energetic breeding has been going on for well over 100 years. Raising seed, selecting the best flowers, and growing selected ones into stocks large enough for one to sell a proportion, is such a long-term job that only dedicated fanciers are going to be tempted to turn their obsession into a business. There have always been amateur growers willing to pay the necessarily high prices for new kinds and so a succession of daffodil-breeding enterprises has succeeded, although no huge fortunes are made.

Many breeders grow daffodils as a paying hobby, and therefore a degree of detachment has been exercised in selecting, showing, and marketing the flowers. Establishing and enhancing a reputation has taken precedence over financial gain.

Novelties appear in catalogues and at shows. Breeders are often fanciers who have succumbed to the fascination of trying to improve and diversify the daffodil. Their interests are dominated by show criteria, and they may deem nameworthy flowers showing an advance, however small, in one or two characteristics. Petals may be a mere fraction wider or half a shade purer in colour than those of the nearest rival; bulbs may bloom two or three days earlier; stems may be two centimetres longer. These things matter little to the average gardener.

For every bulb sold for show purposes, many thousands will be bought to beautify gardens and landscape sites. Important garden characteristics such as flower durability, colour fastness, freedom of bloom, rate of increase, and the amount and tidiness of foliage are all more pressing considerations in these working daffodils. Fortunately a good proportion of show novelties prove themselves fine garden plants as well.

Gardeners notice colour first, but a fancier may well register the form of the flower before its colouring. Those taking an interest in new daffodils may note three main thrusts in breeding. The first is widening the spectrum and combination of colours; the second is improving flower form according to fanciers' criteria; and the third is increasing the diversity of forms and sizes.

Most breeding is done in Britain, America, and Australasia, and the emphasis differs from country to country. British professionals and amateurs look first to the improvement of established types, particularly the long cups, the short cups, and the doubles. American breeders take a wider view. Even in the first three divisions a more empirical approach is adopted. They are ahead in work with cyclamineus, triandrus, jonquil and tazetta divisions, perhaps mirroring the need for adaptation to wider ranges of climatic conditions. There is also great interest in miniatures. In Australia and New Zealand there is movement on a broad front. Established local blood lines are worked, so that each section of the main divisions has native cultivars at least as good as the northern hemisphere ones. Delay in acclimatizing bulbs for opposite hemispheres tends to isolate breeding efforts.

The roles of the RHS, the Daffodil Society and the ADS

The early date at which the Royal Horticultural Society started promoting and guarding the interests of the narcissus indicates how highly it has always been regarded in Britain. The RHS specialist committee for daffodils was one of the first, and has remained an important one. The RHS sponsored conferences as early as the 1880s, published literature, and organized annual shows devoted to daffodils, with the society probably devoting more energy to this than any other individual genus. International responsibility for the registration of daffodil names lies with the RHS, and well over 20,000 names are listed.

The RHS work precluded the establishment of a national daffodil society. However, fanciers in the centre of England founded the Midland Daffodil Society and staged the first Birmingham show in 1897. Members fostered a healthy provincial interest and shows were supported by such growers as Guy Wilson and Lionel Richardson, who often used Midland shows to introduce new flowers. Changing economic and social patterns made it appropriate to reform the society in 1966, when it became The Daffodil Society. It sponsors shows in different parts of the country, and produces publications including annual journals and newsletters.

The American Daffodil Society was founded in 1954. Since then it has done important work for daffodils in likely and unlikely parts. Its journals are a joy, and encourage overseas fanciers to join. Energetic, sensible promotion of shows and annual conventions has meant that anyone in the United States pretending the slightest serious interest must be a member. Geographical scale has demanded the establishment of nine regions, each with regional vice-presidents and directors. Splendid voluntary work has bolstered the ADS as a vital proselytizing organization.

The ADS and the RHS have worked well together. The ADS was the first to establish a definition of 'miniatures'; Dr Throckmorton's fundamental and continuing work has established the Daffodil Data Bank, an invaluable computerized source of information; and the colour coding of the latest classification was pioneered by the ADS and gratefully adopted by the RHS.

Dutch and British governmental research

The importance of ornamental horticulture to the economy of the Netherlands is of such long standing that it is understandable that governmental support should be given through education, training, and research. All aspects of bulb culture and management are constantly updated as the result of new knowledge, technology, and market demands. The limited geographical area in which bulbs are grown has meant that grower and trader co-operation is more easily managed than in other parts of the world. Some research has universal application; some may be of limited value in different climates and soils. The sand base of the Dutch bulb fields allows a feeding regime that could be inappropriate elsewhere. Manipulation of water-table levels is not done elsewhere at present.

British Ministry of Agriculture experimental research stations have done essential work with a wide range of bulbs, but daffodils have been the most important. Recommendations on feeding regimes are based on much work. The management of 'Soleil d'Or' as a flower and bulb crop has been given close attention. At the Rosewarne station in Cornwall, sadly now closed, Miss Barbara Fry undertook a breeding programme aimed at producing better early-blooming cultivars suitable for helping the south-west flower trade. Stocks are being built up of some named and unnamed kinds that could be useful economic kinds. Spin-offs have been some attractive dwarfs including fine cyclamineus hybrids like 'Alliance Party', 'Radical', and 'Tony'.

The public domain

Daffodils crowd florist windows, and are seen in public gardens and at shows local and national. Hitherto there has been little awareness of the vast numbers of cultivars available, and the public is uncertain of the status of the words 'narcissus' and 'daffodil'. When planting time arrives a trip is made to shop or garden centre, where promotions are undertaken of cultivars with large stocks on which profit margins are easily achieved. Inevitably 'Carlton' will be there.

Smaller types are however now making larger sales. Showcases of cyclamineus kinds such as 'Tête à Tête', 'Jumblie', 'Charity May', 'Jenny', and 'Jack Snipe' are being joined by small jonquils such as 'Sundisc' and 'Sundial' and the tazetta 'Minnow'. There is a widening of the perception of the average gardener.

Gardening literature is a mixed blessing. Specialist books can be good, but those claiming encyclopaedic coverage are often disappointing, with sections on daffodils that recommend exciting novelties that were passé 30 or 40 years ago. Gardening press coverage sometimes veers towards the antediluvian but is likely to be more up to date.

Daffodils are one of the world's most loved flowers. Where climate allows they have no rivals in spring. More daffodils are planted than any other perennial ornamental plant.

2

The wild narcissus

To avoid confusion some terms are defined here. The two decorative parts of the narcissus flower are the perianth and the corona. Gardeners call the perianth the petals. Single flowers have six, botanically divided into three outer ones as sepals and three inner ones as petals proper. With flowers like narcissi, where these look alike, they are lumped together as 'tepals'. Strictly speaking, the petals are 'perianth segments'. The three outer ones are normally wider.

The unique feature of the narcissus is its trumpet, crown, cup, or eye, botanically called the corona. Embryo flowers develop in the centre of bulbs during the summer prior to flowering, the main sexual parts being laid down first, with the petals clearly visible before any indication of the corona, which is the last part to develop.

The diagram illustrates the flower parts. Differing forms taken by the main groupings within the genus are shown later.

The scape

This is the stem. It is leafless, and is divided into the main lower part, the peduncle, which reaches as far as the node where the flower bud starts, and the much narrower part that immediately holds the flower. Botanically this is the pedicel, although to gardeners it is the neck. This may be very short, stiff-necked and brittle as in some trumpet kinds, or long as in many poeticus. Stems carry from one to well over a dozen flowers.

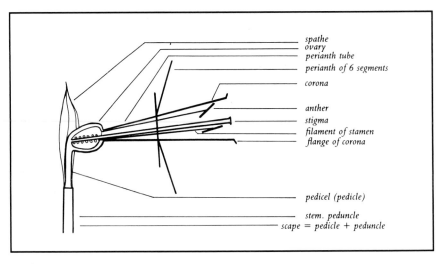

spathe
ovary
perianth tube
perianth of 6 segments

corona

anther
stigma
filament of stamen
flange of corona

pedicel (pedicle)

stem. peduncle
scape = pedicle + peduncle

1 Flower parts

The spathe

The protective casing of the flower bud which splits as the bud swells and opens. The spathe dries to wasted tissue but the point retains a rigidity that can cause damage to a flower if an exhibitor pushes petals back against it when grooming a bloom.

The ovary

The seedbox is outside the flower, inferior, as opposed to superior like the ovary of the lily which is enclosed by petals. The three compartments of the ovary each have a double row of egg cells, ovules, as potential seeds. Pods may contain any number of fertilized seeds – from 1 to over 100. Small species like *N. triandrus* and *N. bulbocodium* are especially prolific.

The tube

Stretching from the ovary to the base of the perianth, the tube usually starts green but may become pale or coloured in the same shade as the flower. It may protrude more or less evenly but can be very fractionally longer below to support a slightly more upward flower pose than is dictated by the pedicel.

The stamens

This inclusive term covers the male reproductive parts: the filaments that hold the anthers, and the pollen-bearing anthers themselves.

The filaments

Six of these arise from the inside base of the tube in most types, and are usually straight and of equal length. In hoop petticoats they curve up at their ends so that the anthers are presented somewhat above and behind the stigma, in the landing area or walkway of visiting insects. *N. poeticus* and *N. tazetta* types have short filaments arranged in two series, three close to the mouth of the tube and three lower. The same double-level arrangement appears clearly in *N. triandrus* and *N. rupicola*.

The anthers

The six anthers vary from the long canoe-shaped ones of trumpet kinds to the small squat ones of other species. They shrink as they split to display the pollen which varies from rich gold to nearly white. In dry weather pollen will remain naturally viable for the whole life of the flower. Stored in a cool dry spot such as a domestic refrigerator it will remain lively for several weeks or months.

The pistil

This inclusive terms refers to the female parts: the stigma, style and ovary.

The stigma

This three-lobed surface area becomes adhesively moist and ideally receptive to pollen which then germinates. Stigmas may be large and bulbous as in some trumpet kinds and most hoop petticoats, or relatively restricted and often concave as in some poeticus, tazettas and others.

The style

This is the shank from the stigma to the ovary down which the germinating pollen projects a tube carrying the male cell to the ovary.

The perianth

This is composed of three outer sepals and three inner petals.

The corona

This projecting ring structure at the base of the petals can be rudimentary, as in the six lobes of *N. viridiflorus* or *N. serotinus*. The small but vivid corona of *N. poeticus* contains in its red areas the highest concentration of carotine known in the wild. Coronas may be lop-sided in some species, most noticeably in hoop-petticoat forms intent on making the lower part into a landing area for pollen-laden visitors. Many trumpet species have coronas which are longer below.

The seeds

Fresh seeds are shiny, jet black, and round. Most wild kinds seed freely and depend on this for dissemination of the species.

The leaves

First seedling leaves are round in section like a rush. Mature leaves, such as those of trumpet, tazetta and poeticus types may be flat, and a midrib is more or less prominent in these. Other species such as the hoop petticoat, triandrus, and jonquil groups maintain the rounded leaf. Some species and forms affect a compromise, with one flat or concave side and one rounded one. Leaves may be rigidly upright or upright and then arching, but are rarely prostrate. The basic green may be highly polished, somewhat duller, or glaucous with a bluey tint. The leaves of the narcissus are unpalatable to animals because the sap that is coursing through them in active life contains raphides (crystals) which cause irritation to soft tissues. Humans may be sensitive to daffodil sap, coming out in a 'daffodil rash'. Sap from cut stem ends can cause this, but so also can the handling of any part of the stem.

The bulb

This is formed of a series of concentric scales, the modified leaf bases, arranged on basal plates, that support the cells promoting the formation of roots below, and the growing buds above that make new leaves and flowers for the following year. New buds are instigated on the basal

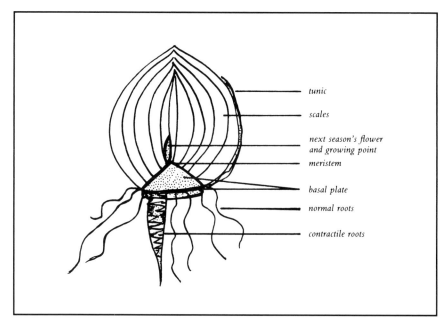

tunic

scales

next season's flower
and growing point
meristem

basal plate

normal roots

contractile roots

2 Bulb parts

plate at its junction with the current or previous season's above-ground growth. The meristem is the growing centre point or points of the bulb. As bulbs grow, one, two, or more buds will be triggered into action, and will be forming embryo flowers before the current year's growth has died down.

Bulb forms in the wild vary from the small rounded ones of *N. triandrus* and those of many little species that are very reluctant to split, to those of *N. pseudonarcissus* that are more like small forms of the usual type of hybrid bulbs widely on sale. *N. pseudonarcissus* bulbs will divide fairly readily, but this does not invalidate the earlier point that all wild daffodils rely primarily on seed for propagation. Some tazetta species have huge bulbs, *N. pachybolbus* being capable of a diameter of 7cm.

Descriptive terms are used for the different-shaped bulbs. The simplest is a 'round', like an onion, with one nose; bulbs with two obvious noses are simply 'double nosed', and are sometimes graded into DNI, DNII, and DNIII, with DNI the largest with two very obvious noses and possibly lesser subsidiary ones, and the other grades progressively smaller; 'mother' bulbs have a proliferation of noses suggesting that parts are nearly ready to split off to begin independent life; parts detached from a bulb which are flat on at least one side, and which are usually smaller than rounds, are termed 'offsets'; and even smaller portions, thinner, flat, or concave segments, are called 'chips'. Fat offsets may bloom, but chips will not.

The botanical status of the genus

The genus is a member of the Amaryllidaceae family, one of the most obvious differences between this family and the Liliaceae being that with the former the ovary is held outside the flower. Its nearest generic relations are the more tender pancratiums. Nowadays tiny *Tapeinanthus humilis* has been included in the genus as *N. humilis* by botanists, and has been thought on at least one occasion to have hybridized with *N. serotinus*. It is brought within the *Narcissus* genus by the *Flora Europaea*. Certainly this and *N. serotinus* are close and apparently primitive species.

In the past various sections have been given generic status: the hoop petticoats for example have been elevated as *Corbularia*. At present there is a consensus as to the limits of the genus, but differences appear in the allocation of specific status to populations within the genus. The

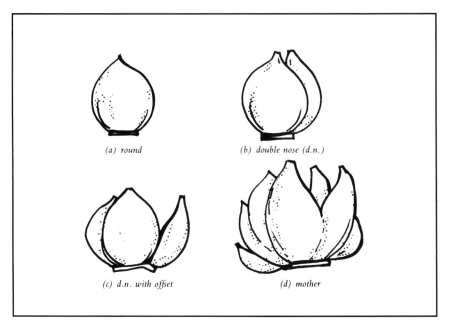

(a) round

(b) double nose (d.n.)

(c) d.n. with offset

(d) mother

3 Bulb forms

two most important contributions to the overall understanding of the genus have come from Prof. Fernandes with his lifetime's work, mostly at the Portuguese University of Coimbra, concentrating on the cytological examination of the genus (see bibliography), and the research represented by the view published in the *Flora Europaea*. There are no startling divergences in the essential balance: it is more a matter of arrangement. Prof. Fernandes gives specific rank to 62 types, whereas the *Flora* lists only 26. Whilst this would seem a dramatic difference, the Flora has many subspecies that go some way towards making up the tally. Both versions are listed in the following chapter.

All generic characteristics are variable, and some more than others. Most obvious are the number of flowers to a scape, and the colours. Some species mark extremes of an evolving genus. Tiny autumn-flowering *N. serotinus* would appear to mark one of the most primitive limits. *N. jonquilla* and the autumn-flowering *N. viridiflorus* are clearly very close and, from these and *N. jonquilla* relatives, it is not difficult to see points of similarity with *N. poeticus* forms. *N. tazetta*, with multi-headed flowers, is close to *N. broussonetii,* which could be seen as a link to some common prototype ancestor species that engendered forebears to it and *N. serotinus. N. tazetta* and some autumn-flowering kinds have different basic chromosome numbers. The genus as a whole has chromosome counts based on 7, so that the diploid is 14; in tazettas the basic number is 10 with diploid species having a count of 20.

There is a recurrent problem in examining any large genus: important work done in a study or laboratory tends to give weight to relatively small variations of habit, form, or structure. Especially dangerous is the viewing of easily vegetatively-propagated plants like a daffodil. Huge quantities of a species may be seen in many gardens, but they could all be parts of a single clone. What looks like a very stable species may be only the propagated result of a selection from the wild. It is likely to be totally unrepresentative of the norm. Even where there is a range of clones in cultivation the gardener may still be getting a severely restricted view – the clones will probably have been picked out for characteristics such as size, colour, and freedom of bloom that may be important horticulturally, but are likely to give a very distorted view of the species as a whole.

One species with little variation is *N. cyclamineus*. Another equally valid species may be tremendously variable. The whole matter is dynamic.

Polymorphic hoop petticoats, whether seen as a single species, *N. bulbocodium,* or as a series of species, would seem to form a multifaceted population in an active state of evolution. Its emphasis on the corona is so exaggerated that one understands the wish of former botanists to disassociate it from the narcissus genus. *N. triandrus* is almost as extreme: both species have almost wasted away their petals in favour of the corona.

N. pseudonarcissus and other trumpet kinds are clearly divorced from other sections. There are no obvious intermediate links between these and species with small coronas. In exploring the dynamic of the family it is easy to acquire a false conception of the value of various species. The tidy parameters laid down by botanists have not been taught to the plants. Within a species such as *N. pseudonarcissus,* there may be populations showing a remarkable degree of uniformity, with any variation being within tight limits. Another population of the same species may seem so changeable that, if one could not see intermediate plants, one could find extremes of variation that would seem to justify specific differentiation.

Some species seem impervious to significant mutation. *N. serotinus* does vary, but very little considering its widespread distribution and large numbers. *N. triandrus,* whilst variable in colour and form, would seem to have arrived at an evolutionary bottleneck, a contrast to the hoop petticoats, the most evolutionarily active. Species like *N. viridiflorus* and *N. broussonetii* may be primitives, with little further evolutionary potential immediately apparent. They have a restricted distribution. *N. pseudonarcissus* and the hoop petticoats seem still to be in an expanding state, both evolutionarily and geographically. It is Man that is going to hinder further diversification of many species by destroying populations and habitats. *N. poeticus* on the hillsides of the Alps and other ranges would seem secure, but even here there are signs of pollution and damage.

The gardener's view of the genus

Gardeners are happiest with plants that grow. Some wild daffodils flourish in gardens; others are homesick, languish, and eventually peter out. *N. poeticus* tempted gardeners to try them in the garden, but most failed, although a few clones did well. Of these, *N. poeticus recurvus,* loved by generations as the 'Pheasant's Eye Narcissus', grew well and became a commercial plant – remnants of pre-1914 plantings can still be found, and I know one where flower crops are still

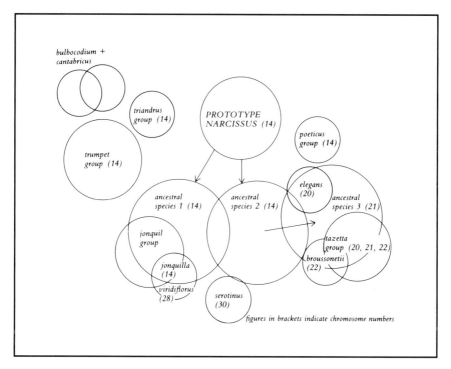

4 Diagrammatic relationship of main groups

A more sophisticated representation would be possible in three dimensions, but even this would not show the time element. The supposition is that a prototype plant engendered ancestral species, one of which gave rise to *N. serotinus* and *N. viridiflorus*. The other gave rise to *N. serotinus* and a further ancestral species that produced *N. elegans*, *N. broussonetii* and *N. tazetta*. *N. triandrus* would have evolved somewhat later and the trumpets and *N. bulbocodium* and *N. cantabricus* would have been relatively modern

harvested each spring; and the smaller but perfect *N. poeticus hellenicus* flourishes but is valued by collectors rather than the average gardener. The white trumpet species from the Pyrenees are usually short–lived in cultivation.

Many familiar plants are unsuitable for commercial growing: they object to being lifted, dried, and then replanted after a period of weeks or months. Most species are only out of active growth below ground for a short while, if at all, and forms of *N. bulbocodium* are almost evergreen. Some tiny species, like *N. cyclamineus* and to a lesser degree the white trumpet species, have bulbs that become dessicated if left out of the ground – *N. cyclamineus* bulbs need to be kept insulated by the surrounding soil, cool and moist, even when not in active growth; others, such as most of the jonquilla group and the tazettas, come from areas and stations where they are inured to prolonged periods of drought, and they can sit waiting for the autumn rains. Normally narcissus bulbs will die if not planted for a year, but some species and even large bulbs of some hybrids, may retain a tenuous grasp on life even if not planted for a season and, after being replanted, will eventually revive.

The 'Lent Lily', *N. pseudonarcissus,* will not submit to normal bulb production methods. Such a well-loved flower is constantly being sought to be grown in wilder garden spots. British wild bulbs are protected by law and nothing should be done to disturb them. However, there are populations growing in parks and gardens, and it may be possible to take a random selection of these to find one or more clones that will adapt to commercial life – 'Bambi' is one already grown, but it is more prolific of leaves than of flowers. An alternative would be to propagate bulbs using the freely borne seed. This could be sown in drills and left alone, apart from being kept free of weed, until the bulbs were ready to harvest. At present however the bulb trader may try to deflect the interest of a potential purchaser to the Tenby Daffodil, *N. obvallaris.*

The 'Tenby Daffodil' is only fractionally larger and blooms as early. Bolder, both in form and in its uniform bright gold, it originally grew in large numbers in fields around Tenby, Pembrokeshire, Wales. In Victorian times and early this century people realized that it was saleable, and collecting nearly eliminated it. The origin of the bulb is unknown. On the only two occasions I have raised seed, it produced flowers which were mainly bicolour and looked more like the 'Lent Lily' than its parent. The uniformity of the plant in the wild and in gardens certainly suggests that we are looking at a vegetatively reproduced clone. On the other hand, one would expect a hybrid to produce widely divergent offspring in the wild, something that does not appear to happen. It certainly produces plenty of seed. The *Flora Europaea* does suggest it may be a hybrid between two *N. pseudonarcissus* forms.

Other wild trumpets that might interest the gardener are the small ones, mainly from the Pyrenees, and *N. asturiensis* from Spain. *N. bicolor,* a larger type, and the similarly large *N. gayi,* are accommodating garden plants but are not planted much now as there are few bulbs in commercial hands, there being little financial incentive to grow them. They are variations of the *N. pseudonarcissus* theme, considerably larger and, in the case of *N. bicolor,* distinctly more dramatically two-coloured. White trumpet species are poor garden plants, now rare in cultivation. *N. asturiensis* is still prolific in the wild and fresh importations keep it in the public eye. It is easy, but its tiny size means that it has to be grown where it is not likely to get swamped by more robust plants or eaten by slugs. It grows readily from seed, and in well-drained soils will split and increase steadily.

Of all species, the most insatiable demand is for *N. cyclamineus.* Those seen at the RHS Gardens, Wisley, tempt many to try them. The difficulty in obtaining bulbs reflects its near extinction in the wild as much as the problems of propagating it commercially. Good bulbs can be raised from seed quickly, and its pods bear plentiful fertile seed. It could be a useful project for someone to take on the raising of substantial numbers of bulbs as a paying hobby.

Other attractive species include the dainty *N. triandrus, N. bulbocodium,* and jonquil types. Most at present on offer are collected wild bulbs. This principle is wrong, since greed is likely to wipe out further populations as collectors are tempted to clear good stands completely. These already face an even bigger threat from agriculture, with land that was formerly lightly employed coming into cultivation. Moreover, even if they have not been mortally weakened by their traumatic treatment, bulbs collected in full growth are going to take time to settle down. Although some *N. bulbocodiums* sold are ridiculously free flowering, others are not all that prolific of bloom even when established, and gardeners can be disenchanted after failing with poor bulbs.

Altogether better results may be obtained by raising stock from seed. *N. triandrus* has pods with huge numbers of seed. From these may be formed perfect round bulbs which get fatter each season, but which are not all that long-lived. Is it too fanciful to imagine someone in Portugal or Spain growing the endemic species as a commercial venture? Under cultivation it should be possible to supply a much better article to bulb dealers and gardeners without threatening wild plants.

Gardeners' attitudes to the species will be different from those adopted toward the modern hybrids. Species need growing; the hybrids will to a great extent look after themselves.

The distribution of the wild narcissus

The narcissus species thought to be the most primitive are found in the Iberian peninsula and North Africa. *N. broussonetti, N. viridiflorus, N. elegans,* and *N. humilis* are found to the south of the peninsula and in North Africa. *N. serotinus* is also present, although it has managed a wider distribution than the others. *N. jonquilla,* which I take to be an early-established species, belongs mainly to Spain.

Geographers' hypotheses of the former joining of the landmasses of Europe and Africa at Gibraltar would seem to have botanical backing in their shared distribution of many plants, including the narcissus. Hoop-petticoat forms are found on both sides of the straits. They grow in the Atlas mountains of Morocco and, in various forms, through Spain and Portugal and into France. They adapt to the different habitats, and as they move from the south with its restricted seasonal rainfall to the lusher meadow conditions in France, the bulbs may change from being tight, round, dark-tunicked ones and become fleshier, paler and longer-nosed. There are *N. bulbocodium* forms that will flourish on alkaline soils, and others that are happier on acid ones. Those that flower for months in the alpine meadow at the RHS Gardens, Wisley, belong to the more northern populations. In the light acid soil they seed themselves happily. As a pod can contain over a hundred seeds, it is not an impossible task to raise large numbers of progeny and achieve a similar naturalized picture.

As a rule wild narcissi grow best in soils slightly on the acid side of the neutral pH level. They do not relish being baked in high-temperature soils. Even where they experience long periods of drought, the worst effects of high temperatures may be mitigated by the coolness of altitude. Having said this, it is amazing to see some bulbs surviving in rock crevices or hollows where there would appear to be little nourishment, and where they are obliged to undergo extended droughts. Moisture from cloud formation and dew may help to lessen some of the apparently unrelieved hardship. Forms of *N. tazetta* around the Mediterranean will expect real summer ripening. In cultivation some, like the miniature tazetta *N. canaliculatus,* grow well enough in the garden but need all the warmth they can get throughout the spring to trigger the formation of the next season's flower buds.

The natural distribution of *N. tazetta* is open to debate. Showy plants will have been moved from place to place by human agency in times past. As with the 'Madonna Lily', bulbs will have been carried by people as they moved homes and travelled over long trading routes.

N. tazetta is listed in floras from the Canary Islands, North Africa, the Iberian peninsula and France, and stretches through Italy and southern Europe to Syria and thence to northern India, China and Japan. Eastern stations could be the result of human distribution.

N. triandrus appears to be restricted to Spain, Portugal, and the Balearic Isles. Various forms of the jonquil complex are confined mainly to the peninsula, being more numerous in the southern half, but some are confined to North African stations, notably in the Atlas mountains. *N. jonquilla* is widespread in Spain and Portugal, and grows wild in the Balearic Isles and North Africa. It will also be found in southern France and other parts of southern Europe; the result of bulbs being moved and naturalizing themselves. It is not impossible that it could have been native to southern France, but the probability is that its occurrences in most places result from deliberate plantings and escapes. It has been grown commercially in France.

Trumpet species are present throughout Spain and Portugal, extending into France across the Pyrenees and northwards to Britain. In Belgium and Scandinavia there are populations thought to be clearly the result of naturalization. *N. pseudonarcissus* is a variable kind, in colour and in form. Normally it is a bicolour with cream petals and a rich primrose trumpet. Petals tend to lean forward, but the angle varies. The range of variation is greater in some populations than in others.

Since the enactment of legislation in Britain to make illegal the removal of bulbs from the wild, and the growing force of the conservation ethos, the stations where *N. pseudonarcissus* was once in danger have seen a good recovery. Unfortunately before this, collecting on a wide scale had wiped out a great many stands in different parts of the country. There is a real need to be vigilant, but the wild daffodil is such an obvious flower and so well-loved, that any major looting is likely to cause immediate uproar.

N. poeticus belongs to the mountainsides of Spain, France, and Italy, and spreads through Switzerland and Austria across to Greece. North of this crescent it is likely to be naturalized, but could have made itself so much at home that it appears native. Plants may be found as modest isolated colonies or massive armies turning hillsides white with blossom in May and June. It is variable, and those dignified by specific names may well only be representatives taken from a wide genetic pool. *N. poeticus recurvus* has not been found exactly replicated in the wild. It is particularly well adapted to vegetative increase under cultivation. *N. p. hellenicus (N. p. verus))* is another grown by clonal increase, and is to be found in Greece.

Wild *N. poeticus* have wide variations of flower form. The shape and width of petals may range from an almost perfect circle to narrow pointed straps in flowers growing within a step or so of each other. It may be difficult to remove a bulb from its mountain lair. They are often quite deep, and shifting soil and detritus will have accentuated the bulb's natural tendency to pull itself low into the ground.

3

Review of the species

This does not pretend to be an exhaustive review of the species. Emphasis is given here to those of greater horticultural interest, and that are either available now or may be so in the future. Neither the classification of Prof. Fernandes nor that of the *Flora Europaea* is followed slavishly. Whichever interpretation seems the more appropriate is followed in each instance, and this is made clear in the text.

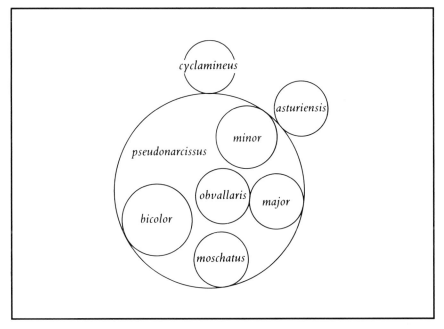

5 Diagrammatic relationship of main trumpet species

The species recognized by the two systems are listed at the beginning of the review of each section. The main differences are the collapsing of the 17 tazetta-type species in Fernandes' section Hermione into four in the *Flora*, together with the compression of Fernandes' 24 species with 24 subspecies, varieties and forms in his section *Pseudonarcissus,* into the six species with seven subspecies and varieties in the *Flora's* section *Pseudonarcissi.*

Botanically, it may be argued that the conception of the genus with the limited number of species in the *Flora Europaea* is sensible, although of course the *Flora* does not cover the species found only in North Africa. Horticulturally, it may be helpful to have a name for vegetatively reproduced clones, so enabling gardeners and dealers to know what is being grown. It makes pragmatic sense, even if botanical nonsense.

Trumpet species

Fernandes
Section *Pseudonarcissus*

N. longispathus Pug
N. hispanicus Gouan
   var. *hispanicus*
   var. *propinquas* (Herb) Pug
   var. *spurius* (Haw) Pug
   var. *concolor* (Jord) Pug
N. nevadensis Pug
N. confusus Pug
N. obvallaris Salisb
N. portensis Pug
N. pseudonarcissus L
   var. *pseudonarcissus*
   var. *platilobus* (Jord) Pug
   var. *insignis* Pug
   var. *montinus* (Jord) Pug
   var. *minoriformis* Pug
   var. *humilis* Pug
   var. *festinus* (Jord) Pug
   var. *porrigens* (Jord) Pug
N. pallidiflorus Pug
   var. *pallidiflorus*

Flora Europaea
Section *Pseudonarcissi*

N. pseudonarcissus L
   subsp. *pseudonarcissus*
   subsp. *pallidiflorus* (Pug) Fern
   subsp. *moschatus* (L) Baker
   subsp. *nobilis* (Haw) Fern
   subsp. *major* (curtis) Baker
   subsp. *portensis* (Pug) Fern
   subsp. *nevadensis* (Pug) Fern
N. obvallaris Salisb
N. bicolor L
N. minor L
N. asturiensis (Jord) Pug
N. cyclamineus DC

f. *pallidiflorus*
f. *asturicus* Pug
var. *intermedius* Pug
N. *macrolobus* (Jord) Pug
N. *gayi* (Henon) Pug
N. *nobilis* (Haw) Schult. f.
    var. *nobilis*
    var. *leonensis* (Pug) Fern comb
      nova
N. *bicolor* L
    var. *bicolor*
    var. *lorifolius* (Herb) Pug
N. *abscissus* Schult. f.
    var. *abscissus*
    var. *serotinus* (Jord) Pug
    var. *graciliflorus* Pug
    var. *tubulosus* (Jord) Pug
N. *moschatus* L
N. *tortuosus* Haw
N. *albescens* Pug
N. *alpestris* Pug
N. *minor* L
N. *provincialis* Pug
N. *pumilis* Salisb
N. *nanus* Spach
N. *parviflorus* (Jord) Pug
N. *asturiensis* (Jord) Pug
N. *cyclamineus* DC

These are the 'daffodils' of common parlance. There are clearly defined species, and others that merge into another in the annoyingly untidy way Nature in which sometimes operates. Both authorities recognize in common five full species by name and concept. These are *N. cyclamineus*, *N. asturiensis*, *N. minor*, *N. bicolor*, and *N. longispathus*.

N. cyclamineus

This engaging dwarf was discovered and illustrated in the seventeenth century, but was lost to cultivation until rediscovered in Portugal in 1885, two and a half centuries later. The extreme fashion of its form as early illustrated, with the very long narrow trumpet pointing down and long pointed petals severely reflexed upwards, led Dean Herbert in *Amaryllidaceae,* 1836, to declare it 'an absurdity which will never be found to exist'. It is little wonder that he reached this conclusion. Every other wild trumpet has petals inclined forwards towards the plane of the trumpet, and none has the slightest reflex. Yet this dwarf not only reflexes its petals, but does so in such an exaggerated way that petal tips touch each other overhead, and may even cross. The trumpet is extruded to an extraordinary length in comparison with any other, being much longer than it is wide. The appearance would look ludicrous in a plant any bigger than the 10 to 15 centimetres height it normally achieves. Variation is minimal. There is little difference in the amount of serration of the mouth and its flanging, but the colour is almost always the same full gold that is made to seem richer by virtue of the thick substance and smooth texture, although I have occasionally grown individuals with paler flowers, a surprising primrose.

In its limited native stations *N. cyclamineus* usually inhabits grassy streamsides or places of ample moisture. It enjoys damp and, rather more importantly, it hates to be dried out. It is best in neutral or somewhat acid soils. Seed which is grown well is converted to

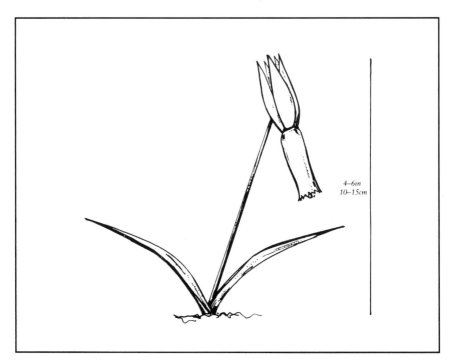

6 *N. cyclamineus*

flowering bulbs in three seasons. Bulbs can grow and split in favourable conditions, but they are slow to do this and clearly prefer to rely on their seed for increase.

N. asturiensis

Although named after the Asturias mountains in southern Spain this diminutive species is much more widespread. It is by far the smallest trumpet. It stands only 5 to 10 centimetres high and opens very early, weeks or months before the large kinds. It varies greatly in flower form: the petals of most tend to fall forwards to the trumpets, but in populations or batches of seedlings some can be picked out with their petals flexed more correctly (in show terms) – nearly at right angles to the trumpet. Petals are narrow and long, and trumpets are usually boldly serrated and more or less flanged. The length of flange and the degree to which it opens is very variable. The depth of serration may be light to very deliberate, resulting sometimes in a rather ragged effect. Stems are slender and almost invariably at a slope, perhaps 45° from the vertical, and leaves are blue-green and flattened like their big brothers, and may be upright or spreading.

The flowers of *N. asturiensis* are usually a rich gold but can pale to a sulphur primose. Their size may depend on the individual or the age of the bulb, but they are always clearly much smaller than any other small trumpet; and although populations vary in their flowering period, most are very early indeed. In Britain this means opening

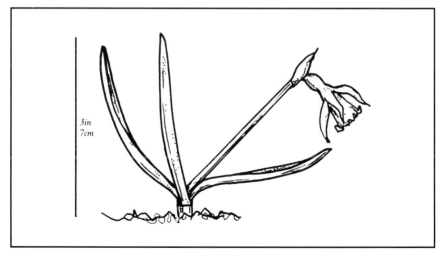

3in
7cm

7 *N. asturiensis*

outside in February, or January in mild locations, and certainly weeks before the next earliest, *N. cyclamineus*.

Bulbs grown in drained soil and kept free from the depredations of roaming slugs will split and divide steadily, just as readily as the giant hybrids. Lifted, split and replanted, they prove longer-lived than many species that depend on seed for propagation. Seed does however germinate easily and grows well.

N. minor

This has long been known in gardens but is not clearly defined in the wild. It is intermediate between tiny *N. asturiensis* and the bold 25 centimetres-high *N. p. obvallaris*. Flowers are a good mid-yellow and formed of long propeller-shaped twisted petals and a cylinder trumpet only very slightly flared at the mouth, but sharply serrated. Our authorities appear to rely on cultivated material and Pugsley's 1933 *Monograph of Narcissus, subgenus Ajax*. It is a steadily increasing, neat plant. Seed sown has not come true, the seedlings varying in form and a significant number being bicoloured.

N. longispathus

This curious gangling species is of interest to botanists and collectors of oddities. It grows much too tall for the relatively small yellow flowers, which do not measure up to the garden claims of competing relatives. The neck of the flower can be 7 to 12 centimetres long, whilst the peculiar spathe often can be some 10 centimetres, so justifying its name.

N. bicolor

Whilst not in general cultivation, this may linger in a few gardens incognito. Larger than *N. pseudonarcissus* and very clearly bicoloured, it has petals which are wide for a wild trumpet and a creamy white, the trumpet being rich yellow. Like other Pyrenees trumpets it is not a robust plant, but it was of considerable interest to early breeders, and produced the fine bicolour 'Horsfieldii' in 1845. It would be interesting to try to cultivate it again now that chemicals are available to combat fungus afflictions.

N. pseudonarcissus

This is the familiar pale bicoloured trumpet flower that poets have praised. In England it is one of the treasures of the Lake District and other parts, including the tops of some Yorkshire dales, and there are notable populations around Dymock in Gloucestershire, near the border with Herefordshire. The same plant is found in the Netherlands, France, the Iberian peninsula, and eastwards, and my own view is that the species is not a true native to Britain, the Netherlands and Scandinavia: the further east one travels through the Pyrenees, the more the type is replaced by stouter plants which are often of more definite two-toned effect. The species is variable botanically, the name being a convenient holdall for a series of plants. Dr Fernandes has the less restricted view of the specific limits of *N. pseudonarcissus*. As seen above, he lists seven varieties and gives specific status to many plants such as the white trumpets *N. abscissus, N. moschatus, N. tortuosus, N. albescens,* and *N. alpestris.* All these pale kinds are reduced in the *Flora Europaea* to coming from a single subspecies, *N. pseudonarcissus* subsp. *moschatus.*

N. pseudonarcissus is an early flower, forming clumps over the years, but spreading by its prolific seed. It is delightful in grass, between shrubs, or in light woodland. Woodland edges are a favourite site, and populations at present growing in meadows may be evidence of woodland or scrub in former times. In full bloom in March and April, well before the trees have broken into leaf, it stands some 15 to 25 centimetres high, with typical flat blue-green daffodil foliage.

The flowers vary in several characteristics, and different populations have their own limits of variation. Petals tend to lean forwards a little, and in some individuals this is taken to excess, with the trumpet emerging from something akin to a cone, and the flange of the trumpet within kissing distance of the petal tips. More pleasing are the majority, which have petals leaning forward shyly rather than at a 45° angle. Petals are long, narrow, pointed and lightly propeller-waved, and petal width is variable, with those whose petals are a fraction wider looking opulent. Colour is usually a pale cream star, with the trumpet a rich primrose. Sensible chaste trumpets are serrated and opened at the mouth, this flanging being noticeably more exaggerated in a minority of individuals. These well flanged ones catch the eye, and although atypical are more worthy plants.

Bulbs may be raised from seed, or from bulbs obtained by sale or by other legitimate means from existing populations in gardens, parks, or churchyards. Their place is in the soil and not stored on a shelf drying out. Good forms can be propagated as one would a large hybrid; clumps are lifted, split and replanted immediately.

The Fernandes varieties differ in these respects:

N. p. pseudonarcissus   Tall, with coronas much cut around mouth but very little expanded.

N. p. platilobus   Tall, with flowers about 5cm long, petals ovate-elliptic, capsules distinctly six-furrowed.

N. insignis   Tall, with flowers about 4–5cm long, petals broadly ovate.

N. p. pisanus   Tall, with corona six-lobed, perianth tube 18–20mm long, flower 45–48mm long.

N. p. montinus   Tall, with corona six-lobed, perianth tube 20–25mm long, flowers 40–55mm long.

N. p. minoriformis   Very dwarf with leaves about 5mm broad. Corona with serrate-dentate margin.

N. p. humilis   Dwarf, flower 35–40mm long, longer stalk than last, leaves 6–8mm.

N. p. festinus   Dwarf, corona with lobate crenate margin, flower 40–45mm long, petals oval and overlapping, capsule about 2cm long.

N. p. porrigens   Dwarf, flower about 40mm long, petals oblong not overlapping, capsule about 15mm long.

Specific status awarded by Fernandes to *N. pallidiflorus, N. moschatus, N. nobilis, N. portesis, N. nevadensis,* and *N. obvallaris,* is reduced in the *Flora* to subspecific status. The *Flora* lists one other subspecies, *N. p. major* which covers such plants as Fernandes deals with under his species *N. hispanicus.*

Most of the remaining wild trumpets are of botanical rather than horticultural interest, with the notable exception of *N. obvallaris.* Alpine and rock garden specialists may think this judgement too dismissive of the charms of the white trumpets, but these tend to be tricky plants.

The *Flora's* classification is followed below, with mention made of the Fernandes species falling within each subspecies' limits.

N. p. subsp. *pseudonarcissus*

N. p. subsp. *pallidiflorus*   Leaves up to 1cm broad, flowers 4–6cm long, uniform cream or bicoloured.

8 *N. alpestris*

N. p. subsp. *moschatus* Dwarf plants, flower 4–6cm long, white or whitish, petals tending to fall forward, flower pose drooping. Fernandes has retained familiar names for white trumpet species apart from his *N. moschatus,* a kind no longer known in the wild. *N. alpestris* is to be found growing in the Spanish Pyrenees. It is a squat plant, at some 10–15cm considerably more dwarf than *N. moschatus* at 20–35cm.

The striking feature of its flowers is the flangeless downward-looking trumpet, and the other obvious characteristic is its difficulty as a plant in cultivation. *N. abscissus* is found in the French Pyrenees, a 30–35cm high plant with rather larger more yellowish flowers than *N. moschatus.*

The tube is noticeably orange-yellow. Forward reaching petals may be white, whitish or any shade to a primrose yellow, and the clipped-cylinder trumpet is cream or primrose. *N. albescens* is another old garden bulb, interesting historically in writings and breeding rather than as a garden plant. It too is unknown in the wild. It is larger than *N. moschatus,* not so hunchbacked in flower pose and allowing a rather more bicoloured effect to the flanged trumpet and the slightly wider and flatter petals. A rough approximation to this species is the early-bred hybrid 'W. P. Milner'.

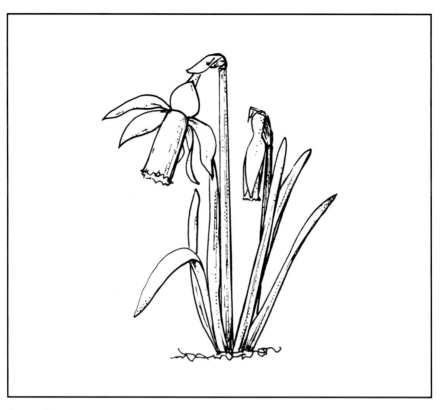

9 *N. abscissus*

N. p. subsp. *nobilis*   Flowers normally between 5 and 7cm long, petals pale yellow or cream, corona golden.

N. p. subsp. *major*   Tall strong, uniform golden flowers.

N. p. subsp. *portensis*   Dwarf, leaves up to 12cm long, stem longer, golden flower 4–4.5cm long.

N. p. subsp. *nevadenis*   Dwarf, flower 3–4cm long, petals flat and somewhat overlapping, more or less uniform gold.

N. p. subsp. *obvallaris*   Remnants of a once large population can be found in Pembrokeshire, Wales, around the town of Tenby. Neither it, nor any plant particularly like it, is to be found elsewhere in Europe. As it is amenable to commercial routines it has been popular as an early blooming naturalizing bulb. Note has already been made of its claim to specific rank (p. 18).

It is slightly taller than *N. pseudonarcissus*, but is clearly stouter in all parts. Leaves in steel grey-green stand more rigidly upright, flower stems are rounder and firmer, and flowers are larger with wider petals much flatter and more inclined to a right angle from the trumpet. Trumpets themselves are wider the whole length, and neatly serrated mouths are well flanged. Colour is a rich uniform gold.

The *N. triandrus* group

Fernandes
Section *Ganymedes*

N. *concolor* (Haw) link
N. *triandrus* L
   var. *triandrus*
   var. *cernuus* (Salisb)

Flora Europaea
Section *Ganymedes*

N. *triandrus* L
  subsp. *pallidulus*
   (Graells) Webb
  subsp. *triandrus*
  subsp. *capax*
   (Salisb) Webb

Gardeners see N. *triandrus* as a well-defined species, and the botanical view may cause exasperation. They are dainty little plants with narrow foliage and slender stems carrying flowers which are completely pendant and with severely reflexed upward-pointing long narrow petals. They are almost totally reliant on seed for reproduction, and individually may not be very long lived. No other species looks similar. Fernandes originally felt all belonged to a single Linnean species, and then distinguished five varieties, *concolor*, *pulchellus*, *cernuus*, *albus*, and *loiseleurii*. This suits the common-sense viewpoint of gardeners. Current views mean losing N. *t. loiseleurii*, although this rare form would seem a distinctive member of the group, with its

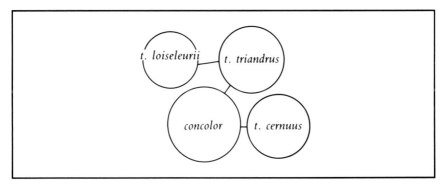

10 Diagrammatic relationship of N. *triandrus* group

white flowers two or three times larger than the others of the species and with dark foliage curled or prostrate. Equally valid arguments could be made for following either the *Flora* or Fernandes. The latter is chosen as more useful and for recognizing the well-defined *N. concolor*.

The evidence of the wild plants in the Iberian peninsula backs the Fernandes hypothesis of their origin. His *N. concolor,* formerly *N. t. concolor,* is seen as the most primitive, closest to the founder type that expanded its territory from a base in southern Spain and engendered the other types to the north in Spain and Portugal.

N. concolor

This looks primitive. Flowering-sized round dark bulbs each produce a thin cylindrical flower stem accompanied to the side, and almost independently, by a single similarly dark rush-like leaf. One, two, or three deep-golden bells hang from the top of a stalk that is clearly going to share the photosynthetic workload.

Populations are in central and eastern Spain as well as in the south, the most southerly being below Granada. It also appears in Portugal, mainly in the centre and not in the north, with the lowest station below Lisbon.

N. triandrus var. *triandrus* This is the white flower of northern Spain with relatively broad leaves some 4–6mm wide and up to 20cm long. With a straight-sided corona measuring up to 17mm long and wide it is proportionately longer than the very variable *N. t. cernuus.* Bulbs bought as *N. t. albus* may include this plant or *N. t. cernuus.*

N. triandrus var. *cernuus* This is found in most parts of Portugal and central Spain. Flower colour is usually cream or pale yellow, but can be white, and there will also appear some with the coronas paler than the petals. Leaves are narrow at approximately 2mm wide. Corona shape is variable with many being somewhat incurved at their margins, most cup-shaped, but with some straight-sided.

N. triandrus var. *loiseleurii* This hails from the Isles de Glenan off the Brittany coast, the most distant outpost of the species which is otherwise not known wild in France. Although variable, those known to gardeners are characterized by their much larger flower and leaf size. Foliage is curled, prostrate and usually shiny dark green rather than the normal glaucous blue-grey green of the species. White, cream

11 *N. triandrus albus*

or pale yellow flowers may have petals up to 30mm long and coronas from 15 to 25mm long.

N. bulbocodium, *N. cantabricus* and *N. hedraeanthus*

Fernandes
Section *Bulbocodium*

N. *bulbocodium* L
  subsp. *bulbocodium*
  var. *bulbocodium*
  var. *nivalis* (Graells) Baker
  var. *conspicuus* (Haw)
    Baker
  var. *serotinus* (Haw) Fern
    comb nova
  var. *citrinus* Baker
  var. *graellsii* (Webb) Baker
  subsp. *praecox* Gatt +
    Weiller

Flora Europaea
Section *Bulbocodii*

N. *bulbocodium* L
  subsp. *bulbocodium*
  subsp. *obesus* (Salisb)
    Maire
N. *hedraeanthus*

N. *cantabricus* DC

var. *praecox*
var. *paucinervis* Maire
N. *obesus* Salisb.
N. *hedraeanthus* (Webb +
  Heldr) Colmeiro
N. *romieuxii* Br–Bl+ Maire
  subsp. *romieuxii*
  var. *romieuxii*
  var. *rifanus* (Emb +
    Maire) Fern
  subsp. *albidus* (Emb +
    Maire) Fern
  var. *albidus*
  var. *zaianicus* (Maire,
    Weiller + Wilczek) Fern
N. *cantabricus* DC
  subsp. *cantabricus*
  var. *cantabricus*
  var. *foliosus* (Maire) Fern
  var. *kesticus* (Maire +
    Wilczek) Fern
  var. *petunioides* Fern
  subsp. *tananicus* (Maire)
    Fern comb nova
  subsp. *monophyllus* (Dur)
    Fern

In these the corona is taken to one of its extreme limits, and perianths are reduced to six narrow wasted strips behind a greatly expanded crown. Corona size is always huge proportionately, but its form is variable. In tiny N. *hedraeanthus* it is a serrated and almost straight-sided miniature imitation of the bucket scoop of an earth-moving machine. In N. *obesus* it can be inflated as if to form a balloon, the mouth beginning to be restricted. In some North Africans the corona expands progressively like the end of a musical trumpet. The extreme position is taken by N. *cantabricus* var. *petunioides,* which can spin out its corona to form a complete disc.

Once again the *Flora* lumps plants together, and Fernandes splits them up. The *Flora* has three species, N. *bulbocodium,* N. *hedraenthus,* and N. *cantabricus,* N. *bulbocodium* being split into two subspecies, the

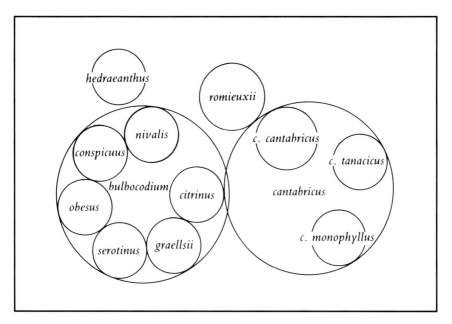

12 Diagrammatic relationship of the *N. bulbocodium, N. cantabricus* group, the hoop petticoats

catch-all *N. b.* subsp. *bulbocodium,* and *N. b.* subsp. *obesus.* Horticulturally Fernandes' section Bulbocodium is the more useful reference work and also covers the African types. It is therefore followed here:

N. bulbocodium subsp. *bulbocodium*   There are at least 11 different chromosome counts to be found within *N. bulbocodium* L. Normal diploid count is 14. These diploids are usually found in stations with definitely acid soil.

N. b. b. var. *bulbocodium*   Narrow leaved (1.5mm), round stems, with dwarf golden yellow flowers up to 30–35mm long.

N. b. b. var. *nivalis*   Slightly broader leaves, stems slightly ridged, bulbs white, flowers smaller.

N. b. b. var. *conspicuus*   A tetraploid with a chromosome count of 28. It grows easily in cultivation with a conspicuous rate of increase, and is similarly conspicuous in producing thin, rush-like erect foliage. However it is less demonstrative with flowers, producing a rather meagre quantity of not over-large deep-gold ones, 30–35mm long.

N. b.b. var. *serotinus*   One of the largest flowers and plants. It can stand 20–30cm high with large inflated flowers 35–50mm long and mid-yellow. It grows strongly and is less clump-forming than the last. Leaves up to 4mm wide, erect growing and longer than flower stems.

N. b. var. *citrinus*   Found in mountains of Asturias and Viscaya, with pale lemon large flowers 35–50mm wide. An attractive kind, not noticeably clump-forming.

N. b. b. var. *graellsii*   Flowers primrose-yellow and smaller, Dwarfer plant. Found in mountains of Castille.

N. b. subsp. *praecox*   A winter-flowering pale yellow form. A strong plant found in Morocco. The type plant has six-nerved segments, and there is a three-nerved variety, *N. b. praecox* var. *paucinervis*.

N. obesus   Plants growing under this name are large flowered but very dwarf: great half balloons of deep gold 2–4cm being somewhat contracted at the mouth are balanced on stalks only 2–5cm high. They split into two forms: one has thick fleshy leaves and leathery flowers, and the other has narrow almost thread-like leaves and normal blooms. Aesthetically I find the second more appealing. Curiously there is another variation: both fat and thin kinds have two forms, one with leaves more or less upright, the second with them pressed completely prostrate over the soil.

Fernandes makes the type plant one with prostrate leaves that are only 1mm wide.

N. obesus is usually fine in the garden if kept clear of slugs. It blooms on very small bulbs and lasts a long time, offering plenty of seed. The chromosome count is the unusual one of 26. Forms with this count do not seem inhibited by any of the usual pH levels, growing well on acid, neutral, or alkaline soils.

N. hedraeanthus   This curious species is rare both in nature and in cultivation, and is miniscule in every way. Bulbs are tiny, often making a garden pea seem gross. Leaves are narrow and can be variously upright, arched, or nearly prostrate. Stems range from next to nothing to a normal 1–2cm. Tiny flowers are a pale lemon colour with little strips or petals and a gaping cone–corona measuring 1–1½cm across. Alpine plant enthusiasts and collectors of oddities will find it interesting, but the sane majority less so. It is best grown in pots or pans where it will not be overlooked.

2½in
6cm

13 *N. bulbocodium obesus*

N. romieuxii subsp. *romieuxii*   Stands 7–10cm with attractive pale sulphur, widely flared flowers with petals as long as the corona. Anthers are pale yellow. Chromosome count of 28. *N. r. r.* var. *rifanus* differs in having perianth segments longer than the corona and darker yellow anthers. Flared coronas are usually shorter.

N. romieuxii subsp. *albidus*   Flowers are white, or whitish to lemony. *N. r. a.* var. *albidus* has petals with a basal width of around 2.5mm and longer than the corona. *N. r. a.* var. *zaianicus* has white or very pale lemon flowers with petals of only around 1.5mm at the base and no longer than the corona.

N. cantabricus subsp. *cantabricus*   Flowers are white and open in December and January. Stems 7–10cm. Bulbs usually have more than one leaf. *N. c.* var. *cantabricus* has narrow prostrate leaves and wide, bowl-shaped flowers. *N. c.* var. *foliosus* has more restricted funnel-shaped flowers and upright leaves. It is more vigorous with perhaps up to half a dozen leaves to a bulb. *N. c.* var. *kesticus* has only a couple of leaves to a bulb and small ivory flowers.

The outstanding plant in the gardener's eyes is *N. c.* var. *petunioides* with, in its best forms, each white corona spun out completely flat to make a slightly pleated disc around the narrow tube and projecting stigma and anthers. Raised from seed, flowers vary a little, some having coronas shaped like shallow dishes. Its sparkling purity, unique form, and free-flowering habit make it one of the most sought after of all alpine house bulbs. It blooms late winter and is then quite magical. Its dark green thin foliage arches over, and the flowers end their life by collapsing backwards over the tube, a piece of acrobatic behaviour unique in the genus. The name suggests the likeness to a petunia flower. It came from the Atlas Mountains.

N. cantabricus subsp. *tananicus*   This is a lively little bulb with upright leaves, up to five per bulb, with flared white or whitish flowers. It also hails from the Atlas Mountains.

N. cantabricus subsp. *monophyllus*   This is a beautiful white wide-crowned flower usually with only one leaf per bulb. It is found in limited areas in the south eastern tip of Spain, and in the mountains of Morocco and Algeria.

N. jonquilla and *relatives*

Fernandes
Section *Jonquilla* DC

N. viridiflorus Schousb
N. jonquilla L
   var. *jonquilla*
   var. *henriquesii* Samp
   var. *minor* (Haw) Baker
   var. *stellaris* Baker
N. fernandesii Pedro
   var. *fernandesii*
   var. *major* Fern
N. willkommii (Samp) Fern
N. requienii Roem
   var. *requienii*
   var. *pallens* (Freyn ex Willk)
     Fern comb nova
N. gaditanus Boiss + Reut
N. minutiflorus Willk

Section *Apodanthae*

N. calcicola Mendonca

Flora Europaea
Section *Jonquillae* DC

N jonquilla group

N. jonquilla L
N. requienii Roem
N. willkommii (Samp) Fern
N. gaditanus Bois + Reut
N. fernandesii Pedro

N. rupicola group

N. rupicola Duf
N. cuatrecasasii Casas
N. calcicola Mend
N. scaberulus Henriq
N. viridiflorus Schousb

N. scaberulus Henriq
N. rupicola Duf
  subsp. *pedunculatus* (Cuatr)
    Lainz
  subsp. *marvieri* (Jahand +
    Maire) Maire + Weiller
N. watieri Maire

In the Fernandes list *N. rupicola pedunculatus* would now be recognized as *N. cuatrecasasii, N. jonquilla* var. *henriquesii* has become *N. cordubensis,* and as described below *N. requienii* should now be known as *N. assoanus.* The species *N. atlanticus* needs adding to the Apodanthae section.

There is little difference between the species listed by the *Flora* and Fernandes, but the latter authority recognizes an extra species in *N. fernandesii,* and elevates *N. minutiflorus* to specific rank, rather than keeping it within *N. gaditanus* as might most gardeners.

We shall use the more complete roster of the two Fernandes sections, Jonquillae and Apodanthae. The most obvious difference between

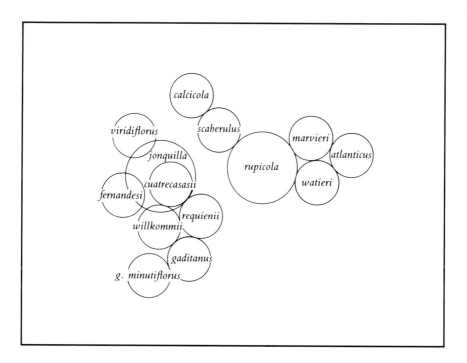

14 Diagrammatic relationship of Jonquillae and Apodanthae sections

plants of the two sections is the foliage, Jonquillae species having dark green, shining rush-like leaves, while the Apodanthae's leaves are like those of garden daffodils, flat rather than rounded, glaucous, with a grey or blue-green effect. Flower stems of the Jonquillae species are rounded; those of the Apodanthae more or less flattened. Seeds of the Jonquillae types are angular and less shiny than the round ones of the Apodanthae, which are also distinguished by the presence of the white tissue that formerly held them to the ovary.

N. viridiflorus   Clearly this is close to *N. jonquilla*. Cytological examination shows chromosomes of *N. viridiflorus* matching those of *N. jonquilla* but doubled in number. *N. viridiflorus* may have arisen from the chromosome doubling of an *N. jonquilla* individual or, more likely, from the doubling of those of a common ancestor of both species. *N. viridiflorus* may look closer to this postulated ancestor and the imagined prototype of the genus, or perhaps *N. viridiflorus* is a regressive species with its very rudimentary corona. It grows at Spain's southernmost tip, at Gibraltar, and along part of the Morocco coastline heading southwest on the Atlantic seaboard.

Of all species this is the most eccentric. It is unusual in having a corona reduced to six tiny lobes, having uniform green flowers, blooming in autumn, and in rarely having leaves if flowering. Flower stems grow on after blooming to twice their length, and labour as leaves.

Autumn rain stirs the dark tuniced bulbs into growth. One, or occasionally two leaves are pushed up, or a single flower scape. At 15–20cm two to seven dark green stars are opened. Narrow, straight-sided thin triangular petals point flat away from the six minute arcs that form the corona. Occasionally petals lie slightly forward, but more often they tend to reflex a little. Overall width of flowers is 2–3cms. Held at right angles to the stem, they may be more noticeable for their powerful perfume than their appearance: a whiff is exciting, but more can soon be overpowering.

This botanically interesting species will only grow outside in warm parts with summers akin to those of North Africa.

N. jonquilla   This familiar well-differentiated species must have evolved early. It is found through the southern half of the Iberian peninsula, but in other parts of Europe it is probably an escape from cultivation. It is late into flower, and we have had it opening in June (Midlands, Britain). It contrasts in this with *N. viridiflorus*. Firm dark polished rush leaves are normally upright. Rounded stems carry three to seven or eight bright golden starry flowers. Shapes vary: small coronas may be rather wide, small-lobed cups, or more widely bowl-shaped, while petals can be of impoverished narrowness or quite wide, and sometimes dramatically spatulate – with the widest part at the petal end furthest from the corona. They are deep gold and powerfully scented.

Some clones are a free-flowering joy, but others may be cause for continual complaint because of their lack of flowering intent. They like drained warm soils, and can continue to flourish for years. The most annoying clones are those that, with a mass of foliage, are phrenetically splitting bulbs down below so that none is ever large enough to start forming flower buds.

N. cordubensis (N.j. var. *henriquesii)* is distinguished in having larger flowers possibly deeper in colour and with coronas longer and wider than *N. jonquilla.* Bulbs appear to be more robust.

N. fernandesii This is more dwarf than *N. jonquilla* with petals 1cm long and cups half as long, the lobed coronas being more conspicuous than those of *N. jonquilla* and the perianths being more informally twisted in all the stock we have grown. Stems from 10 to 20cm long carry several bright golden flowers.

N. wilikommii Semicylindrical leaves are up to 2.5mm broad, and they are more upright than those of *N. assoanus.* It has been distributed under the name *N. juncifolius* in the past, although this familiar name is more usually thought of as the synonym of *N. assoanus.* Six-lobed cups are 5–6mm deep whilst petals are about 8–10mm long. Plants stand only about 8–10cm high.

N. assoanus Part of the former *N. juncifolius* which was then known for some years as *N. requienii,* a name that now has to give way by rules of precedence to the earlier published one, *N. assoanus.* Leaves up to 2mm wide. The type has flowers of primrose yellow with corona a similar or darker shade. There are paler forms but they hardly warrant the botanical distinction sometimes thrust upon them. The species is an attractive little plant usually some 6–7cm high with two or three blooms to a stem. Bulbs normally increase quickly in warm well-drained soils.

N. gaditanus A little plant from scrubland towards the coast of southern Portugal and Spain as far as Cadiz, its stems carry one to three small deep golden flowers with straight-sided bowls 5mm deep to the petals' length of 6–7mm. It is often a frustrating little plant producing a mass of small bulbs with scarcely any of them strong enough to bloom. A clump of the thread-thin leaves can only have limited attraction.

Comparison of the chromosomes of *N. gaditanus* and *N. assoanus* show them to be similar, but with a fragment missing from one of those of *N. gaditanus*. Possibly the species arose from *N. assoanus*.

N. minutiflorus This rarity is found in the same range as *N. gaditanus* in the southern part of the Iberian peninsula. It is very similar to *N. gaditanus* to which it has often been assigned, being tiny, only about half the size, with petals a mere 4–5mm long and coronas 2.5–3mm deep.

Fernandes section *Apodanthae*

Found in North Africa and the Iberian peninsula, these plants are characterized by relatively broad blue-green leaves and keeled stems. These are some of the most enchanting of all the miniatures. North African kinds found in the Atlas Mountains pose a slight problem

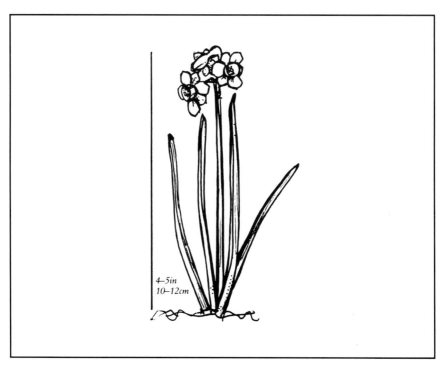

4–5in
10–12cm

15 *N. calcicola*

about their origin. Cytologically and taxonomically they appear to have come from *N. rupicola* or a common ancestor species, but as yet no populations of these have been found in Africa.

N. calcicola   This extraordinarily smart plant, almost too dandified for a wildling, has very erect, clean steely foliage and strong stems of 10–15cm carrying between one and an exceptional six or seven blooms, with four the most usual number. Having raised thousands under cultivation it would have been difficult to pick one that did not please, although they are variable in form. Normal petals are flat and broad, almost square, at right angles from bold, straight-sided, bowl-shaped coronas which can often be wider than deep. Odd individuals may hold their anthers in an untidy gappy fashion, but normally all is parade-ground smartness. Colour is a gold bordering on orange. With good drainage, bulbs grow well.

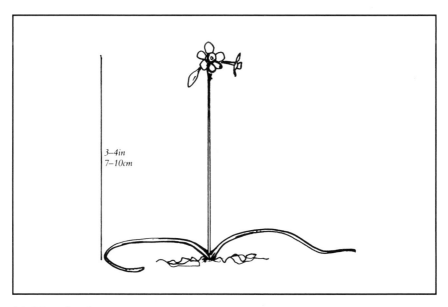

3–4in
7–10cm

16 *N. scaberulus*

N. scaberulus   This is a poor country cousin to *N. calcicola*, being half the size and lacking the good-mannered foliage. Fewer and meagre leaves usually arch over or grow flat on the ground. Slimline stems carry two to four flowers. It usually grows on Portuguese mountainsides in granite detritus with plenty of under-surface moisture.

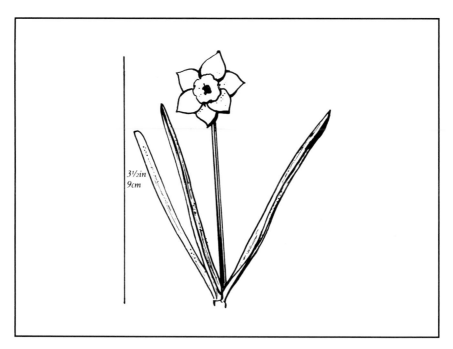

17 *N. rupicola*

N. cuatrecasasii   This has been grown under the name *N. rupicola pedunculatus,* but it seems sensible to have it as a separate species, and certainly clear of the *N. rupicola* name. It usually has solitary flowers, but may occasionally have twins. They are a uniform bright yellow but differ from *N. rupicola* in having a cup-chaped corona often inclined to be restricted at the margins, unlike the flared and crenellate typical *N. rupicola* corona. It differs also in having a clearly marked pedicle of around 1cm, whilst this feature is absent or very nearly so in *N. rupicola.* Foliage is upright unlike that of *N. scaberulus,* and its usually solitary flowers contrast with the habit of *N. calcicola* which very rarely has fewer than three flowers except on very small or immature bulbs.

N. rupicola   This is one of the loveliest of species, neat in bloom and habit. Fernandes divides it into three subspecies: *N. r.* subsp. *rupicola, N. r.* subsp. *pedunculus,* and *N. r.* subsp. *marvierii.* The last is a North African plant which, it is suggested, arose from the type *N. rupicola.* Subsp. *pedunculatus* is now *N. cuatrecasasii.*

The type stands 8–10cm high with neat leaves held at 45° or more from the stem. These keeled stems carry the mid-yellow flowers, so often remarkable for their perfect show form. Petals are occasionally narrow, but this is an unusual exception as the norm is a nearly perfect circle. Coronas are like wide plates or shallow-lobed bowls. Flowers measure approximately 2cm across – large for the size of the plant.

The main populations grow high up in the hills of the northern half of Portugal well above Lisbon, and in Spain mainly to the north of the river Tagus, and not to the east of Madrid. In cultivation it likes the good drainage it enjoys in nature. It will be happiest on a sunny slope in the rock garden, or making a fine little bulb in the alpine house.

N. r. subsp. *marvierii* is variable but is larger than *N. rupicola* and, whilst enjoyable, has a less finespun appearance. Colour is a deeper gold. Petals vary in width but unlike typical *N. rupicola* can be broad and often pointed. Foliage is larger and more or less erect.

N. watierii   This is a gem. The plant looks like a more robust *N. rupicola* with blue-green leaves held quite rigidly and at similar angles. The keeled stem is usually at an angle and not bolt upright. Flowers are much larger than those of *N. rupicola*, being twice the width, but of similar silken texture. Their pure white is untouched by any hint of cream or yellow, something rivalled only in some *N. poeticus*. Petals are held in a flat plane or slightly reflexed behind the wide almost disc-like lobed corona. Overall width may be 2–3cm. Growing in a warm pocket in the rock garden, or as a treasure in the alpine house, it can look enchanting. Fernandes suggests it may have arisen by chromosomatic mutation or mutations from *N. marvierii*.

N. atlanticus   This rarity from the Atlas Mountains is more or less the same stature as *N. r. marvierii* and as grown under cultivation is a creamy white flower with good broad petals and a definite cup a shade or so darker than the petals.

N. poeticus types

Fernandes
Section*Narcissus*

N. poeticus L
    var. *poeticus*
    var. *verbanensis* Herb
    var. *hellenicus* (pug) Fern
    var. *recurvus* (Haw) Fern

Flora Europaea
Section *Narcissus*

N. poeticus L
    subsp. *poeticus*
    subsp. *radiiflorus* (Salisb) Baker

var. *majalis* (Curt) Fern
N. *radiiflorus* (Salisb) Baker
   var. *radiiflorus*
   var. *stellaris* (Haw) Fern
   var. *poetarum* Burb + Baker
   var. *exertus* (Haw) Fern. comb
     nova

Fernandes follows Pugsley's paper *Narcissus poeticus and its Allies,* 1915 Journal of Botany. Pugsley's two series become the two species, and his species are reduced to varieties. The *Flora's* conception would keep most observers happy. Walking the hills, the polymorphic state of the species is more obvious than by the study of botanical literature.

All have in common very flat leaves, conspicuous white perianths, and very restricted, brightly coloured coronas. Bulbs tend to be narrow and long-nosed. Flowering is towards the end of the season, which in Northern hemisphere gardens means April and May, and in their native hills the end of May until July.

Following Fernandes' nomenclature, obeisance is made to Pugsley, but this is being adopted as a matter of convenience. In part the classification is no doubt justified, but in detail it is surely open to attack. Dividing into two species may be a sensible stratagem on the divide and rule premise, making it easier for gardeners to identify clones of plants, but varieties have been somewhat arbitrarily taken from the varied wild populations. A compressed version of Pugsley's criteria and their use in differentiating species is as follows:

N. poeticus. With stamens unequal, perianth segments usually shortly narrowed and overlapping towards the centre.

A: Corona flat:

                                       1 *N. poeticus* var. *poeticus*
     Corona more or less cupular:

B: Flower small:
C: Stature dwarf:

                                       2 *N poeticus verbanensis*

       Stature tall:

                                     3 *N. poeticus* var. *hellenicus*

     Flower large:

                                     4 *N. poeticus* var. *recurvus*

D: Corona red margin with adjacent white zone:

                                     5 *N. poeticus* var. *majalis*

N. radiiflorus. With stamens subequal, perianth segments usually narrowed below

A: Corona cupular, small:
          Corona 2.5mm deep, 8mm wide:
                                            6 *N. radiiflorus* var. *radiiflorus*
          Corona 2mm deep, 10mm broad:
                                            7 *N. radiiflorus* var. *stellaris*

      Corona flat or nearly so when mature:

C: Corona colour wholly red:
                                            8 *N. radiiflorus* var. *poetarum*
D: Corona flat, discoid:
                                            9 *N. radiiflorus* var. *exertus*

N. poeticus var. *poeticus*   These flat-eyed narcissi are found in millions of guises from the high pastures of France and Spain across to Italy and Switzerland and the mountainsides of Austria. Flowers vary most noticeably in the width and form of their petals. Some are starry, others are fit for the show bench. Petals can be frenetically twisted or lie in a flat plane with a yellow eye red–rimmed. Petals may lean back, or, more rarely, be slightly forward. Do not be deceived if you think you have found a white-rimmed one; the sun will have burnt out the carotene and left white tissue.

N. poeticus var. *verbanensis*   This small-flowered dwarf could be worth a place in the garden if a good clone could be found that would take to garden life. It seems loath to leave its home in south eastern France and neighbouring northern Italy.

N. poeticus var. *hellenicus*   This tough little flower is one of the founder members of the modern hybrid families. It is a tall wiry-stemmed flower with small but very perfect blooms of waxy texture. Opening cream, it soon becomes snow-white with many forms having perfect overlapping petals which form a good rounded perianth, flat to start with but tending to reflex later. It used to be known as *N. p. verus,* a late-flowering kind from Greece. The clone I grow is a good garden plant, probably the one used as the basis for Pugsley's botanical description.

N. poeticus var. *recurvus*   The 'Pheasant's Eye Narcissus' is the most widely grown poeticus, and one of the few collected in the wild that have found cultivation to their liking. Huge quantities have been grown from the beginning of the century. It makes good long-nosed bulbs that manage out of the soil better than most. Apart from the fact that it does not die, points that have made it such a favourite are its powerful scent, its very late flowering time, the clean lines of its gracefully recurving petals, and its eye of citron-rimmed dark red. Its flowers are long lasting for the time of year at which it blooms, the end of May and, on occasion, into June.

It is best in cool moist conditions with at least 10cm over its nose. Once planted it should be left alone. It will be mid-summer before its leaves can be cut back. It is important to pick a site where the foliage can be left in peace. A shrubbery or woodland edge seems the ideal.

N. poeticus var. *majalis*   I do not think I have seen the authentic plant. Pugsley's description of it as having a red rim with a white zone below makes me uneasy: I need convincing that there are poeticus types with coronas which have areas devoid of carotene when fresh.

N. radiiflorus var. *radiiflorus*   This small-cupped one is said to belong to mountainsides north of Lake Geneva, and in Austria and Yugoslavia. I believe we have found it in a few spots on the French side of the Jura range. Perianths of several degrees of regularity or informality seem possible.

N. radiiflorus var. *stellaris*   This is described as having starry perianths and wide eyes of yellow with a scarlet-red edge within which there is supposed to be a thin white zone, but I suspect this description is of flowers which have been bleached by sunlight.

N. radiiflorus var. *poetarum*   This was a selection from the wild, but an exact match of the plant has not been located. Petals were twisted and gappy but it had an eye of solid red which was exploited by early breeders via such seedlings as 'Will Scarlett'. It was an early-flowering kind, but is probably no longer in cultivation.

N. radiiflorus var. *exertus*   This is a Swiss plant with a very flat corona of yellow-edged red.

Fernandes
Section *Serotini* Parl

N. serotinus L
  var. *serotinus*
  var. *emarginatus* Charbert
  var. *deficiens* (Herb) Baker

Flora Europaea
Section *Serotini* Parl

N. serotinus L

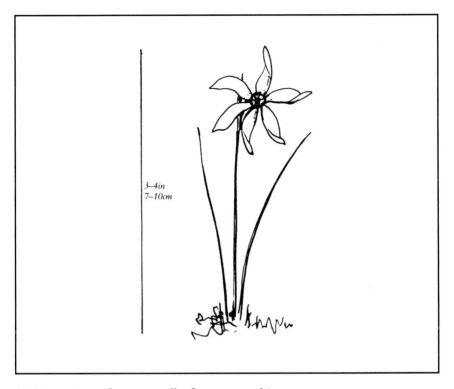

3–4in
7–10cm

18 *N. serotinus* (flower usually faces upwards)

N. serotinus   I have grown this successfully and achieved good rates
of increase in number and weight. Bulbs in well-drained compost in
containers were left out during the summer and brought under
unheated glass in the autumn as the flower buds and thin bright green
leaves began to show. Bulbs are quick to bloom with slender stems
some 6–10cm high. Usually solitary, twins are not infrequent and
there are reports of plants with several blooms on a stem. They look
upwards, with six relatively large white petals pointing outwards, and
in the centre of this star is just discernible a corona made up of six tiny
lime-coloured lobes.

This successful species seems a clearly differentiated one. From a base
in southern Spain it travels along the African coastline to Benghazi in
Libya; it inhabits the whole Atlantic coastline of Morocco; and its
widest base is around Seville over the lower ground to Cordoba from
where it fingers its way into the Algarve coastline. Eastwards it covers
the Spanish Mediterranean coast and all the islands of the Mediterranean; it lines the western Italian seaboard and around the foot up as

far as Barletta; and it grows in parts of Yugoslavia and around southern Greece. All this geographical spread is managed with a very minimum of variation.

Flora Europaea Section *Tapeinanthus*

N. cavanillesii Barra + Lopez *(N. humilis)*   The first species and section of the genus in the *Flora,* under the name N. *humilis,* this plant is not listed in the Fernandes review. It belongs to southern Spain and Morocco, and is often listed as *Tapeinanthus humilis (Carregnoa lutea).* It lives on the generic borderline. Its nearest ally is *N. serotinus,* and it would certainly belong in Fernandes section *Serotini.*

On the same scale as *N. serotinus,* it has thin rushy leaves either with the flower stems or immediately after. Flowers are produced singly in late autumn. Sometimes two little yellow stars will be carried. They appear to be without a corona at first glance, but on close examination a rudimentary structure of six tiny lobes or scales can be seen ringing the throat above the stamens, three of which are on view and three held in reserve. Corona variation can be such that some have little more than a slight protruded ridge while others approach *N. serotinus's* six little arcs or tiny crenellated sections.

Fernandes Section *Aurelia*

N. broussonettii Lag.
   f. *broussonettii*
   f. *grandiflorus* (Batt. + Trab) Maire

N. broussonettii   Found only in a restricted Moroccan area, this species therefore does not appear in the *Flora Europaea.* Fernandes gives it pride of place in his first section, the monotypic one, Aurelia, which is followed by Hermione which includes N. *tazetta* types.

It lives on the Moroccan Atlantic coastline from near Larache down to below Agadir. It reaches inland from Rabat on the lower ground and inland from Agadir in more mountainous terrain. Fernandes suggests it arose from a lost ancestral triploid species that also engendered *N. tazetta* forms and *N. elegans.* Chromosomes of *N. tazetta* and *N. broussonetii* are similar, one showing an additional section and one losing a fragment.

The large round bulbs are dark, like tazettas. Autumn growth is quick. Flowers are carried on 30cm stems. From two to six snow-white flowers are similar to tazettas but for their very sketchy effort at a corona. A circular ridge appears behind protruding anthers with bright yellow pollen. Foliage is flat and below the flower level when in bloom. By being grown in pots that are allowed to dry out in the summer below a greenhouse bench they may be given the right impression of native heat and drought. A dousing of water in autumn brings them to life.

N. tazetta types

Fernandes
Section *Hermione*

N. corcyrensis (Herb) Nym
N. tazetta L
N. ochroleucus Lois
N. patulus Lois
N. cypri Sweet
N. italicus Ker-Gaw
N. bertolonii Parl
  var. *bertolonii*
  var. *algericus* (Roem)
    Maire + Weiller
  var. *primulinus* Maire
  var. *discolor* Batt
N. aureus Lois
N. cupularis (Salisb)
  Bert ex Schult. f
N. pachybolbus Dur
N. canariensis Burb
N. dubius Gouan
  var. *dubius*
  var. *micranthus* (Jord + Fourr)
  Aschers = Graeb
N. panizzianus Parl
N. barlae Parl
N. polyanthus Lois
N. papyraceus Ker-Gaw
N. elegans (Haw) Spach
  var. *elegans*

Flora Europaea
Section *Tazettae*

N. tazetta L
  subsp. *tazetta*
  subsp. *italicus*
    (Ker-Gaw) Baker
  subsp. *aureus*
    (Lois) Baker
N. papyraceus Ker-Gaw
  subsp. *papyraceus*
  subsp. *polyanthus*
    (Lois) Asch + Graeb
  subsp. *panizzianus*
    (Parl) Arcangeli
N. dubius Gouan
N. elegans (Haw) Spach

f. *elegans*
f. *aurantiicoronatus* Maire
var. *flavescens* Maire
var. *fallex* Font-Quer
var. *intermedius* Gay

No tazettas are of undoubted hardiness in any except the mildest parts of Britain. Even *N. canaliculatus* can be lost in severe winters. In warmer places, such as parts of the USA, Australia and New Zealand they can flourish. Hardiness is tricky to measure, especially with bulbs that grow below ground and can be insulated with snow in some of the worst weather. In America tazettas should be hardy in zones seven and above. In Britain zones F and G should be easy, and E normally all right (see maps).

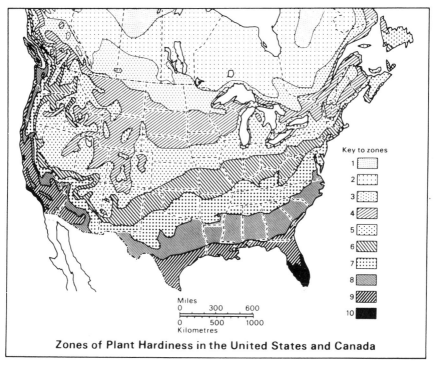

Key to zones
1
2
3
4
5
6
7
8
9
10

Miles
0   300   600
0   500   1000
Kilometres

Zones of Plant Hardiness in the United States and Canada

18a & b The zones are based on the degree to which plants will withstand frost. Plants hardy in zone A will be hardy throughout the UK. Plants hardy in zone D will be fine in E, F and G but will need shelter and protection in C. In the USA zones range from 1 – the most severe, to 10 – the warmest and most frost free

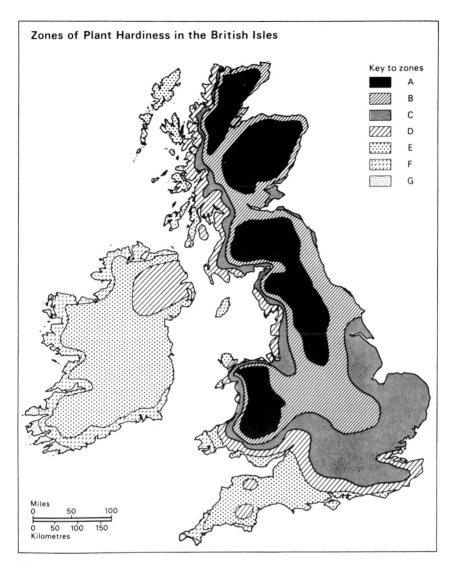

Zones of Plant Hardiness in the British Isles

Key to zones

A
B
C
D
E
F
G

Miles
0   50   100

0   50   100   150
Kilometres

18b

N. elegans This autumn flower is native to the part of North Africa pointing to the link with Spain. It spreads only a short way westwards, but to the east follows the coast to Libya. It is found in Corsica and Sardinia, and on the Italian coast opposite Corsica, and south including Sicily, and reaching the same limits northwards as *N. serotinus.*

It is larger than *N. serotinus,* measuring perhaps 4–5cm across, with longer wider white petals which are considerably more waved and propeller-twisted. Very small coronas, tiny entire cups, are olive, deeper at the rim and then losing the green tint and becoming orangey. Flowers are usually single, but twins are possible. Leaves are flat, and two or more appear before flower buds.

N. dubius   This is one of the rare stable species derived from the hybridization of two distinct species. It has a chromosome count of 50 derived from parents *N. tazetta* and *N. assoanus (N. requienii, N. juncifolius)*. Fernandes has shown that haploid chromosomes of *N. dubius* reproduce the combined haploids of *N. tazetta* with 11 chromosomes and the diploid form of *N. assoanus,* giving a total count of 25. The parents were probably *N. papyraceus* with a normal diploid count of 22 and a tetraploid *N. assoanus* with a count of 28. Joining the two haploids was followed by chromosome doubling, giving the count of 50 and enabling the new plant to produce viable haploid cells containing full genetic material in pollen and egg cells.

N. *dubius* is found in a continuous area on the Mediterranean coasts of Spain and France, from Tortosa below Barcelona to Toulon beyond Marseilles, and travelling some distance inland.

It is a perfect miniature tazetta some 10–15cm high with neat upright blue-green foliage quite dissimilar to that of *N. assoanus.* Stems carry three to six white flowers with rounded petals at right angles to a relatively broad straight-sided cup. Outside it needs a climate similar to its home stations where it is usually found on rocky ledges, but it is a good alpine house plant given a summer baking. It seeds freely.

N. tortifolius Casas   The unusual derivation of *N. dubius* is echoed by that of the newly discovered Spanish *N. tortifolius. N. tortifolius* with a chromosome count of 2n = 50 originates from a hybrid between a tazetta form, probably *N. papyraceus,* and *N. gaditanus*. The chromosome doubling that followed hybridization ensured that a stable fertile species resulted. Neat white flowers are very similar to those of *N. dubius* with stems 20–30cm high and carrying from 5 to 16 blooms. The coronas are possibly shallower, and may incurve a little at the rim. The distinctive feature is the twisting of the two or three leaves.

A compressed key to the Fernandes Hermione section follows:

Corona yellow/orange
Petals white

Flowers 19–40mm diam.

Petals subequalling tube

Petals narrow not overlapping, may be reflexed; corona
  yellow or orange. S. France, Iraly, Balkans   *N. corcyrensis*

Petals shorter than tube, ovate or obvate, overlapping; corona
  lemon or orange.

Plants tall; leaves erect

Flowers 25–50mm diam; corona 4–5mm deep, yellow or orange.
  Mediterranean.   *N. tazetta*

Flowers 25–30mm diam; corona about 4mm deep, lemon. S. France.
  N. ochroleucus

Plants dwarf, flowers 18–24mm diam; corona golden about ½ petal
  length. S. France, Italy, Mediterranean islands, Balkans   *N. patulus*

Flowers 40–50mm diam; corona cream yellow, mouth expanded.
  Plant robust. Cyprus, Syria, Italy.   *N. cypri*

Petals yellow/yellowish

Petals oblong, pointed, very little overlapping; flowers 23–50mm
  wide.

Flowers 40–50mm diam; petals yellowish, slightly overlapping;
  corona pale yellow. S. France, Italy, Sicily, Sardinia, Corsica.   *N. italicus*

Flowers about 35mm diam; leaves glaucous.   *N. bertolonii*

Flowers uniform bright yellow. Blooms Nov–Feb. Italy.   *N. b.* var.
  bertolonii

Flowers two-toned, gold, corona orange. Dec. Morocco, Algeria.
  N. b. var. *algericus*

Petals sulphur   *N. b.* var. *primulinus*

Petals yellowish white   *N. b.* var. *discolor*

Petals ovate, much overlapping; flowers 25–35mm diam.

Corona yellow, slightly darker than petals. S. France, Italy, Balkans
  N. aureus

Corona deep orange/yellow, petals yellow. S. France, Sardinia,
  Italy.   *N. cupularis*

Corona and petals white

Flowers 12–20mm diam.

Corona entire, less than $\frac{1}{3}$ petal length

Petals ovate oblong, about $\frac{1}{2}$ tube length; large bulbs. Algeria, Morocco. *N. pachybolbus*

Petals ovate lanceolate, pointed, less than $\frac{1}{2}$ tube length; smaller bulb. Canary Islands. *N. canariensis*

Corona more or less lobed, about $\frac{1}{2}$ petal length, ovate and overlapping. *N. dubius*

Flowers about 20mm diam; leaves up to 6mm broad. Catalonia, Aragon, S. France. *N. d.* var. *dubius*

Flowers about 15mm diam; leaves 9–12mm broad. S. France. *N. d.* var. *micranthus*

Flowers 20–40mm diam.
Flowers 20–25mm diam.
Petals pointed, shorter than tube; leaves and stems green. Jan–Apr. Portugal, Spain, S. France, Italy. *N. panizzianus*

Petals obtuse, subequalling tube; leaves and stems glaucous. Italy. *N. barlae*

Flowers 25–40mm diam.
Stem slightly flattened, stems and leaves green; corona entire; flowers 25–35mm diam. Mediterranean. *N. polyanthos*

Stem flattened, stems and leaves glaucous; corona more or less crenellate; flowers 33–40mm diam. Portugal, Spain, S. France, Italy, Morocco, Algeria. 'Paperwhite' *N. papyraceus*

Corona cup or saucer-shaped, 1.5–2mm deep; petals long narrow; 2–10 flowers; leaves flattish, up to 9mm broad.
Corona conic or cylindrical, only 1.5–2mm deep, entire, crenate or 6-lobed; petals 12–18mm long, 3–5mm wide, slightly reflexed; thin stems, 2–7 flowers. *N. elegans*

4

History in cultivation

Early lists of medicinal and apothecary's plants include daffodils. Monastic sites often still retain populations of old-established kinds outside their normal limits. These presumably were introduced centuries ago. It is arguable that even the well dug-in English 'Lent Lily', *N. pseudonarcissus*, could be an introduced plant. Such a good colonizer could spread widely in a relatively short period.

N. tazetta travels around the Mediterranean eastwards through the Middle East to the Himalayas, China, and Japan, appearing to follow the old overland caravan trading routes too closely to disallow the probability of human agency aiding their dispersal for a combination of aesthetic and trading purposes.

From the sixteenth century written records show how interest in daffodils grew in Britain and mainland Europe, especially in the Netherlands. Turner, in his *A Few Narcissus of Diverse Sports*, lists all known to him in 1548, amounting to 24 species and varieties.

In 1581 Lobel (Lobelius), Mathias de l'Obel, working in the Netherlands, but travelling extensively in Germany, Hungary, and Spain, energetically collected plants to forward his work of classification based on the characteristics of leaves. Much of his work depended on illustrations; the observer was to recognize in the arrangement of these pictures the natural affinities of plants as conceived by this early botanist. 21 drawings of narcissi were reproduced from wood blocks and published by the great printer Plantin. The wide-leaved included *N. tazetta, poeticus, elegans*, and *ajax* (trumpet form). Narrow leaved ones included *N. bulbocodium, triandrus, jonquilla, juncifoliius*, and *serotinus*. These illustrations were used in other works, including most notably that of Clusius.

Clusius, Charles de l'Ecluse, having been driven from his French home by religious persecution, spent most of his life working in Germany and the Netherlands. His *Rariorum Plantarum Historia* was first published in 1576, and was revised and republished in 1601. It was the best of such compilations, following the contemporary practice of arranging classifications in 'books'. Clusius produced six books, on trees and shrubs, bulbs, sweet-smelling flowers, scentless flowers, poisonous and narcotic plants, and finally plants with milky juice. He worked with living material and in the above publications, together with various appendices, he sorted out the narcissus genus as he found it in this manner:

1 Single flowered:

    A. Wide-leaves.   4 *tazetta* forms.

    B. Narrow-leaved   *jonquilla, intermedius*, and possibly *odorus*. Plus from appendices, *juncifolius*, and *triandrus*

2 Double flowered: 3 *tazetta* forms, 2 *poeticus*. Plus from appendices, *pseudonarcissus plenus*.

3 Leafless: *serotinus*

4 Pseudo-narcissus: *eyestettensis*, 2 trumpet kinds from Spain, 2 *bulbocodium* (listed as *N. pseudo-narcissus juncifolius*) being a white and a yellow form. Plus from appendices, *moschatus, incomparabilis*.

The 1588 herbal produced by Tabernaemontanus, Jacob Theodor, was followed by illustrations in 1590, and further editions in 1613 and 1664. Some of the assorted illustrations were curious in the same way as are medieval drawings of fabulous beasts, being imaginative rather than representational. Gerard's *Herbal* in 1597 used the Tabernaemontanus illustrations. Fifteen narcissi were shown with English names by Gerard, and a second edition in 1633 had 30 kinds.

John Parkinson's *Paradisi in sole Paradisus Terrestris* of 1629 is the most quoted early source. Whilst apothecary to King James I of England Parkinson was diligent in collecting plants and collating previous writings. His compendium is interesting and readable but neither the text nor the poorly copied illustrations are reliable sources of information. Just short of 100 narcissi are described and classified mainly on flower form, especially by the corona, with the aim of dividing the true from the false Pseudonarcissus. 'Many idle and ignorant gardeners ... doe call some of these Daffodils Narcissus, when as all know that know any Latine that Narcissus is the same thing, and therefore alone without any other epithite cannot properly distinguish severall things.' It is a moot point whether he helped to clear confusion, but his work held prime place till the arrival of Linnaeus.

Modern systematic botany is dated from Linnaeus, Carl von Linne, who was born in Sweden and did most of his work there, although he spent time in the Netherlands and travelled in France and England. From childhood he was fascinated by all living things and their classification. Despite being directed towards the ministry by his parents his devotion to his plant and animal studies meant that his life, despite recurrent financial problems, was spent researching with the greatest dedication all matters concerning the classification of living things, and especially of plants. In his old age he was revered by most of his countrymen. His two-word nomenclature, giving generic and specific names, swept away former names that had tended to grow into miniature descriptions. His idea of narcissi in his *Plantarum* of 1753 was a 'lumper's' delight, giving only six kinds. Having worked in Holland in the 1730s he would have known the many forms, but even in the second edition of 1762, only 13 are listed, and two of these are not true narcissi.

Whilst early plant collections may have been for medicinal and culinary purposes, it is difficult to imagine that this remained the sole driving force for long. With the dissolution of the monasteries there would have been extra incentive for private collecting in Britain. Here and in the Netherlands the amassing of all types of bulbs accelerated as international travelling and trading increased and expanded. Being so easy to handle, bulbs stole a march on other plants. Species, unusual forms and mutations were collected, propagated and distributed. Double forms were especially prized.

The old favourite early double, now burdened with the official name *N. telamonius plenus*, was probably being grown in the 1500s, well before Vincent Van Sion is recorded by Parkinson as flowering it in London in 1620. Bulbs were given to Parkinson and to George Wilmer who, to Parkinson's disgust, grew and distributed it as 'Wilmer's Double Daffodil'. I can remember baskets of bulbs being offered as 'Wilmer's Double' although they were better known as

'Van Sion'. Lesser bulbs have their golden doubling confined within the trumpet, while stronger ones belch out in Falstaffian good humour, fully doubled.

Two other doubles known before 1601 are associated with Queen Anne of Austria. 'Queen Anne's Double Daffodil' is officially *N. eystettensis* (formerly *capax plenus* when *capax* was used for *N. triandrus loiseleurii*). It is thought to be a double of a triandrus and trumpet hybrid. No perianth tube or corona is present: all is subserved by a series of straw-coloured narrow pointed petals laid row upon row, and so becoming progressively smaller towards the centre and forming a six-pointed star. 'Queen Anne's Double Jonquil' is a rounded little flower like a golden carnation, obviously a doubled early *N. × odorus*.

Ireland was made for daffodils. It rains almost every day, and large parts of it are influenced by the surrounding seas and the Gulf Stream, so that the climate is rarely very harsh. Many old kinds have made this their second home. 'Van Sion' grows in ditches and banks as freely as a dandelion. Rarer types also do well. W. E. Hartland, in the second half of the last century, gathered many kinds and grew them into stocks. The writing and illustrations of his catalogues are a joy, the work of a real enthusiast. *Hartland's Original Little Book of Daffodils* first appeared in 1886, and at least five editions were offered to the discerning public. He writes, 'this little book of daffodils is given to the public regardless of personal labour and additional expense. . . . The woodcuts etc, alone of this work cost over one hundred and thirty pounds.'

> The *polyanthus* group (*N. tazetta*) may be described as tender, for on cold soils and on exposed situations they certainly do suffer in a frosty spring. And the same may be said of the *bulbocodium* group (*N. corbularia*) which requires a dry sandy soil, and shelter against the keenest wind; but, it is never-the-less true that the whole of the *narcissus* (*tazettas* and *corbularias* included) may be grown to perfection in all parts of these islands when suitable provisions are made to ensure for them the proper comforts of a garden. The species and varieties number six hundred, the smallest of these that are generally known is *Narcissus pseudo minimum*, the largest is *Narcissus incomparabilis* 'Sir Watkin'. The first may be thrust into a lady's thimble, and the second will require for safe carriage, nothing less than a carpet bag, or a peck measure. When cut for a button hole it should only be for the largest man in the country.

In 1819 A. H. Haworth had brought together all his thinking on narcissus in *Narcissorum Revisio*, and later updated it in the

'Monograph on the Suborder V of Amaryllideae' published in *Sweet's British Flower Garden* of 1831. The Linnean Narcissus was replaced by 16 genera, and 148 species were recognized, some based only on the evidence of indifferent drawings.

Dean Herbert is given credit as the first to encourage the breeding of daffodils. His *Amaryllidaceae* of 1837 cut the Haworth proliferation down to six genera, and the species to 45 with some 130 varieties. Species based on illustrations alone were summarily dismissed. Ironically in doing this he deleted *N. cyclamineus*, 'an absurdity which will never be found to exist.' His paper 'On crosses and Hybrid Intermixtures' instanced some crosses he had performed. He ended with a rallying call: 'It is desirable to call the attention of the humblest cultivators, of every labourer indeed, or operative, who has a spot of garden, or a ledge at his window, to the infinite variety of narcissi that may be thus raised and most easily in pots at his window, if not exposed to too much sun and wind, offering him a source of harmless and interesting amusement, and perhaps a little profit and celebrity.'

Some fanciers may have taken note. Edward Leeds, a stockbroker, started to hybridize and soon had many fine flowers, but being in poor health he offered his collection of 24,000 for sale in 1874 for £100. Peter Barr formed a small syndicate which bought them.

William Backhouse of County Durham raised daffodils from 1856, wishing to produce better-coloured flowers. He was successful. The famous 'Emperor', 'Empress', Weardale Perfection' and the small pale trumpet 'W. P. Milner' were all from his stable, and the first two can still be found growing in parks and gardens today, and looking well. His collection was more important than that of Leeds, and was also bought after his death by Peter Barr.

Peter Barr enlisted J. G. Baker, then head of the Kew Herbarium, to instill order into the collection of 360 kinds that he had growing under his control. Baker had written authoritatively in his 'Review of the genus Narcissus' in F. W. W. Burbridge's *The Narcissus: its History and Culture*, 1875. Baker was not befuddled by previous writings and saw the confines of the genus clearly. Haworth's fanciful genera were banished, and the Linnean single genus firmly established.

Baker's classification of garden hybrids had sections named after prominent daffodil personalities: Barrii, Engleheartii, Leedsii, Backhouseii, Nelsonii, Bernardii, and Burbidgei. His 1888 *Handbook of Amaryllidecae* was a masterly account and is still today regarded as the basis of the botanical view of the family. Three main sections divided the genus Narcissus:

Magnicoronati:	Corona funnel-shaped or cylindrical, as long as perianth segments.
Subsection Ajax:	1 species
Subsection Corbularia:	1 species
Mediocoronati:	Corona cup-shaped, about half as long as the perianth segments.
Subsection Ganymedes	
Subsection Queltia	
Parvicoronati:	Corona small, obconic or saucer-shaped.
Subsection Hermione:	corona uniform in texture
Subsection Eunarcissus:	corona scariose at the edge
Subsection Aurelia:	corona nearly obsolete

Baker brought order out of chaos.

Peter Barr's energy ensured that the daffodil's importance was recognized quickly. He inspired others with a vision of its potential. With the RHS he organized a daffodil conference in the spring of 1884, and he exhibited his Leeds and Backhouse flowers together with other established kinds. At this conference an RHS committee, a forerunner of the society's Narcissus Committee, passed a sensible resolution:

> Proposed by Mr Elwes, and seconded by Mr J. G. Baker, that in the opinion of this Conference uniformity of nomenclature is most desirable, and that garden varieties of narcissi, whether known hybrids or natural seedlings, should be named or numbered in the manner adopted by florists, and not in the manner adopted by botanists.

The same autumn Peter Barr published a wonderful catalogue, really a small book on the narcissus family, to be purchased for one shilling and 'Solde by Peter Barre and hys Sonne, at their Shoppe in King Strete, by ye Covent Garden, nigh ye Strande, in the Parish of St. Paul's, Westminster.'

Interest in raising new kinds was stimulated by the conference. Apart from Barr and Son, some of the others who started to raise seedlings were the Rev. G. H. Engleheart and Mrs R. O. Backhouse. Other British fanciers were joined by some Dutchmen. S. A. de Graaff bred from bulbs purchased from Peter Barr. His 'Madame de Graaff' was given a First Class Certificate by the RHS in 1887, and the following year's bulbs were on sale for the huge price of over £5 each.

In 1890 a second major conference which lasted for four days was held by the RHS at their Chiswick gardens. With all leading experts present, papers were read on many aspects of the cult, and the work of the Narcissus Committee was fully detailed. The daffodil had become a dominant ornamental plant, and new kinds now commanded big prices.

Being a lengthy process, raising daffodils is an expensive one. Since the 1880s there have always been fanciers in Britain willing to pay high prices for the latest hybrids, and around the turn of the century a monied class was happy to subsidize the raisers' efforts. In gardening circles there was a certain cachet to having some novelties in one's garden.

The halcyon days were those up to the outbreak of the First World War. 'Daffodilmania' was not restricted to Britain: Americans were becoming interested, and wealthy visitors would arrange to have leading cultivars sent home. Between the two Wars interest continued despite the Depression. Now bulbs were being dispatched to Australia, New Zealand, the USA and Canada – the cult had become world-wide.

Milestones in breeding

Over the last 150 years and more, breeding seems on the face of it to have been a process of steady diversification and improvement. A closer look suggests a more erratic history, with outstanding novelties leaping ahead by virtue of one or a combination of characteristics. Painstaking work in one direction has often produced a surprise demanding effort in previously unenvisaged directions.

In the beginning each new seedling was an exciting surprise. Soon time, energy, and space demanded clear aims. Herbert crossed species all ways. It was an explicit aim to produce an orange trumpet daffodil. His crossing of trumpet and poeticus types was the fundamental strategy producing the base for the huge modern races of long and short cups. His example was followed using potentially better parents like *N. poeticus hellenicus*, *obvallaris*, and *hispanicus*.

Most early breeders kept no records. William Backhouse did not know the parents of his famous duo, 'Empress' and 'Emperor'. He thought *N. bicolor* was a seed parent and this could have been correct with a *N. pseudonarcissus* form as the other parent. Hybrid vigour made these two, 'Emperor' tall in yellow and darker livery, and 'Empress' in milk-white and yellow, much more successful garden plants than their parents.

In 1845 *N. bicolor* gave John Horsfield a seedling that became an important market flower as *N. horsfieldii*. I remember seeing a bunch of it in the 1970s that Alec Gray brought to a RHS meeting. With pointed white petals and dark chaste chrome yellow trumpet it looked astonishingly good, and made one wonder how much progress we had made in the intervening 130 years.

Everyone knows 'King Alfred' by name. Bred from 'Emperor' by *N. hispanicus* it was given a First Class Certificate in 1899 and was for decades a major force. 100 bulbs were sold then for over £5 each – the total would have bought a street of houses. 50 years in the limelight embedded its name in the public consciousness to such an extent that it is still used as a label to sell many later-raised kinds. Despite this huge advance it was not always the easiest of plants to grow.

At the turn of the century the long cups were being led by such as the large yellow 'Sir Watkin' named by a Mr Pickstone in 1884, having been found by him in many Welsh gardens where it had been long established. It deteriorated, probably due to viruses.

William Backhouse's seedlings provided the working capital for the next generation of breeders. Short cups 'Barrii Conspicuus' with *N. poeticus recurvus* as one parent, 'Duchess of Brabant', and 'Minnie Hume' from *N. ps. albescens* × *N. p. radiiflorus* were named in 1884, together with long-cupped whites 'Mrs Langtry' and 'Duchess of Westminster'. Many of today's leading kinds trace their parentage back to these, a limited number of cultivars.

Rev. G. H. Engleheart　Engleheart's work traversed the early times of the 1880s until the daffodil was an established modern plant in the 1930s. He died in 1936. From *N. poeticus ornatus* × *N. p. poetarum* he raised a series of poets. 'Horace' won the Barr Silver Gilt medal as best seedling of the year in 1894 and was a leading market flower until the outbreak of the Second World War. Then stocks were destroyed to make way for food production. 'Horace' did not give good seedlings, its offspring having inordinately long necks, but others like the red-eyed 'Chaucer' were more useful. 1920 saw the introduction of Engleheart's 'Dactyl' which can still be bought as flower or bulb.

Poets are admired, but are, and were, a minority interest. More important things were happening. Engleheart's short cups 'Beacon'

(1897) and 'Firebrand' (1902) together with long cup 'Will Scarlett' (1898) led the way to bright flowers. As one of the cornerstones of breeding, 'Beacon' was used for decades and was still in the collection of Guy Wilson in the late 1940s. I remember it as a small smooth flower with primrose-yellow pointed petals and a small cup rimmed with orange. Mated with a seedling it had given the very important sisters 'Mitylene' and 'White Sentinel' which between them feature in almost every pedigree of white-petalled long cups and many other types as well. 'Beacon' had all the attributes of the angels; 'Will Scarlett' on the other hand was a flamboyant scoundrel that should perhaps have been outlawed like its namesake. Its colour, which it passed to its progeny, astounded, but manners it lacked. Petals were of the 'pulled-through-the-hedge-backwards' type, and this sartorial vacuity it also readily passed on. It had come from the small white trumpet species *N. abscissus* (Fernandes) by the red-eyed poet *N. p. poetarum* with highly suspect perianth.

Engleheart worked with all types. An important series of white and pale-coloured ones were led early on by 'White Queen' (1898), 'White Lady' (1898), and 'Lady Margaret Boscawen' (1898). A later success was 'Tenedos' (1923) with long triangular petals and a long crown only lightly expanded. 'White Sentinel' (1923), and 'Mitylene' (1926) in white and pale yellow were used to produce some of the most promising pink cups. 'Rosary' (1926), a bicolour trumpet, showed hints of pink described by Engleheart as having 'pinky,-citrony,-buffy,-apricotty,-tawny,-topazy,-inside-of-a-melon, colouring'.

Engleheart trumpets were famous in their day. His early trumpets 'Magnificence' (1914) and 'Forerunner' (1927) are still grown, but undoubtedly his most famous trumpet was the epoch-making 'Beersheba' (1923), still a white trumpet to be reckoned with well after the Second World War.

Fortune Breeding better orange-cupped flowers was every breeders' preoccupation. It received its biggest boost in 1923 when 'Fortune' was first shown. It astonished with its wide flat perianths and large bowls of good tangerine. It was obviously of better form than all predecessors. Happily a good bulb, many tons are still sold today. It would have given way to better things if it had not been such a early kind and although used a lot in breeding its influence was not dramatic.

The Backhouses Mr and Mrs R. O. Backhouse lived at Sutton Court, in a small village outside Hereford, and started raising daffodils in 1888. Both carried on until their deaths, Mrs Backhouse in 1921 and Mr Backhouse in 1940. There was no connection with William Backhouse of 'Emperor' and 'Empress' fame. The husband-and-wife team worked with many types, but their brightly coloured ones, owing much to *N. poeticus poetarum* and its seedling, 'Will Scarlett', made the greatest impression.

Mrs Backhouse took the lead and had to her credit a string of successful kinds, many now only names. 'Lord Kitchener' (1905) was an early success and was for a long time a leading pale long cup, bred from 'Minnie Hume' × 'Weardale Perfection'. By the 1920s she had established a fine series that became well known and important kinds after her death. 'Sunstar' and 'Coronach' are two vivid white-and-red short cups. 'Galopin' (1927) was altogether larger with a wide ivory perianth and large bowl the colour of red lead. From our present vantage point it is easy to pick 'Hades' (1925) as one of her most important kinds. Introduced by Lionel Richardson it became for decades the benchmark against which new kinds were measured for depth of corona colour. Petals were ivory and by today's standard lacked something in width. Used extensively by Richardson it was a parent to 'Kilworth', from which almost every modern white-and-red flower is descended.

Backhouse kinds were bought by Dutch growers. For many years 'Scarlet Leader' (1933) in primrose and orange was a familiar bulb in catalogues and in shops, and still more famous was 'Texas' (1928), the double yellow-and-orange. Both were introduced by De Graaff. The public will always associate her, appropriately enough, with 'Mrs R. O. Backhouse' (1923), the important pink. This long-cup trumpety kind has petals that look quite respectable on opening but become very windswept. Crowns, starting chrome yellow, soon take on various shades of pink, which in some seasons and climates are very rich. It features in the pedigree of many modern pinks.

P. D. Williams   Daffodils were, and still are, of considerable importance to the economy of the south-western peninsula of Britain. Early flowers from the Isles of Scilly and Cornwall were marketed in huge quantities, and in Cornwall there was a number of people interested in breeding daffodils. Pre-eminent amongst these was the noted horticulturalist, P. D. Williams, who started working at Lanarth, St. Keverne, Cornwall, in the 1890s and continued till his death in 1935.

It is almost impossible to overemphasize the value of his contribution to the daffodil story. He maintained the highest standards, insisting on healthy constitutions for anything thought worth naming. His importance may be gauged by the huge quantities of his cultivars still being commercially grown well over 50 years after his death. A roll-call of his seedlings shows his work to have been commercially by far the most important. The acreages of his 'Carlton' (1927) make the point immediately.

He must have had an exceptional eye for a good flower and an almost mystical feeling for the game, as his methods were often the opposite of methodical. Walking amongst his flowers with a favoured flower in hand or buttonhole he might see a possible seed parent. The flower would be taken and pollination effected immediately. No proper records were made.

The background to much of the Williams breeding was the trumpet *N. hispanicus*. Lasting quality, strong bulbs, and tough blue foliage were all things that came to be expected of his cultivars, *hispanicus* hallmarks. His yellow long cups were unbeatable, and the rich 'Crocus' (1927) and 'Havelock' (1927) were leaders for years. 'St. Egwin' (1927) had a smaller corona and was exceptionally smooth in mid-yellow. Alongside these were being bred orange cups that owed nothing to the likes of 'Will Scarlett', which 'P.D.' would not allow on his grounds. 'Folly' (1926) in ivory and tangerine was splendid with perianth gently recurved, and 'Killigrew' (1907) was an early yellow-and-orange that was still being grown decades later.

1927 must have been a great year. Apart from those mentiond, many others were named. Soft yellow 'Sulphur' was one. White-and-yellows 'Polindra', 'Niphetos' and 'Penvose' all belonged to that year, and 'Polindra' features in some American breeding, whilst 'Niphetos' was used by all serious breeders. As early as 1907 the jonquil 'Lanarth' was introduced and others followed, with the perfumed 'Trevithian' belonging to the *annus mirabilis*, 1927. Cornwall's soft climate made it possible to work with tazettas. 'Scarlet Gem' in yellow and orange was introduced in 1910, whilst the precocious 'Cragford' made its debut in 1930. Cyclamineus hybrids such as 'Peeping Tom' had been raised years before its introduction by Matthew Zandbergen in 1948, and 'Bartley', similar but better, was registered in 1930.

The Brodie of Brodie   Brodie Castle was the home of a very dedicated breeder. It was almost unheard of for him to leave his flowers in the daffodil season. From 1898 until his death in 1943, the Brodie of Brodie worked with a wide range of flowers using mainly those of his own raising. Many of his appeared in the catalogues of his friends Guy Wilson and Lionel Richardson. 'Hunter's Moon' (1941) in haunting lemon-sulphur tones was much in demand for a decade before the Wilson and Mitsch lemons became more numerous and available.

Some perfect small flowers with tiny cups enchanted gardeners from the twenties until overwhelmed by sheer numbers of new things in the fifties and sixties. 'Fairy Circle' (1921) with a little rimmed eye, 'Silver Salver' (1922) in pure white green-centred, and 'Samaria' (1923) with snowy petals and citron eyes, all cast their spell. His pink-crowned flowers were eagerly looked for and often entered breeding plans before being named; indeed some never got beyond seedling numbers because advance was so rapid. 'Suda' (1927), from 'Nevis' × 'Lord Kitchener', was a strong plant with bold flowers of well-flushed pink. It stood the test of time better than many.

Brodie's work as a breeder was recognized, and without advertisement, or writings, or show stands, his flowers made their way into major collections. His meticulous records make a fascinating study. None of his kinds had a greater effect than 'Seraglio' (1926). This melded the influences of the unruly grandparent 'Will Scarlett', with the civilizing ones of another grandparent 'Princess Mary'. Both these were white petalled although the immediate parents of 'Seraglio', Brodie's 'Mozart' (1915) and 'Gallipoli' (1923), had yellow in their petals. 'Seraglio' was father to 'Green Island'.

Whites from 'Nevis' (1916), 'White Nile' (1920), and the large 'Askelon' (1923) were used by all breeders, especially by Guy Wilson.

Guy L. Wilson   Guy Wilson started breeding as a child in 1906 and continued until his death in 1962. He saw and helped a revolution in the daffodil genus, a change from the wildling and primitive hybrids he grew as a schoolboy, to the state of near perfection in the 1960s. He began with plants like *N. obvallaris* and *N. hispanicus*, and ended with glorious things like 'Empress of Ireland' and 'Panache'. His whites are his memorial. Starting with wretched weak little plants, he had by the end of his life brought them, almost single handed, to perhaps the greatest degree of perfection of any type, and to be strong robust plants.

By the 1930s he had world-beating ones like 'Samite' (1930), 'Slemish' (1930), 'Ave' (1935), 'Trostan' (1938), and the wonderful 'Chinese White' (1937). A major breakthrough was 'Kanchenjunga' (1934) with very wide petals and hugely flanged trumpet. 'Broughshane' followed in 1938, and then what was perhaps his favourite, 'Empress of Ireland' in 1952. Some even topped this, and his 'Panache' (1962) was named by the fancier and breeder, F. E. Board, in the year of Guy's death.

Short-cupped 'Cushendall' (1931) and 'Frigid' (1935) with green eyes are still treasured by gardeners.

Although associated with pale flowers, Guy Wilson made significant contributions in most sections of the main divisions. His 'Preamble' (1946) was the leading bicolour trumpet in its day, and he also produced traditional yellow trumpets like 'Slieveboy'. However it was his 'King of the North' × 'Content' flowers that broke new ground and gave birth to most bewitching lemon flowers like the huge ghostly 'Moonstruck' (1944) and 'Maraval' (1945). Most famous is 'Spellbinder' (1944), which opens a biting rich lemon, before allowing the inside of the trumpet to fade to white in a metamorphosis resulting in a reversed bicolour. It remains a favourite. Long-cupped yellow-and-orange flowers received a significant boost with his early 'Armada' (1938). Short cup 'Chungking' (1942) had a clear run of show successes for at least 20 years and was still winning 10 or 15 years after that.

Wilson pinks were high-quality ones, often of a purer pink than those of his competitors. Rimmed 'Interim' (1944) gave him banded flowers and also ones with pink solid to the base. 'Irish Rose' (1953) was an advance, but the finest of all was 'Passionale' (1956) combining a flower of perfect form, colour, and texture with a plant of rumbustious vigour. It is now grown by the ton.

Lionel Richardson   Beginning only a year or so after Guy Wilson, Lionel Richardson bred flowers until his death in 1961, and Mrs Richardson carried on for a number of years thereafter. All main types were bred at Waterford, their Southern Ireland home, but the orange cups were their speciality. The first catalogue appeared in 1922, and in 1928 Jack Goldsmith joined as foreman at a point when breeding was beginning to show results, and proved the ideal man to take the work forward. By the end of the 1930s there was a wide range of important kinds.

Significant stages in daffodil development were marked by such flowers as yellow trumpet 'Kingscourt' (1938) and the smaller 'Goldcourt' (1937). 'Green Island' was another landmark; mated with Guy Wilson's 'Chinese White' it spawned a whole race of fascinating beauty, and it was also important in breeding pinks via 'Rose Caprice', giving extra strength.

Richardson pinks stemmed mainly from the introduction of 'Rose of Tralee' (1937). 'Salmon Trout' (1948), hailed as a world beater, was soon challenged by flowers like 'Rose Caprice' (1952), 'Infatuation' (1954), 'Debutante' (1956), 'Salome' (1958), and 'Romance' (1959).

'Galway' (1943) was for years the top long-cup yellow, though it looks like a trumpet. Yellow-reds were constantly being improved, a big step forward being 'Ceylon' (1943), sturdy and with metal-strong flowers of deep gold, the goblet cup opening dullish but becoming a very rich shade. It marked a major improvement in sunproofing – for years at Waterford 1,000 or so seeds were sown of tough 'Carbineer' bred by A. M. Wilson, a kind that helped resist the effects of the sun. 'Vulcan' (1956) had neat rich fast colours, but the most outstanding was 'Falstaff' (1960). Not only was this a finely-modelled flower but its colour was without parallel, and it opened very early.

Almost all leading white-and-reds came from Richardson's 'Kilworth' × 'Arbar' and their descendants. They established new standards for both long and short cups.

History will show which Richardson flowers last longest in the public esteem, but I would put my money on the doubles. All recent advances have stemmed from his weakly 'Falaise', raised from a seed or two found on normally sterile 'Mary Copeland'. 'Falaise' was not fully double and was fertile. It was used as seed parent to a wide variety of pollen parents. One result was 'Gay Time', a much improved double white-and-red that is also very fertile and gives excellent double seedlings. Leading Richardson doubles include white-and-red 'Acropolis' (1955), large white-and-orange 'Gay Challenger' (1962), and white-and-yellow 'Unique' (1961).

Alec Gray Whilst other breeders concentrated on mainline types Alec Gray's interest was captured by the small ones, and he worked with these from 1927 until the 1960s. He made crosses of all sorts successfully: tazetta, cyclamineus, triandrus, jonquil, and trumpet kinds. If for nothing else he will be remembered for his 'Tête à Tête' (1949) and sister seedlings 'Jumblie' (1952) and 'Quince' (1953).

W. J. Dunlop Willie Dunlop started breeding in 1937. He lived in Ballymena, Co. Antrim, only a few miles from Guy Wilson, and later moved to a farm the other side of Guy Wilson's village of Broughshane. He bred mainly quality flowers and was not afraid to repeat a cross made by another breeder, realizing that the potential of the cross was not exhausted. His bicolour trumpet 'Newcastle' from the same parents as Wilson's 'Preamble' is an example. For years it was the only possible winner in its class. He had a series of fine red-and-whites including 'Glenwherry' (1947) and 'Irish Splendour' (1962).

John Lea John Lea raised leading show flowers from 1949. He made his mark early, but the introduction of 'Canisp' (1960) made his position secure. He followed this lovely white flower with another, 'Inverpoly'. His race of tall strong yellow-and-orange flowers with rather restricted coronas had 'Loch Hope' (1970) from a seedling × 'Vulcan' as flag flyer, although it was not sunproof. He concentrated on show flowers of the first four divisions, and this enabled him to win the prestigious Engleheart Cup for 12 seedlings on 12 occasions. His contributions to the race for the best white-and-pink double included several fine kinds. 'Delnashaugh' from his double 'Kimbrace' by the dark pink 'Romance' is a large well-balanced bloom of white and rich pink.

D. and J. Blanchard John Blanchard is a highly successful breeder who is unusual in being at least as fervently interested in the small daffodils as he is in the large hybrids. His father had made very good progress in producing flowers of many divisions, and John now has a whole gamut – the widest range in types in Britain. What a good idea to establish a daffodil-breeding family succession! Quality is as high in the small as in the winning large flowers. Even hoop petticoats have not escaped his pollinating brush. Named kinds were selected from a *N. cantabricus foliosus* × *N. romieuxii* cross and a further generation raised. Mixed white clones were named 'Nylon' by Alec Gray, and are now being grown on in Holland.

Brian Duncan Irish breeders have an advantage – daffodils grow so well there. Brian Duncan takes full advantage of this and makes an annual foray to London with a group of friends to exhibit a collection of beautifully-grown flowers. He has raised flowers of many types. His pink cyclamineus ones from 'Foundling' are noteworthy. His double 'Pink Paradise' is a wonderful round paragon, and only one of a number of fine doubles. In addition to many excellent flowers of his own he has marketed the products of other important breeders such as Tom Bloomer.

Kate Reade Daffodil breeding is infectious. Living close to Guy Wilson and Willie Dunlop, Kate Reade caught it easily. With the co-operation of her husband and family she built up a fine collection and has brought forth a steady stream of fine flowers. Her 'Foundling' is a delightful pink cyclamineus. 'Gin and Lime' is as refreshing a flower as it is a drink, being a very fine reverse bicolour trumpet from 'Goldcourt' × 'Moonstruck'. 'Fool's Gold' is an intriguing double from 'Daydream' × 'Egg Nogg'; white petals form a background for inner segments that are lemon on opening but fade to white with golden edges.

Barbara Abel-Smith Using stock from several sources, but especially from George Johnstone, Mrs Abel-Smith has raised attractive kinds of many types but with a special emphasis on the pinks. The quality of her flowers shows how much may be achieved without allowing the whole enterprise to become too huge or cumbersome.

Barbara Fry At the Ministry of Agriculture experimental station at Camborne, Cornwall, Miss Fry undertook a long-term programme to get early flowers useful for growers, especially those in Cornwall and the south-west, who need improved early bloom for the cut-flower market. Collecting a wide selection of cultivars and a few early blooming species such as *N. cyclamineus*, Miss Fry made a series of crosses. Some useful garden kinds have been a handsome by-product of the programme. 'Radical' is a vastly better cyclamineus trumpet to replace 'Peeping Tom' and 'Bartley'. 'Alliance Party' is a smart early little cyclamineus in gold, useful in the rock garden or border.

Some of Miss Fry's most interesting work may eventually prove to be that concerned with the raising of new tazetta types for the cut flower trade of the Scilly Isles and Cornwall. At present over 60 of her seedling clones are being grown on, and some of these will surely make a big impact on the flower market and could enter garden cultivation, even if only as pot plants in cooler areas.

Cultivation in Holland

As far as daffodils are concerned, whilst the Dutch have concentrated on growing bulbs rather than trying to breed new ones, they have not entirely neglected the art. In the early days de Graaff produced 'Mme de Graaff' (1887) followed by 'White Knight' (1907) and 'Mrs Robert Sydenham' (1907). M. van Waveren and Sons introduced a big yellow trumpet in 1900, 'Van Waveren's Giant', for some decades an important garden plant.

In 1912 E. H. Krelage and Son introduced the stately 'Mrs E. H. Krelage', classified as a white trumpet but really a pale bicolour. It was well thought of up until the outbreak of the Second World War.

Dutch priorities were different from British ones: the plant must be good both as a garden and as a cut flower, and finer show points were secondary. A series of useful yellow trumpets included 'Rembrandt' (1930) from Lubbe, the early lemon 'Mulatto' (1931) from Van Tubergen and, most important of all, 'Golden Harvest' (1927) from Warnaar. This became renowned, and is still the dominant trumpet in the commercial market, despite worries about its susceptibility to basal rot. Warnaar introduced 'Joseph MacLeod' in 1946, a robust fine golden trumpet that I believe has never received the recognition it deserves.

Large cups were welcome – the larger the cup the better. G. A. Vit den Boogaard registered 'Duke of Windsor' in 1937, and after the war every bulb was eagerly sought. I remember a notice in a shop window producing a queue. With wide white petals and a very broad crown of rich apricot salmon it was not going to be overlooked. A series of similar flowers were marketed under the name 'Weatherproof Narcissi', a marketing style that was only moderately successful.

Dutch eyes have always been ready to spot any double mutations. 'Golden Ducat' (1947) was a sport from 'King Alfred', and 'Dick Wilden' (1962) appeared in 'Carlton'. Like many doubles so discovered, their stems are scarcely adequate for the increased flower weight. This criticism does not apply to the doubled tazettas like 'Cheerfulness' or the doubled sport found in 'Treamble'. This was noticed while a float was being decorated for a carnival in Holland. The bulbs whence the flower came were left unlifted for another year and the odd mutated bulb located. It was later introduced as 'White Marvel' (1950), the doubling being restricted to the cups.

The successful garden plant 'Ice Follies' was introduced in 1953 by Koynenberg and Mark, also known to the public for their gladioli. Its huge vigour and floriferous habit made it very popular. Crossed with 'Binkie' it gave this firm the fine garden daffodil 'St Patrick's Day', a very telling lemon kind with a wide crown that fades but retains a shining lemon rim.

Jaap Gerritsen has worked consistently at his breeding. His main contribution has been the race of split coronas sometimes called 'Collar' daffodils. Initially no vituperation was too damning from fanciers, but flower arrangers thought differently: they recognized their dramatic appeal. Some fanciers still regard them as anathema, but they are now part of the daffodil scene, the newer kinds being more refined and pleasing.

Cultivation in America

There is a considerable history to the cultivation of daffodils in America and their breeding. Now their cultivars are the equal to any, and in some directions lead the world, and no one has done more for the flower than Grant Mitsch.

Grant Mitsch   Grant Mitsch started in Oregon in 1934. He spent almost the whole of his life working exclusively with daffodils, and was the first American to achieve a truly international reputation. A very modest, sincere man, he worked hard and set himself the highest of standards. The flowers that first made his name abroad were his lemons. He repeated Wilson's 'King of the North' × 'Content' cross but, instead of being satisfied with around 100 seeds, he sowed 10,000 and so gave himself a chance of realizing the genetic potential of the cross. The lemon trumpet seedlings were backcrossed onto the long cup 'Binkie' to expand the range. His 'Honeybird' and 'Daydream' are still world leaders.

Mitsch flowers are represented in every division and every class. Lovely cyclamineus and jonquil hybrids jostle with tazettas, doubles and even split coronas. In the first four divisions his kinds stand comparison with any, and some lead the way, and his pinks have a depth of colour approaching red.

Happily the enterprise is now being carried on energetically by his daughter and son-in-law. The Havens are raising high-quality flowers with the same dedication.

Dr T. D. Throckmorton   Most of the flowers bred by Dr Throckmorton are those opening one colour and developing others. He has used extensively the Mitsch ones 'Aircastle', 'Old Satin', and 'Irish Coffee', but has brought in more or less unrelated genetic material by way of such types as 'Russet' and 'Altruist'. The lovely quality of his flowers is obvious, and their changing ways make description hard but admiration easy. He is one of the few breeders to have established a definite new race, 'Throckmortonii'.

There have been, and are at present, plenty of keen raisers in America. Some, like Dr Throckmorton, have taken a particular aspect to exploit, while others have worked on a broad front. The late Mr M. Fowlds and others have conjured up some magical miniatures and dwarfs, and Bill Pannil, Murray Evans, Bill Roese, and others have flowered seedlings of the highest possible quality – judged by any standards they must be with the world leaders.

5

Classification

Maintenance of order amongst impending chaos is what gardening is about. Dedicated people have ensured that the swelling numbers of new daffodils has not brought total confusion. The work of early herbalists and botanists was useless when confronted with the daffodil population explosion from the 1850s. An *ad hoc* classification grouping flowers of similar character under names of leading daffodil personalities held sway for a while: 'Backhousei' housed hybrids from trumpets crossed with tazettas, and 'Bernardii' was home to those between *N. abscissus* and *N. poeticus*. Proliferation of kinds and more involved parentages soon made this obsolete, and J. G. Baker's classification of 1888 was thankfully adopted.

Baker had three groups based on the relative lengths of petals and coronas, a criterion that has stood the test of time, but which has been deployed rather differently as the years have passed, the proportionate lengths being changed. A simplified classification was adopted in 1909 and has been kept under review since then by the RHS Narcissus Classification Committee.

In 1943 an overhaul was needed. A revised system was approved in 1947, and started in 1950. People's names were no longer used for any divisions. Division 1 was for trumpets. 1A denoted a trumpet with perianth and corona coloured; 1B indicated trumpets with white petals and coloured coronas; 1Cs were all white; and 1D was the catch-all class for other colours, and became home for reversed bicolours.

Relatively recently American fanciers led by Dr Throckmorton suggested that main divisions based on flower proportions were perfectly in order, but that it made more sense to use letters following division numbers to give some idea of the colour make-up of the flower. This sensible arrangement was agreed.

The official classification as authorized by the RHS is as follows:

The classification

1 The classification of a daffodil cultivar shall be based on the description and measurement submitted by the person registering the cultivar, or shall be the classification submitted by such a person.

2 Colours applicable to the description of daffodil cultivars are abbreviated as follows:

W = white or whitish   P = pink
G = green   O = orange
Y = yellow   R = red

(The definition of orange or red lies, like the estimation of beauty, somewhat in the eye of the beholder – daffodil enthusiasts are apt to regard a healthy orange as red.)

3 For the purposes of description, the daffodil flowers shall be divided into perianth and corona.

4 The perianth shall be described by the letter or letters of the colour code most appropriate.

5 The corona shall be divided into three zones; an eye zone, a mid zone, and the edge or rim. Suitable coded descriptions shall describe these zones, beginning with the eye-zone and extending to the rim.

6 The letter or letters of the colour code most accurately describing the perianth shall follow the division designation.

7 The letters of the colour code most accurately describing the zones of the corona shall then follow, the eye zone to rim separated from the perianth letters by a hyphen. In Division 4, the letters of the colour code most accurately describing the admixture of petals and petaloids replacing the corona shall follow in proper order using 3, 2, or 1 colour codes as appropriate.

8 If the corona is substantially of a single colour, a single letter of the colour code shall describe it.

Using these basic requirements, daffodils may be classified as follows:

DIVISION 1   Trumpet Daffodils of garden origin
Distinguishing characters: One flower to a stem; trumpet or corona as long as or longer than the perianth segments.

DIVISION 2   Long-cupped Daffodils of garden origin
Distinguishing characters: One flower to a stem; cup or corona more than one third, but less than equal to the length of the perianth segments.

DIVISION 3   Short-cupped Daffodils of garden origin
Distinguishing characters: One flower to a stem; cup or corona not more than one third the length of the perianth segments.

DIVISION 4   Double Daffodils of garden origin
Distinguishing characters: One or more flowers to a stem, with doubling of the perianth segments or the corona or both.

DIVISION 5   Triandrus Daffodils of garden origin
Distinguishing characters: Characteristics of *Narcissus triandrus* clearly evident: Usually two or more pendant flowers to a stem; perianth segments reflexed.

DIVISION 6   Cyclamineus Daffodils of garden origin
Distinguishing characters: Characteristics of *Narcissus cyclamineus* clearly evident: Usually one flower to a stem; perianth segments reflexed; flower at an acute angle to a stem, with a very short pedicel.

DIVISION 7   Jonquilla Daffodils of garden origin
Distinguishing characters: Characteristics of the *Narcissus jonquilla* clearly evident: Usually one to three flowers to a rounded stem; leaves narrow, dark green; perianth segments spreading not reflexed; flowers fragrant.

DIVISION 8   Tazetta Daffodils of garden origin
Distinguishing characters: Characteristics of the *Narcissus tazetta* clearly evident: Usually three to twenty flowers to a stout stem; leaves broad; perianth segments spreading not reflexed; flowers fragrant.

DIVISION 9   Poeticus Daffodils of garden origin
Distinguishing characters: Characteristics of *Narcissus poeticus* group predominant: Usually one flower to a stem; perianth segments pure white; corona usually disc-shaped, with a green or yellow and a red ring; flowers fragrant.

DIVISION 10   Species and wild forms and wild hybrids
All species and wild or reputedly wild forms and hybrids. Double forms of these varieties are included.

DIVISION 11   Split-corona Daffodils of garden origin
Distinguishing characters: Corona split rather than lobed and usually
for more than half its length.

DIVISION 12   Miscellaneous Daffodils
All daffodils not falling into any one of the foregoing divisions.

I believe those responsible for drawing up this classification are to be
congratulated. It is precise and clear, with all the weight of obvious
legality but without any of the legal profession's specialized vocabulary.
It delights me to find the last division retained, to catch all that
otherwise might fall outside the law.

6

Cultivation:
Growing daffodils in the garden

Of all garden plants, the daffodil must be one of the easiest to grow. Plantings 100 years old continue to flourish. It may seem that the sum total of their cultivation is to scratch a hole, tip in the bulbs, cover them, and leave well alone, for they are hardy and persistent plants. When growing professionally, it was our practice when lifting to have a sack to receive any damaged or doubtful bulbs. Human nature being what it is, the odd bulb would get tossed hedgeways, if the hedge was nearer than the sack. Some would root, pull themselves down, and quickly form a clump of healthy leaves and flowers. However there is a dictum that suggests that the more one puts into an activity, the more rewards one receives. Whilst not wishing to argue its universal truth, it is often accurate in gardening. It is worth giving your bulbs some care, for a basic minimum of work will give excellent results.

Planting times

Bulbs belong in the ground, but we pluck them from their environment for our convenience, to examine their health, split them, replant them or trade with them. They do not need a ripening or resting period out of the soil, but some may appear 'dormant' without leaves or functioning roots. This applies mostly to natives of North Africa or the Mediterranean coast. Tazettas and African hoop petticoats enjoy a dry period. Poeticus kinds are rarely if ever without working roots, and the closer the hybrids are to the poeticus the more they are likely to be busy underground most of the time. Certainly new roots can be emerging around a poet's basal plate before the current years' leaves have finished. Usually most kinds will be rerooting for certain by

August, but may have started in July. In the southern hemisphere this activity will be under way by January or February.

The longer the rooting time, the better the bulbs are likely to grow. The best planting months are August, September, and October, but most growers will have planted bulbs much later on occasion and been pleasantly surprised by the results. To plant after October is to forego possible bulbous increase, and the later they are planted the more chance of losing stem length and flower size. Overlooked bulbs, or some received from the opposite hemisphere, can be planted between January and July and will still give flowers and leaves, so maintaining life. They will however need a season or so to re-establish the correct routine, since they live off stored energy and will have only a small chance to make good lost time.

These cultural notes are aimed at the broad mass of hybrids. The specialized needs of some small species will be detailed separately.

Soils

Daffodils grow well in a variety of soils. Outstanding collections have been grown on chalk, as well as on sands and clays. They do well within a wide band of pH values, but may be at their happiest just on the acid side of neutral. Some species are more fussy.

The soil's physical structure is important for bulbous health. To make the best use of the moisture it likes while it is in active growth, a lively root system needs to be established and kept going, which cannot be done in sodden ground. Free drainage is important.

New ground is best deeply dug. Some enthusiasts dig their special beds two spits deep – double the depth of the spade's blade. Incorporating humus helps to improve fertility, aids its structure, and helps to maintain a reservoir of moisture. Raw farmyard manure, if available, is best not brought into immediate contact with the bulbs, so heavy manuring of ground some while before planting or for a previous crop is helpful.

Once bulbs are planted the ground will begin to establish its natural drainage. Soil composition, plant roots, and earthworm activity all help to create a working system. Mulching soil with well rotted compost after the leaves have died helps to boost humus content and keeps bulbs cool.

The role of daffodils in the garden

There are few places where some daffodils will not improve the site, and it is difficult to find a spot where they will be incongruous. Wild trumpet kinds often grow on the edge of woodland or light scrub, while the poets belong to hillside meadows and grassland with a ready supply of water below the surface. Daffodils look right growing in grass or light woodland. A group of trees and shrubs giving a woodland effect is an ideal venue, since the failing foliage is no great distraction, and other growing things mask possible untidyness. Clumps of daffodils in grass in small gardens where normal routine means the mower going its rounds every ten days or so are going to look untidy. They will have to go into the border.

Planted in beds and borders as part of an integrated plan, daffodils bring colour and life early in the year before many herbaceous plants and shrubs have got into top gear. Following vegetation masks dying daffodil foliage, and a useful partnership is set up. Remembering where bulbs are planted is not a difficult problem, since if labels are not allowed, sites can be marked by surrounding plants. Any danger of a bare patch developing after the spring can be averted by sprinkling a pinch of a summer-flowering annual. We do this frequently, using some simple things such as Candytuft or Love-in-the-Mist.

Smaller bulbs are fine in the front of the border, in the rock garden or rock beds, and in odd corners. Some grown in containers can liven up the most desolate spot, and have the advantage of being moveable so that they may be replaced by later-flowering things such as geraniums or lilies. Inside, or under even a little glass, bulbs can be forced to bloom from October through until the spring is in full swing outside.

Keen enthusiasts may feel it necessary to have a bed or beds devoted entirely to daffodil culture. A few shrubs planted in these will avoid them looking like a desert when the bulbs are not in bloom.

Naturalized bulbs

Few things capture the spirit of spring so well as naturalized daffodils. Many will flourish in natural conditions, but some cultivars will not do well and must be avoided. It is often best to restrict one's choice to the earliest kinds, which are doubly welcome after the winter, and die down early so that the grass can be mown and all is tidy before summer. Some early kinds are very persistent in bloom and seem almost weatherproof.

Showy modern kinds are unlikely to look natural; something closer to the wild ones is preferable. *N. pseudonarcissus*, as a wild plant, is naturally perfect. Its size is not too large and this some gardeners will feel is an advantage, though others will want to maximize the impact by planting something larger. In the end personal choice dictates. Factors in favour of *N. pseudonarcissus* and the golden relative *N. p. obvallaris*, the 'Tenby Daffodil', are earliness and foliage which is in scale with the plants and not a dominant feature dying down. On this small scale there are cyclamineus hybrids like 'February Gold' that are early and very persistent in bloom, and that adapt well to naturalized conditions.

Choice will depend on the colours you want. The 'Lent Lily' is cream and primrose, while the 'Tenby Daffodil' and 'February Gold' are bright yellow. Smallish cyclamineus kinds include 'Charity May' in sulphur yellow, 'Dove Wings' in white and primrose, and 'Jenny' in white and cream becoming white with age. All the cyclamineus hybrids are excellent naturalizing plants. It may well be best to pick only these.

The colours mentioned are obvious spring ones. It might be thought that yellow and orange flowers would brighten the picture, but this is not necessarily the case for the green of grass, a complementary colour to the orange, can make it look muddy. This is certainly so with orange seen at some distance in grass, although orange in the foreground close to the observer may look perfectly satisfactory.

Larger kinds worth trying are the indomitable 'Brunswick' in white and lemon, 'Binkie' in lemon, 'Rembrandt' in gold, and in good soils the triandrus kinds like 'Tresamble'. Doubles are rarely good, but an exception is old 'Van Sion', clumps of which can be very effective. Also the double white 'Mrs Wm. Copeland' is not too tall, and with pointed petals has been for us a great joy.

A few rules are suggested. Plant groups or drifts of one kind only – a mixture within a group looks untidy and terribly disappointing; plant only those kinds known to be good naturalizers; and avoid, like the worst of plagues, advertisements for naturalizing daffodils when it is obvious that surplus bulbs are being offered that would be unsaleable at normal prices. Trying cheap bargains can be the most expensive deal one ever undertakes – bulbs may bloom the first year but be unsuitable for the rigorous life and give up flowering. One is then faced with the problem of lifting the bulbs and disposing of them – the foliage growing each year without flowers is too much of a constant reproach to be left alone.

Designing natural effects may seem paradoxical. Aim to get the bulbs looking natural whilst making the maximum effect. Random distribution will give a disappointing effect – bulbs should be in drifts or groups. These can be positioned to look their best from the most frequent vantage point. 20 or 30 bulbs, and up to several hundred can live in a drift the shape of a fish or eclipse; one or more smaller, subsidiary groups some distance away suggest that odd bulbs have managed to break away to establish the beginnings of new kingdoms; and bulbs may be planted closer towards the centre of the drift to give the effect of a nucleus to an expanding population. Spreading bulbs too widely will exacerbate grass mowing problems.

Planting is best done in early autumn just as soon as the ground is reasonable. At the end of a dry summer it may be wise to wait until the ground is moistened and easier to penetrate. Leaving it too late means cold miserable weather makes planting a penance rather than a pleasurable task. The rough shape of drifts can be marked with labels, and bulbs lobbed gently from a short distance to give the impression of random natural distribution. A concentration towards the centre may develop. If too close they will be overcrowded and for this reason fail to bloom freely. There should therefore be at least 10 centimetres between bulbs at the centre, and half as much again towards the outside of the drift.

Planting depths are vital. The most frequent cause of failure with naturalized bulbs, apart from using unsuitable cultivars, is too shallow planting. Being close to the surface stimulates splitting into many parts, but none of these is likely to be big enough to bloom. The converse is true; the deeper the bulbs the more inhibited they are about splitting. There should be at least 10 centimetres of soil over their tops. Naturally small bulbs such as those of *N. bulbocodium* and *N. cyclamineus* will not however need this depth – 4cm cover should suffice. When starting to plant a quantity such as 500 bulbs it is easy to plant the first one correctly, but the attraction of the job can pall so that the 499th gets less than its fair topping of soil.

Every so often a new 'miracle bulb planter' is marketed. So far all have been variations on a theme: a metal cylinder is pressed by hand or foot into the ground, and is then removed with a neat plug of soil. The hole allows the dropping in of a bulb, and the soil can then be neatly replaced. It rarely works so well in practice. Fate ensures that stones or rocks bar the way, and even without stones it can be difficult to push the tool into many soils, and then it may or may not remove the plug of soil intact.

I prefer the old-fashioned spade. Two insertions are made into the turf to form a right angle. The next side of a square is formed by a third insertion and it becomes possible to ease up the turf. One, two, three or more bulbs can be inserted and the turf returned. Alternatively the turf can be removed from the drift area, the ground dug over, general fertilizer added, the bulbs planted, and the turf replaced.

Normal garden soil should provide plenty of nourishment to maintain good health. If the bulbs need a tonic, a dusting with potash in the spring and autumn will be appreciated, and the autumn one could be combined with a general fertilizer. Foliar feed is used by some, but this must have a good spreader added or it will be repelled by the leaves.

Naturalizing failures may be diagnosed as follows: if there are plenty of leaves but no, or very few flowers, either unsuitable cultivars have been used or bulbs have been planted too shallowly; if bulbs disappear, they may be suffering from the depredations of daffodil fly; and if you notice distorted leaves and flowers, the problem will be eelworm.

In beds and borders

Early daffodils will open in February but, failing this, a March début will still beat the majority of all other plants. The bulbs will give early colour and excitement. Yellow, the colour of youth and rebirth, vibrates in the border. Otherwise only a few kaufmanniana tulips and a handful of small auxiliary bulbs join the winter heathers to celebrate the first day of spring, although soon everything will seem to be happening.

Bold groups are hugely more effective than scattered kinds and, although this may go against the powerful collecting instinct, it is best in the garden to restrict one's choice. A splash of early 'Falstaff' will set the border alight with gold and flaming red. 'Brunswick', although old, looks well between shrubs, especially amongst dark rhododendrons that will contrast with the flower's shining whites and lemons. 'Bartley', or the newer 'Radical', will open early and last for weeks or months, with long cyclamineus coronas trumpeting their golden message. Other kinds can continue the succession until June.

Depending on garden and bed size, the number in a group will vary. Three bulbs of a special kind will soon become a dozen and a dozen quickly 50. Ten bulbs will give a good account of themselves and in their second year provide 20–60 flowers. We try to group 20 or so together to give an immediately opulent effect.

Prior to planting, the soil should be well dug and a sprinkling of fertilizer added. Deep planting prevents excessive splitting and helps to keep them safe from surface cultivation after dying down. A simple rule of thumb for planting daffodils is to take the depth of the bulb from nose to base as 1 unit, and then plant in holes $2\frac{1}{2}$ units deep. In other words $1\frac{1}{2}$ units of soil should cover the bulb noses. With most this means that around 10cm of soil tops the bulb. In parts of the world where prolonged hard frosts penetrate deeply into the soil it is sensible to plant deeper with 15cm over the bulbs.

A space of 10 to 15cm is allowed between bulbs. If they are planted for one season only and a thick effect is required, they may go closer. If bulbs are to be left down for three or four years they are going to need the 15cm gap.

Labels lack aesthetic appeal, but sometimes they are essential. When flowers are in bloom it seems child's play to remember which lot grows where, but by the middle of June, when a decision to lift them may be made, it may be an altogether different matter. Permanent plastic labels can be indelibly written and depressed into the ground so that they are hardly seen but can be fished up and read after a surprisingly long time. Labelling will help to make sure that bulbs are unmolested and their territory defined. Alternatively ringing with clumps of primulas, heucheras or other herbaceous items that are not too rapacious will provide permanent reminders.

Space may be at such a premium that after blooming, bulbs may be filling sites earmarked for summer or autumn acts. Bulbs to be moved in growth should be thoroughly soaked beforehand. Then if dug and lifted with plenty of soil, they can be replanted temporarily in a less obvious spot, just as deeply as before, and given another soaking. It is not ideal but the best compromise available, and here they will die down naturally.

Bulbs may be left two, three, or four years before their increase will dictate uprooting. Left alone they can quickly become so thick as to provide only foliage. They may be lifted before all sight of the leaves has gone and it is difficult to locate them – in the second part of June or the first half of July. If possible lift, inspect, split, and replant the same day. Obviously it is best to move the bulbs to a fresh site, but if all is healthy there is no overriding reason for not replanting in the same spot. The opportunity may be taken to thoroughly dig over the site, incorporate some humus, and apply a dose of fertilizer.

Considerable increase should take place in two or three years. Depending on space and their importance, the largest will be replanted and the smaller ones planted in nursery rows to fatten up and be given away to the local gardening club, or be discarded. If space and time allow all to be replanted, they need space to expand. Good offsets broken from parents may bloom their first year – they will certainly grow fast to adult size with full floral responsibilities. All bulbs that are damaged or showing signs of disease should be rejected.

You may decide against the rapid lift and replant plan, feeling it better to dry bulbs so that they may be easier cleaned, inspected, split and then replanted. Shaken free of soil they may be laid out in trays in a dry cool airy spot and allowed to dry, making sure they are adequately labelled. After a week or so they will be bone dry, and then are easily cleaned. Removing almost detached offsets is simple, and bulbs can be given fungicide treatment more easily – 'Tulisan' or a similar preparation will help clear and check possible infections. Alternative fungicides include Benomyl (Benlate) and the newer thiabendazole available in the UK and the USA. If they are not then replanted they may be stored in small plastic mesh bags such as are sometimes used for fruit and vegetable packs. These keep bulbs together but allow air all around. Again make sure your labelling is efficient.

Rock gardens and beds

The shrinking size of gardens helps to channel interest even more towards small plants. There are hundreds of little daffodils than can belong to such a collection. Some wild ones are charming, although some are difficult in the open in climates so different from their native habitats. Infinitely more amenable are the miniature hybrids, almost all plants of exceptional ease of culture: increase can be almost embarrassing. The definition of 'small' when applied to daffodils in the rock garden will depend on the scale of the whole, and of the other inhabitants. Larger-scale creations will accommodate plants and flowers up to 30–40cm high, and 'Peeping Tom', but more likely the somewhat smaller 'Jenny' and 'February Gold' are going to be the biggest; moving downscale a stage would make 'Sundial' and 'Sundisc' at 15–20cm the tallest permissible; and where only the smallest things are grown, the choice will be restricted to the miniscule *N. rupicola*, *N. watierii*, *N. triandrus*, *N. bulbocodium* and *N. asturiensis*.

Some gardeners feel the bugbear of daffodils in the rock garden and elsewhere is the foliage after flowering. All small species have such thin little leaves that they occasion no trauma. Larger ones like *N. obvallaris* are more obvious, but die down early and are really not too bad. The smaller hybrids are similarly discreet, and plants such as 'Jenny' may be grown behind some small shrub that becomes active as the daffodil foliage begins to die, thus disguising a potential eyesore.

A few groups of *N. asturiensis* are almost essential in slug-proof corners so that the tiny flowers can perform their miniature trumpet voluntary in January and February before even most alpines have bestirred themselves. *N. cyclamineus* is another persistent little early one which is ready to settle down and increase in a moist spot perhaps a touch on the acid side. Different hoop petticoats are fun, and then the perfection of small jonquils such as *N. rupicola*, and *N. requienii* are a joy. They do however have their likes and dislikes. Jonquils enjoy good drainage and do not object to a little baking in the summer. Hoop petticoats and *N. cyclamineus* are happiest with moisture around at most times, although they do not like being drowned in sodden airless soil.

Small species look well with tiny creeping plants such as thymes, raoulias and the less rampant saxifrages. Slightly larger kinds need the company of more expansive plants, and 'Tête à Tête' and *N. obvallaris* look well with winter-flowering heathers which will be in bloom with them – the yellows and mauve-pinks make a pleasing contrast.

In containers

Bulbs are almost too easy to grow in pots and bowls. They often get scant attention and are handled in an offhand manner just because they are so easy and are expected to do their party piece with little help.

The obvious advantage of containers is that they are mobile and bulbs may therefore be brought to their flowering stations just when they are ready to give of their best, and then retired to the wings. Such places may be outside, or in the living room or conservatory. Outside, containers may be used on the patio, in the yard, by the house entrance, or at a strategic position in the garden, perhaps flanking a path. They may also be sunk in pots in positions in the garden border for their flowering period. Later they will be returned to decorative duty. Garden centres in the USA will usually carry large stocks of containerized mature plants ready to give of their best, and thus the almost instant garden is a real possibility. In Europe more plants are being sold in this manner and bulbs, led by daffodils, suit this treatment perfectly.

The usual idea is to use the containers to provide an artificial environment to persuade bulbs to bloom precociously. Cheap bulbs are forced hard, their strength sapped, and then thrown away, although after blooming they may be planted out in the garden to spend two years recuperating.

Sometimes flowers are needed for an early show or for early pollen. These are likely to be more important or more expensive bulbs and will need less cavalier treatment.

A few enthusiasts grow important bulbs in large pots to give them controlled environments and so encourage maximum increase and monitor health. This is an interesting approach to daffodil culture, and may teach us useful lessons for growing in more orthodox ways.

Bowls and pots for the house

From childhood onwards planting indoor bulbs is a popular annual ritual helping to foreshorten the winter. Fresh flowers may smile at us in the deep midwinter, even on the Christmas table.

The first decision to be made is whether the bulbs are to be recycled. If so all must be done to promote strength, for there is life after the container; if not, cheap ones may be grown in easy mediums that do little but provide moisture and anchorage. The second decision is the choice of container. It needs to be big enough to take the bulbs comfortably and provide enough weight to prevent the centre of gravity of the fully-grown entity being too high. It is far easier to grow bulbs in containers with drainage holes, and nowadays many bowls have holes, some plastic ones being marketed with matching saucers. The third decision is the choice of cultivars.

Bowls without holes may use mediums such as pebbles, grit, rough sand, bulb fibre, or soilless compost. Apart from the last, none of these will provide any food. Pebbles might be thought a shifting and unsure base, but once bulbs have rooted extensively they help form a cohesive whole. These or clean grit are often used for quick growing early ones like 'Paperwhite', 'Cragford', or other tazettas that, once planted and allowed a drink, propel themselves up like rockets. The problem may be to prevent them shooting up too far before blooming. Bulb fibre is still the most popular medium. Traditionally this is mainly peat, normally fibrous, with charcoal and crushed oyster shell added. Nowadays a similar constituent may take the place of shell, and some packs contain a modicum of fertilizer either integrated or in coloured pellet form. It is important that the peat is fibrous since this makes it more open and allows air to stimulate root activity.

The number of bulbs per bowl depends on bowl size and whether one is aiming at a crowded opulent effect or something more restrained. Bulbs can touch each other or, if depth allows, a second layer can nestle between the noses of the first layer. More bulbs mean the container drying out quicker. Bulbs in full growth sup avidly, especially in a warm environment, so that watering should be done regularly.

The earlier the planting, the earlier bulbs may be given the warmth deceiving them into thinking that spring is on the way. The usual target date for the first batch of bloom is early in the New Year. There may be enough colour at Christmas without extra bowls then, but some may want that bit of freshness to add to the festival decorations, and a few kinds can be easily brought into such early display.

For Christmas flowers

'Paperwhite', many-headed white-scented tazettas.

'Scilly White', like 'Paperwhite' but with pale lemon cups.

'Avalanche', a much improved 'Scilly White'.

'Soleil d'Or', tazetta with many golden and orange sweet-scented flowers. Use only bulbs guaranteed virus-free – the results will be spectacular.

'Cragford', a tazetta hybrid with several cream and orange flowers, scented.

'Tête à Tête' and 'Jumblie', dwarf cyclamineus hybrid siblings with a tazetta grandparent. Need to be started early.

'Early Sensation', a traditional yellow trumpet, easily the earliest. Needs starting early.

Other early kinds responding well to forcing are likely to be tazettas, but avoid naturally late-flowering ones like 'Cheerfulness' and 'Geranium'. This last is excellent in containers, but blooms well after Christmas.

Cooled bulbs

Gross deception may be practised on bulbs by manipulating their environment. Lifted bulbs are stored at a temperature of 9° Celsius for a period of nine weeks. They are then planted and, convinced the winter has come and gone, the hurrying flowers can save from three to four weeks up to a very useful ten. Cultivars respond differently – 'Geranium' reacts favourably. Cooling has little or no detrimental effect on the vigour of the bulbs. Bulbs to be treated are lifted and allowed two or three weeks drying, then they are ready for cooling for the nine weeks before planting. Domestic refrigerators may be set at 6–9°C and used to cool a small parcel of bulbs.

Bowls planted early are going to be best, and August is a good month. Place them in a cool spot and keep them moist for a minimum of eight weeks before allowing them any warmth. Energetic extensive root systems must be established before there is any hint of forcing, and it is better to extend the cool rooting time and get this mass of white thirsty roots than to apply warmth too early. Too sudden or too early heat results in the collapse of less robust plants: their roots give up and they come to an undignified halt, never to be restarted.

Each cultivar has its own metabolic pattern. With some the problem is to keep them reined in so that all is not spent before Christmas. 'Cragford' and 'Paperwhite' are two such rapid growers: 'Cragford' I have seen in full bloom outside in September and October with no help. There is therefore no desperate urgency in planting these two. However 'Early Sensation' and 'Tête à Tête' should be planted early to ensure success by making extensive root growth as quickly as possible.

The eight to ten-week cool rooting period may be spent in a shaded corner outside with pots or bowls sunk in the ground, in ashes, or under straw. A covering of 15cm helps to keep all cool. Constant moisture is needed, but not sodden wetness. Bowls with no drainage holes are likely to be flooded quickly, and even those with holes will need careful watching. A piece of plastic sheeting may be helpful. Bulbs in a watery morass will fail, since roots rot.

The bulbs must be persuaded of the cool winter. If this is not possible outside, the coolest spot inside should be found. In the garage or next to the wineracks in the cellar, where they are unlikely to be forgotten and allowed to dry out, could be the answer. The airing cupboard or a position near the central heating boiler must be avoided.

Rooting may be examined carefully. After eight or so weeks the roots may be seen chasing round the surface perimeters of the bowls without it being necessary to upturn one and remove the container. This athletic activity is what we want. Leaf buds may be pushing up from noses. If there are seven or eight centimetres of yellow leaves it is best to introduce the bowls to light gently, since placing them immediately in strong sunlight may cause burning.

Sudden transition from cool to heat can cause problems. Double cultivars may abort, the buds appearing as dry papery tissues. From modest warmth the first week they may move to 12°C, and then forward in seven or ten days to 15–17.5°C. Finally they may enjoy the luxury of your living room at 20°C. This is the equivalent of a commercial forcing routine.

Two common causes of failure are almost too obvious to mention, but may nevertheless get overlooked. First, the bulbs must not dry out, since once they are thoroughly dried there is no instant way to resuscitate them (valuable bulbs can however be planted outside to allow time to exercise its healing touch). The second thing to avoid is not quite so obvious. Human eyes may find the living room beautifully light, but it may seem as gloomy as the middle of a dense jungle to the bulbs. They start straining upwards looking for the missing sun, and their stems grow tall and weak. Even with support the flowers look incongruous on very elongated stalks. Move the bowl as close to the windows as possible.

Pots

Daffodils do well in pots. Here we assume that the bulbs are to be retained. One to three bulbs in a 15cm pot can be managed easily. Small pots are more difficult to manage, drying out quicker, being more vulnerable to frost, and having soil temperatures which fluctuate more erratically. 20cm pots are excellent for growing three to six bulbs. They are heavy in full growth and wet, but if you want to see flowers at their peak this may be the way to achieve it.

Compost may be soilless or John Innes. Peat-based ones are easier to work with and have few drawbacks, provided they are not allowed to dry out. Sensible nutrient levels should be ensured. J.I. potting compost No 3 is excellent if well made. There are also bark-based mediums likely to be launched on the amateur market before long. They may be of:

50% sphagnum peat and/or Perlite
25% granulated pine bark
25% coarse grit
plus slow release fertilizers.

Fertilizers are likely to be locked into slowly decaying resins. Such a mix will have a healthy airy porosity, a moisture impregnated openness that will lead to healthier root production and do away with the stagnant congested masses often found in poorly managed John Innes composts.

Bulbs can be placed on a cushion of compost so that when the rest is added the level is just below the pot's rim, and the noses of bulbs just covered. The covering helps to maintain an even temperature for the living tissue and to prevent damage or the curbing of the growing potential of plant and flower.

Criteria for judging compost are its ability to provide a healthy rooting medium, its water-retaining ability, and its supply of balanced nutrients. Any peat used must be fibrous not dusty, and grit or sharp sand should be clean of clay.

Bulbs potted in August or September will be well rooted before the cold slows activity, and October or November will be still all right provided one is not aiming to force too early in the New Year. If you want flowers just a few weeks early, relatively late planting is not too great a handicap. Lionel Richardson's potted bulbs were not dealt with until this late stage, and their perfection under Jack Goldsmith's handling was second to none.

Growing for show is unlikely to mean any undue haste, a few days gained being all that is required. The procedure may be:

1   Pot bulbs August, September.

2   Plunge pots in ground, or better still in a bed bounded with substantial boards, walls or railway sleepers. Cover with weathered ash, peat, or forest bark, and allow for drainage.

3   Leave until the New Year and then bring pots into a cool greenhouse as required.

4   Maintain airy, buoyant, frost-free atmosphere with plenty of moisture.

5   Keep bulbs moist. As they grow, increase quantities of water. Capillary matting on which to stand pots is a useful aid.

6   If leaf-cutting insects are a problem all ventilators should be covered with fine netting.

7   Use shading when the sunlight becomes strong. This is a worthwhile precaution against flower colour being scorched or faded.

8   After blooming, remove pots to plunge bed outside and ensure adequate watering.

The greater the degree of forcing the bigger the toll on the bulb's reserves. Gentle forcing will produce immaculate blooms without affecting bulbs. Untouched by the vagaries of the weather buds reveal their full potential, and there is no better way of producing show blooms if schedules allow such growing. A careful eye must however be kept on temperatures, and automatic ventilation is a godsend.

Growing for show is not an exact science. Each cultivar behaves differently, and so do different growers. Cultivars under glass sometimes differ significantly in colouring. Newcomers find this means less colour depth. Solid orange cups outside may be rimmed ones with heat under glass. Long-necked ones outside may become inordinately elongated inside.

A cool greenhouse has many advantages. Pots may be on a bench for easier examination; flower textures are often smoother and more crystalline; whites can be whiter; flowers grow larger and bloom a few days earlier; and whatever the weather outside, under cover one can pause, wonder, admire, and tend without hindrance.

Potted bulbs depend on the grower for their needs. Roots that in the garden travel astonishing distances make several circuits of the pot, but will be happy provided they find plenty of moisture and nutrients. Most peat-based and John Innes composts start with plenty of food but daffodils enjoy such copious amounts of water that there is a danger of food shortage later – the bulbs use a lot, but drainage of surplus water will leach more away. It is therefore prudent to augment diets with a fertilizer. Balanced ones, rather high in potash, are likely to be most suitable, and tomato ones at half strength can be useful. Care is usually taken of bulbs up until flowering, but afterwards there is a tendency to be less caring. They do however need water and feed at this stage to prevent the bulbs being badly checked.

After they have bloomed it may be best to turn out the pots and plant the bulbs in the garden in the site where they are to grow the following year. They need planting deeper than they were in the pots. Alternatively they may be returned to the plunge bed and allowed to die down naturally. Then one can see how good a job has been done in growing them. Plump hard bulbs gain top marks, but if some seem wasted and soft their culture has probably been at fault.

7

Propagating your daffodils

The four basic methods of propagation are by seed, by natural bulb division, by inducing small bulbils from sliced pieces of bulbs, and by tissue culture.

By seed

Species depend mainly on seed for increase. Hybrids, with mixed genetic material, do not breed true, but may give improved or quite different flowers. A species is not a series of manufactured look-alikes, but an expression of a theme within the governing confines of their genetic inheritance. There is variation in many characteristics, with more in some than others, and sometimes vastly more within one species than another. Populations within one species can be far more volatile than those within others.

N. triandrus is almost exclusively dependent on seed for its increase, spread, and survival. *N. bulbocodium* and other hoop petticoats are heavy seeders and, though some forms make clumps, others are less vegetatively prolific. Pods may have 50–100 seeds, and as clumps may give anything from a single bloom to perhaps a few dozen, a clump has the potential to instigate a population explosion. Rates of survival in the wild must be low. To find a stand of a species not freely seeding suggests that it is the result of a single clone spread by cultivation or by shifting mountain soils moved by erosion or the scrambling feet of goats or sheep.

Clones of wild daffodils are to a degree inhibited from setting seed by their own pollen. Pollination by another clone of their species helps to preserve a healthy pool of genetic material. Hybrids may not set seed readily, though some do.

Fertilization is followed by swelling pods, but fat green pods do not always mean seeds within – false-pregnancy routines are not uncommon. Normally seeds are ripe some six to eight weeks after the flowers have faded.

If the harvest is to be safely gathered in, the pods must be watched, for split seed scatters widely and is difficult to find. The answer is to harvest the pods just as soon as you can hear the loose seeds rattling inside.

Viability starts high, and remains good for some weeks or months, but the longer seed is out of the ground the lower the rate of germination and the more erratic it is in timing. It is best to sow it quickly after collection.

In some parts it may be permissible to sow in drills in the open. In Britain this can only be done if the germinating seed is protected from winter frosts. Freezing and thawing of soil raises the top few centimetres into the air. This may bring up the germinating seedlings to be left high and dry afterwards. It is easier to sow in containers and keep these under cover at least through the winter, or to sow in frames that can be insulated.

Any container provided with adequate drainage may be used if the compost is a healthy one. As seed and seedlings are going to remain here for two seasons before planting out, the containers should be strong enough to stand this time. Very large ones are difficult to handle, but very small pots dry out too quickly and soil temperatures fluctuate too much.

Seed germinates by growing downwards and then bending to come vertically up, eventually breaking the soil surface as a thin round rush-like leaf in the New Year. The U-bend is where a swelling starts and becomes the bulb. By July strong hybrid seedlings may have a bulb about pea-width but an elongated bottle shape. Tiny species will be smaller, often white and rounded.

Hybrid seedlings make their second year's growth at the same time as mature bulbs. A single flattened leaf is normal. Another year will see a couple of leaves, and the fourth or fifth year may produce a flower.

Some species grow with a will and in favourable conditions bloom in their third year, and we have had lots of hoop petticoats in bloom in eighteen months. These can be kept in almost perpetual growth. Once started, and kept moist and free of pests and weeds, the young bulbs thrive. Home-grown species bulbs may be a revelation compared to the miserable collected wild ones so often sold. Jonquils and African hoop petticoats may benefit from a few weeks of drought in the summer, but even these are soon back expanding their bulbous strength.

Differences between growing in open aerated composts and badly consolidated ones are seen in the size of bulbs and their rates of increase. Young plants need moisture and air in the soil. Once possessed of a healthy root system they will take some gentle feeding. Half-strength tomato fertilizer works wonders – Phostrogen and others can be good.

Species seedlings can be turned out after their second year, but they may be small and care needs to be taken. These are best grown on in fresh containers or frames until they reach flowering size, in their third or fourth season.

Hybrid seedlings are planted out in nursery rows in the summer of their second season. Here they remain for three years. The site should be free from perennial weeds, and the bulbs, although small, should be given plenty of space – 7–8cm apart in the row is the closest one can plant them, and the rows should be far enough apart to allow free access. The better they are grown the higher will be the proportion blooming the fourth rather than the fifth year. Saving a complete year is a huge advantage, and the easiest time to try to do this is in the first two seasons when the young plants can be encouraged to achieve rates of increase that are proportionately much greater than are ever likely to happen again.

As with most gardening activities, each gardener is likely to evolve personal procedures. Of paramount importance is a foolproof labelling system, since there is a long period without any clue to identity.

Increase by bulbs

Rates of increase for species vary from very, very slow as with *N. triandrus concolor*, to hugely prolific with some such as *N. requienii* and *N. willkommii*. Clones within a species vary dramatically. Kinds such as *N. obvallaris* and *N. poeticus hellenicus* may be treated in the same way as hybrids.

Expectations of bulbous increase will vary according to treatment, climatic conditions, and cultivar. Left more or less to their own devices, bulbs will increase their weight by between 50 and 100 per cent during a season. Complicated mathematics are not needed to show that several years are needed to accumulate reasonable stocks of a new individual seedling. It is good sense to do all possible for an important new kind. On a small scale this can be managed – commercial stocks are another matter.

The Ministry of Agriculture's Rosewarne Experimental Horticultural Station at Camborne in Cornwall undertook variety trials for a prolonged period and published two reports about the performance of many cultivars. One of the factors reported on was the percentage increase in the weight of bulbs over a two year period. The general results were summed up as cyclamineus, jonquil and poeticus kinds being very prolific, large and small cups being prolific, and trumpets and tazettas being moderate. From the second report covering the years 1964–67 the following results were obtained for the following kinds (my selection):

Cultivar	% weight increase in 2 years	Cultivar	% weight increase in 2 years
Actaea	220	Kilworth	255
Beryl	270	King Alfred	154
Binkie	281	Mount Hood	217
Brunswick	158	poeticus	
Carlton	223	recurvus	325
Cheerfulness	328	obvallaris	373
Dutch Master	211	St Keverne	182
Early Sensation	243	Van Sion	208
February Gold	208	Thalia	205
Golden Ducat	127	Unsurpassable	183
Golden Harvest	201	White Lion	212

Healthy bulbs and healthy soil will give the maximum increase if provided with adequate moisture and food. Optimum conditions will produce increase vastly exceeding the average expectations, and will involve feeding regimes which rely heavily on potash (potassium) which has a striking influence on the health and increase of bulbs. Response to extra nitrogen and phosphate is very muted.

In garden conditions a general fertilizer with a NPK formula approximating to the following will be effective:

N:Nitrogen: 10
P:Phosphorus: 10
K:Potassium: 20

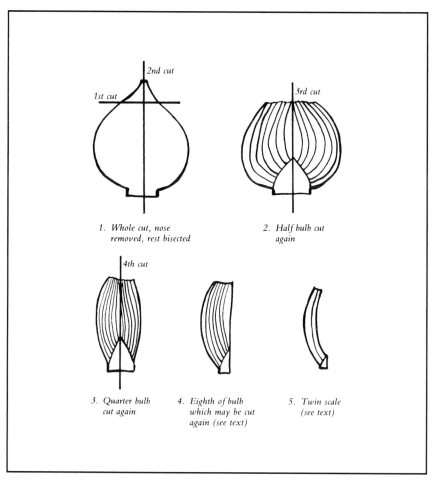

1. Whole cut, nose removed, rest bisected

2. Half bulb cut again

3. Quarter bulb cut again

4. Eighth of bulb which may be cut again (see text)

5. Twin scale (see text)

19   Diagram of bulb cut for chipping

Twin scaling and chipping

Cutting bulbs to make them produce adventitious bulbils is not a new idea – damage to bulb bases will sometimes cause a series of small bulbils to form. Experiments many years ago showed this was possible but it remained impractical knowledge until the advent of systemic fungicides that prevent ever-present organisms from rotting the damaged tissue.

Chipping, sometimes called chitting, and twin scaling are variations on a theme. Chipped bulbs may produce from around 20–70 small bulbs after a 12-month period. Well grown, these may be of flowering size in two years, and in three years should all be flowering.

The procedure is as follows:

1   Select and label healthy bulbs in active growth. If possible isolate such bulbs from main stocks.

2   At lifting time, raise selected bulbs and sort out undamaged round ones. All may be used, but it is easier to work with onion-shaped ones. The best time to operate is June and July.

3   Cleanly cup off the nose end of each bulb leaving the major three-quarters to two-thirds.

4   Retained portion is cut in half and then into quarters vertically. It is imperative that each section has its fair share of the basal plate, for without the base no bulbils will form. Depending on the size of the original bulb, the quarter section may be divided into two or more segments. Final segments should not be less than around 5–8mm wide.

5   Segments are immediately immersed in a solution of a systemic fungicide such as Benlate for a period of 20–30 minutes.

6   Segments are placed in damp clean vermiculite in a plastic bag that is closed to make it airtight, but with a good bubble of air inside. Dry vermiculite takes up huge quantities of water when soaking. To prepare it it should be left half an hour or so in a container of water, which may then be turned on its side and the surplus water allowed to drain away. It may be left for an hour or even overnight. Do not add further water to moistened vermiculite as it will then collapse and become useless. Two or three handfuls of the damp vermiculite in a bag measuring 20 × 25cm will be sufficient. Bulb segments can be joggled around to effect an even distribution, and one or two close to the edge will allow progress to be monitored.

7   Plastic bags of any size are fine, but must be clean. Smallish sizes are easier and more prudent – it is better to have two small ones than one large one. Even with every care, sometimes infection can start and then it is good to know there is a second bag left with valuable propagating material.

8   Labelling is vital. One slice of bulb looks like any other. Using waterproof pens or pencils, a plastic name label is enclosed with the sections, and bags should also be written on.

9   Bags are placed where the temperature remains as close as possible to 21°C. This may or may not be a light area.

10   After seven or eight weeks each section will have formed at least one, two or three fairly substantial bulbils. Sometimes a leaf appears. They may have started to form roots, and are ready to be planted out.

11   Bulbils should not be allowed to dry out. Their treatment will depend on your own resources of time and equipment. It is legitimate to plant them outside in nursery rows in well dug and worked soil, and watered well and covered with polythene they should be all right. Five centimetres of soil over the small bulbils is necessary; their vulnerable time is during frosty weather when they can be pulled up by frost, and nursery rows outside are practicable only where frost protection is possible.

One effective way of dealing with small quantities is to have containers with compost ready for bulbils to be planted in immediately, 2.5cm or more deep and about 2.5cm apart. They are kept moist. Compost should be open, with good drainage and plenty of air. Good results have been obtained by using equal amounts of John Innes No 1 or a soilless compost with equal volumes of Perlite (traction grit) – inert inorganic granules of expanded mineral that improves drainage whilst helping to retain moisture and nutrients. Compost depth is not less than 10cm.

Commercial quantities are likely to be planted under polythene tunnels.

12   Planted and watered, the containers may be enclosed in large plastic bags to preserve moisture and create a helpful microclimate. In a cold frame or cool greenhouse as the warm weather passes the bulbs start to grow and the bags can be removed and the plants kept moist and free of frost.

13   Foliage will appear with other daffodil foliage in early spring if the bulbils are outside, but an eye ought to be kept on them, because sometimes they can be precocious and will need frost protection. Under glass bulbs grow earlier, and the idea is to make sure they have as long a growing period as possible.

14   In June or July, after a year growing, young bulbs can be planted out in nursery rows and left for two seasons until they reach flowering size.

Twin scaling

Initially this got greater publicity than chipping, which is much the more popular method. This takes chipping a stage further. Instead of leaving the final chipped segments complete, these are divided further. It means one starts with more viable parts and large numbers of bulbils can be achieved – 100 from a bulb is possible. Two main problems are the greater care needed to subdivide the segments, and the greater chance of infection and rotting. Bulbils may be more numerous but smaller.

In the diagram of a bulb cut for chipping a section of bulb as used for chipping shows six scales. The aim in twin scaling is to divide these into three pairs by cutting through the basal plate at the bottom of every other scale. Three pairs of scales with attached bit of basal plate should then be ready to be treated with a systemic fungicide and the same subsequent treatment as the chipped sections.

Tissue culture

This is still an expensive laboratory technique not normally suitable for the amateur. The growing point, the meristem, is isolated from the bulb, and placed in a culture to grow lots of undifferentiated tissue that can later be divided and allowed to form small bulbs. Meristems are cut out in the aseptic conditions of an enclosed air-filtered cabinet. Each is introduced into a flask of culture medium and kept at the optimum temperature to initiate the maximum rate of cell division. The tiny fragment soon becomes a sizeable mass. This is retrieved and divided into many pieces each as small as the original. Each fragment then forms the starter tissue in a fresh culture flask.

In theory the process may be repeated until enough material for the required number of individual plants has been grown. In practice it is wise to return to the original source material after a few divisions, and use the meristem of a fresh bulb or bulbs. This lessens the danger that if a mutation occurs in the flask, this mutated material may be propagated unknowingly. Mutations can be discovered only when tissue has been taken from the culture and allowed to grow differentiated tissue of bulbs, and these have grown on to flowering size. This may take three or more years with daffodils, and involve a great deal of time, labour, and expense.

If you have sent bulb material to a laboratory for tissue culture, it is convenient to arrange the return of the resulting plantlets in the early spring, perhaps February. I have found this best, with the young being grown on under cover for a few months before dying down in the summer, and being treated like any other small young bulbs thereafter.

8

Exhibiting daffodils

In Britain two main shows are organized by the Royal Horticultural Society. Others are sponsored by the Daffodil Society, and there are countless local shows featuring daffodils heavily. The different branches of the American Daffodil Society run shows in their various regions, so that by moving around you can be knee deep in daffodils for months. New Zealand and Australian fanciers are just as keen and their shows maintain the highest standards (see appendix for details of societies).

The RHS daffodil competition and its daffodil show are both held in April, for the former some time in the first ten days of the month, and the latter two or three weeks later. Each is held in conjunction with a show of general interest and is open to the public for two days. Competitors may stage exhibits the day before or, if they have only a limited number, on the first day of the show before the judging at ten o'clock.

The Daffodil Society's main show is usually held in Birmingham or within easy distance of the city. In many years it may suit some flowers and growers better, being usually a week later than the RHS show. Competitions are also held at Harrogate, with the North of England Horticultural Society's marvellous spring show. These Harrogate competitions are organized by the Daffodil Society, and are becoming more important each year. Growing numbers of local shows have standards reaching or already at national status.

RHS, Daffodil Society, and ADS show schedules are comprehensive. Being under constant review they reflect the interests of growers and the availability of various types of flowers (for schedules see addresses in appendix). Basically, there are classes for single flowers of each colour class of each division; there are classes for collections of flowers within one division or for several divisions; popular collection classes may call for three blooms of each of three cultivars; and there will be classes for floral effect. Fanciers take the keenest interest in classes for seedlings raised by the exhibitor, for top novelties are likely to make their début here.

Showing

Experienced judges can usually see clearly how prizes ought to be allocated amongst competing single blooms. There will be close contenders, and in the very, very last resort the judge's personal preferences may tilt the balance. This final weight thrown in the balance is infrequently used, and very much less than competitors may believe. At national level judging is almost always excellent.

Accepted scales of points are laid down. One scale is for single blooms, and another for classes with three or more blooms in a vase.

The RHS scale of points:

In a class for single blooms:

Colour	5 points
Form	5 points
Condition	4 points
Size (for cultivar)	3 points
Texture	3 points
Poise	3 points
Stem	2 points
total	25 points

In a class with three or more blooms in a vase:

Condition	4 points
Form	4 points
Colour	4 points
Size (for cultivar)	3 points
Poise	3 points
Stems	2 points
Uniformity	2 points
total	25 points

The American Daffodil Society scale of points:

Condition	20%
Form	20%
Substance & Texture	15%
Colour	15%
Pose	10%
Stem	10%
Size	10%
	100

These scales may guide exhibitors.

Colour Everything else being equal, the best-coloured flower wins. Clean uniform colour wins over muddied shades; there should be no fading or burning; and in whites, the whiter the flower the better.

Form Flower balance should feel right. The corona of a trumpet or long cup should not be so wide as to look ungainly and out of proportion with the perianth; perianths should be flat in all the first three divisions; and petals should be broad and even, with many judges preferring rounded to triangular or pointed petals.

Condition Flowers need to be fresh, and as far as possible without flaw, natural or unnatural. They should neither show signs of ageing nor look as if they have been picked too early. Blooms need time to acquire proper character. If a bloom threatens to come to its peak a few days before the show date it may be cut and kept in a cool cellar, the domestic refrigerator, or in a cold store kept at just above freezing point – frozen flowers are useless. We have kept flowers in cold store for 14 weeks and had them on our Chelsea stand at the end of May for several days in good order.

Size Flower size should be in character for the cultivar. Except sometimes in miniature or intermediate-sized kinds, the bigger flower gains points.

Texture Not the most obvious characteristic to a newcomer. Flowers should be of firm substance and look like silk rather than coarse linen. They should be as far as possible without creases or wrinkles.

Poise Some good flowers are spoilt by long necks that do not hold the flower firmly enough. Some point slightly upwards naturally, and this is permissible provided it is not taken to extremes, but a tendency to look downwards severely in flowers of the first four divisions loses them points. Flowers are for seeing, not hiding.

Stem   Stems should be strong without looking grossly stout. They should be unmarked by disease or physical damage, and dark green is preferred to a yellowy shade.

Even excellent blooms may not get just recognition if poorly staged. Ideally a bloom should stand vertically, looking boldly at the judges. Long and short cups need to look squarely to the front. If a bloom tends to look down it may be persuaded to correct this by being left in a bucket at a slope facing down. Left in this way for a few hours in a position where it needs to make an effort to reach for light, it may well move through several degrees. It is also possible to improve the angle of presentation by gently bending it backwards at the neck, but there is a limit to the amount of this type of manipulation that is practical, and care needs to be taken especially with short necked ones as they are often brittle. It is one of life's rules – the better the flower the more brittle the neck.

Trumpet kinds have a natural inclination to look slightly downwards – a perfectly correct and sensible posture that saves them filling up with rainwater, and of course the characteristic triandrus and cyclamineus pose is downwards. With multi-headed stems it is worth looking at the disposition of individual florets and perhaps teasing one away from another if they seem too crowded.

The traditional material used for arranging blooms in narrow vases is clean fresh moss. Having placed a little in the neck of the vase, the flowers and leaves can be added and more moss worked in to keep all steady in parade-ground stance. The moss may be neatly trimmed with scissors. Others will find Oasis easier, cleaner, quicker, and tidier. It is essential to soak it thoroughly before use.

Blooms will be accompanied by clean upright disease-free foliage that may be picked from any variety. Stocks of a healthy-leaved cheap kind can be kept for foliage. In vases the upright foliage will look most natural with its tips about 2–4cm below the level of the blooms. With flowers and leaves correctly arranged in clean vases, all that remains is to look to the finer points. Exhibits must be correctly and neatly labelled. It is worth double-checking with the show schedule to make sure every entry is in its correct place. It is easy when dealing with many classes inadvertently to leave a vase in the wrong area. Few things equal the annoyance and upset to one's ego caused by arriving after judging to find scrawled on your entry card 'NAS' – not according to schedule. Make sure that there is enough water to satisfy the needs of flowers and leaves.

Finer points could include a little grooming of the blooms. Surprising improvements can be engineered by gentle persuasion. One can help petals to lie flat by lightly brushing back offending segments with a large soft-haired brush such as are used by watercolourists. Gentle massaging with finger and thumb is permissible if done with very great care – no bruising or breaking of cells must disfigure the bloom. The aim is petals lying in one flat plane at right angles to the stigma. When working with the petals, care must also be taken not to push them back onto the brittle point of the dried sheath behind the flowers.

Individual show blooms look best with the top petal centrally positioned, and this top petal should be for preference one of the inner three. Usually the flower achieves this naturally, but slight adjustments can be made by delicately twisting the flower from the rear. Where three or more blooms are in a vase, the best bloom is normally picked for the top leading one, provided it has a stem long enough for the role. In trios the two supporting blooms will be equally spaced below, and there will be air between all the flowers now arranged as an equilateral triangle.

Much work will have been done before the show date. Bulbs grown in pots may have been brought into the cool greenhouse – sometimes only to be shunted out again and placed in a cool area to try to delay blooming. An eye is kept on potential blooms in the open, and kinds that lose their best colour in the sun are picked just on opening or are shaded from the sun's rays.

Exhibitors build up collections so that if one kind for a certain class has passed its peak there is another later cultivar just ready to enter the lists. It is possible to split stocks in order to have one lot of bulbs growing in a warm early spot, but some others in cool conditions which may make a difference of a week or more to the flowering time. Later planting can also influence flowering dates a little, and two-year-down bulbs usually bloom earlier.

Flowers are better for a long drink before starting their journey to the show – overnight in water helps to harden them. If you are going by car, it is best to have the flowers safely in buckets that are wedged so that they cannot slide or tip when you have to brake suddenly. Flowers need to be kept from rubbing against each other. Some Oasis, flower arrangers' foam, in the bottom of the bucket will provide a firm base for the stems. A grid over the bucket top, even if it is only a carefully bent-over piece of chicken wire, will mean that each bloom can be kept clear of its neighbour. However anything like chicken wire must have all sharp ends bent safely over to prevent your best flower being speared.

Travelling by train or aircraft means packing flowers in boxes without water. Get firm flower boxes, line them with tissue paper, and pin a pillow of paper across the top of the box so that the first row of flowers can be laid in with their upper petals resting on the paper pillow – a further roll of tissue may be pinned below the lower petals. The blooms are now stable. Further rows may be added and each made firm. Although it is possible to pack rows alternately at the top and bottom of the boxes, it is wiser to work from one end only, even if this means using extra boxes. It avoids the extra chance of accidents. Once at the show the flowers are retrieved and placed in a bucket with some water. Slivers are cut off the bottom of stems whilst under water so that they can imbibe freely.

The temptation to list good show kinds is resisted here since a few seasons will make such a list out of date. Most fanciers will make the best choice within their financial budget – the sternest competition and the highest prices reign in the first three divisions. Expensive novelties are not always winners – it is easier to find good flowers from a number of bulbs of a proven show kind than to depend on the one or two buds of a single newly purchased one. A good stable of likely winners can be got together for all divisions from 5 to 11 without undue expense.

Notes on show-worthiness will be found in chapters devoted to reviewing cultivars. Past show results published by the RHS and other societies will give prospective exhibitors real pointers towards cultivars worth considering.

It is part of the fun of the hobby to see how others manage their daffodil affairs and to evolve your own winning methods. Winning may or may not be relevant to you, but certainly the care you have taken with your flowers will have encouraged an even greater appreciation of their beauty.

9

Trumpet daffodils

These are daffodils with a long history of breeding, but they remain some of the most stubborn to improve significantly. Reasons for this can be found. Basic crosses between trumpets and poeticus types started the continuing avalanche of novelties. A mass of genetic material was stirred up in a large pot. As early diploids gave way to tetraploids scope for variation increased dramatically, and it became apparent that a series of genes governed the length of the corona. Producing full length trumpets from the mixed progeny was not easy, even by backcrossing onto trumpet types, whilst restricting breeding to trumpets severely limited the gene palette.

Various species and forms were grown well before breeders got to work in the the 1850s. By our standards they were not impressive. *N. pseudonarcissus* types proved poor breeders. There were no good white species – pretty and dainty they may have been, but they were small miffy plants with flowers looking severely downwards. There were however a couple of useful yellows in *N. hispanicus* and *N. obvallaris*. The former was then known as *N. maximus* or *N. maximus superbus*, appropriate names for an outstanding plant unapproached in size and vigour by any except good forms of *N. bicolor*. Botanists had a fine time with *N. hispanicus*. It is officially now *N. pseudonarcissus* subsp. *obvallaris* var. *maximus*. Gardeners and some botanists will find this name confusing. *N. p. obvallaris* is totally distinct, with its flowers in form and character almost as far as possible removed from '*hispanicus*' whilst still remaining a yellow trumpet. We retain the more sensible name *N. hispanicus* for the sake of clarity.

Breeders played with other species like *N. minor* and even *N. asturiensis*, but basically the trumpet breeding stock was *N. hispanicus*,

N. obvallaris, N. moschatus as defined by the *Flora Europaea*, and *N. bicolor*.

Each founder species had strengths and weaknesses to contribute. *N. hispanicus* had deep-gold bordering on orange, strong stems, and blue-green foliage all very much on the credit side, but with a suspicion of capriciousness about growing, and the propeller twist of petals could also be a problem; *N. obvallaris* contributed good form and a neat habit but was a trifle small; and whites provided smoothness of texture, a leavening process for offspring of mixed colour parentage. These white founding species were poor bulbs.

N. bicolor provided a more fleshy strength and vigour than *N. hispanicus*, giving size, usually good form, and very definite bicolouring. The deep-yellow pigment of the trumpet tends to run into the white of the petals, something not liked by fanciers, and genetic linking between the dark trumpet colour and the spillage onto the petals still provides breeders with problems. The choice seems still to be between a clean division of white petals and pale yellow trumpet, and a rich contrast in colour but less clearly defined margins between white and yellow.

None of today's leading trumpet kinds are bred from pure blood lines. Yellows have some white blood, the best whites have yellow or bicolour blood in their make up, and the bicoloured ones are likely to have both yellow and white ones in their ancestry. Reversed bicolours owe allegiance to all three strands.

The greatest impacts early on were made by the white 'Mme de Graaff' (1887) and 'King Alfred' (1899).

We review the trumpets by colour.

Yellow trumpets

N. hispanicus is the dominant species in the history of yellow trumpets, and is important for many others too. It is now rarish, ousted by its descendants which grow rather less capriciously. Large, dark tuniced, round, hard bulbs produce a plant with firm upright leaves with a characteristic twist. Tall, strong stems hold the deepest gold blooms in a bold jutting pose. Groups make attractive early pictures, the blue-green foliage augmenting the rich flowers with their informal propeller twisted petals and notched trumpets. These are noticeably long in comparison with *N. obvallaris* and proportionately much longer than they are wide. The twist of the petals looks fine in this flower but it is something breeders have since been trying to iron out. The flowers are very durable.

'King Alfred' was a major leap forward. Its breeding is unknown but it must have inherited its good colour, stems and durability from *N. hispanicus*. For many decades it was the standard yellow, and it remains the one name known by people who know no other. There is only a handful of genuine 'King Alfred' bulbs now grown, though many other kinds are offered under this name. It inherited some of the fastidiousness about growing of *N. hispanicus* – fat Dutch bulbs would do well the first year, and then dwindle year by year. The same behaviour may be seen in its double sport, 'Golden Ducat', still widely available .

Many early bulbs of 'King Alfred' were sold for the astronomical price of £10. Engleheart introduced other *N. hispanicus* seedlings. 'Magnificence' (1914) is an early one still to be found on sale, an obvious *hispanicus*, and other smoother flowers had this same species as parent, 'Sulphur' and 'Godolphin' being two.

Refinement was added by using white and bicolours. 'White Emperor' × 'King Alfred' gave the well formed mid-yellow 'Hebron' (1923), and this in its turn gave the very neat 'Cromarty' (1933). Earlier Dr Lower had produced a smooth mid-yellow called 'Royalist' with pointed petals and overall chaste form.

P. D. Williams bred his daffodils in Cornwall where *N. hispanicus* flourished. It backed many of his trumpet and long-cupped kinds. Deep-golden long cup 'Crocus' (1927) from P. D. Williams was crossed with 'Cromarty' to produce Richardson's 'Goldcourt (1937). This is only medium-sized but of a thick velvety texture with very deep colour in its narrow trumpet, and neat petals. The following year Richardson introduced his 'Royalist' seedling, 'Kingscourt', a kind that is still a flower to reckon with. Much larger than 'Goldcourt', it is not so deep, but its wide flat petals and well-balanced trumpet make an ideal traditional flower.

Intercrossing 'Goldcourt' and 'Kingscourt' gave a fresh generation of excellent golden flowers. 'Arctic Gold' (1951) is like an improved 'Goldcourt' with a wider-flanged mouth and wide petals, but the same rich colour, and 'King's Ransom' (1950) and the later flowering 'Spanish Gold' (1948) were two other fine flowers of this lineage. 'Viking' from the same parents is like a larger 'Kingscourt' but with a less flanged mouth.

Deep-golden flowers are always welcome, but the use of bicolour and white blood produced paler sorts. Most important of these were

lemon ones that came from the famous cross 'King of the North ×
'Content' first essayed by Guy Wilson. 'King of the North' (1927) was
a Brodie flower from 'King Alfred' by the bicolour 'Glory of
Noordwijk'. 'Content (1927) was a P. D. Williams pale one from the
yellow 'Lord Antrim' crossed by the fine white 'Beersheba'. Guy
Wilson must have been highly delighted when he saw his progeny.
They ranged from delightful self-lemons to the intriguing ones that
after opening lemon had trumpets that faded to white and so became
reversed bicolours like 'Spellbinder'. One of the largest of the series
was 'Moonstruck', a huge bloom of impressive form with flat
triangular petals and a well-balanced trumpet, nobly flanged. In pale
lemonade shades it looked ghostly, but it was a sufficiently substantial
flower to stay the course well. 'Maraval', a few tones darker, was in
various vibrant tones. Somewhat newer is 'Lemon Cloud', a large
flower with pointed petals and long trumpets, all in pale-lemon shades.

Repeating the Wilson cross, Grant Mitsch in Oregon produced a
new race. Some were reverses, while others were shades of lemon.
'Moonmist' is useful for its early flowers with pointed petals and well
flanged trumpets, and is impressive but not too tall. 'Moonshot' is one
of the finest, with a perfectly balanced flower with a flat perianth of
wide petals and neatly serrated not-too-long trumpet. A day or two
after opening it may show buffiness in the trumpet.

There are a number of flowers raised in New Zealand and Australia
that equal the best northern hemisphere ones, and at present leading
golden ones would include the American 'Inca Gold'. Colour, earliness
and durability make it first-rate in the garden. 'Prosperity' (1978)
comes from two long-cupped parents, the reverse bicolour 'Nazareth'
crossed by the golden 'Butterscotch'. It is an excellent show type in
shining golden lemon.

Red trumpets

An early dream was the idea of an orange trumpet daffodil. Trans-
forming the dream into reality took well over 100 hundred years.
Trained geneticist W. O. Backhouse, the son of famous daffodil
breeding parents who had themselves being trying for the same goal,
started work. His parents had only managed three-quarter-length
flowers such as 'Backhouse's Giant' and had singularly failed to get
any coloured trumpets. W. O. Backhouse crossed a yellow trumpet
with a red-cupped kind and raised a generation of three-quarter-length
ones all of which were yellow. Intercrossing these he raised a further

generation of some 400 plants. Some were trumpets, but none were coloured. The original generation were now numbered and each was backcrossed with the red-cupped parent. Each parent had between 20 and 40 seedlings. Of this generation only 2 to 15 per cent had red colouring, and no full-length trumpets were coloured. Of the first generation No 17 proved the most useful. It eventually gave a number of red-trumpeted seedlings and from these were bred the red trumpets such as 'Brer Fox'. This was a largish flower with broad ribby petals and a flanged trumpet of rich orange. Unfortunately the stem was weak. When Mr Backhouse died I was happily surprised to find that he had left me the bulbs of 'Brer Fox' in a codicil to his will. We have used it to produce further flowers of which the best yet is 'Hero', with trumpets of tangerine. We have found the red trumpets chary of producing seed, but remain hopeful that more interesting flowers will arrive. Good full trumpets of gold and orange-red will make attractive garden plants.

Bicolour trumpets

Many of the first white trumpets introduced were really pale bicolours. Others were genuine bicolours like 'Empress' (1865) bred from *N. bicolour* × *N. pseudonarcissus*. This can still be found growing contentedly in old gardens and churchyards. Milk-white petals back bright yellow trumpets. The next real advance came with the flowers of P. D. Williams. His 'Content' (1927) was one that opened a pale lemon overall but soon faded to white, with the trumpet left only a tone or so darker lemon.

It was the Williams long cups that really brought about significant advances in the show qualities. 'Niphetos' was a tough plant with durable long-cupped flowers white petalled and with crowns of cream. Crossing it with large white trumpet 'Kanchenjunga' produced some excellent bicolour trumpets. 'Preamble' (1946) would still be a leading kind today if its bulbs had been a more sensible size. Silken smooth white perianths backed carefully flanged trumpets of a rich chrome yellow. 'Newcastle' (1957) from the same parents still holds its place as a show flower, and is still winning more prizes in this showclass than any other cultivar even though it has the annoying habit of partially twisting an inner petal to give a slightly hooded effect.

'Frolic' (1958) (seedling × 'Kanchenjunga') from America is one of the cleanest two-coloured flowers, with flat triangular petals shining snow-white and bold trumpets somewhat goffer-crimped at the mouth a bright lemon. 'Descano' (1965) ('Frolic' × 'Polindra') is an elegant clean flower, with flat pointed petals and a narrow trumpet of clear primrose lemon.

White-and-yellow bicolours have never engendered the excitement produced by white and pink ones, although these have not proved any too easy to breed. 'Rima' (1954) (Kenmare × Dawnglo) was one of the first to make an impact with very rich pink trumpets. 'Candyfloss' (1985), due to the sheer size of its blaring trumpet of pink, cannot be overlooked but truth to tell it is showy rather than refined. However refinement is now being added to colour. 'At Dawning' (1975) is like a better-formed smaller 'Rima', its father-mother was 'Radiation' (White Sentinel' × 'Mrs Backhouse'). From 'At Dawning' × 'Graduation' came 'Pink Silk' (1983), a larger and more brightly coloured flower. Wide perianths of clean petals back a chaste trumpet lightly flared at the mouth and a good pure pink.

'Memento' (1979) has mixed colour that makes classification difficult. At present it is listed 1YW-P. As explained in the chapter on classification, the number 1 refers to the form of the flower which is of the trumpet division, the letters before the hyphen indicate petal colour, and the letter after the hyphen gives the corona colour. Pale lemon petals shade down to ivory white and make a good perianth behind a narrow trumpet of apricot pink. 'Prophet' (1975), bred from 'Spellbinder' × 'Maiden's Blush' is a beautiful shape, a lemon 'Cantatrice' with long pointed petals and slender trumpet. The whole flower is a cool lemon, but the trumpet fleetingly flushes pink. Some of the flowers from Australia and New Zealand have these interesting colours – 'Red Conquest' has creamy lemon petals and a large flanged trumpet strongly suffused peachy pink – and more flowers of this type are now appearing.

White trumpets

Wild white trumpets are small hunchbacked flowers from around the Pyrenees. Most are palely bicoloured. There is no absolute botanical truth about them: depending on the temperament of the botanist reviewing them they are looked at as a series of species or as a single variable one. *Flora Europaea* has them all as *N. pseudonarcissus* subsp. *moschatus*. Some have been grown for centuries in European gardens, and were treasured when there was little competition. By vegetative increase clones became widely distributed and rather rigid conceptions were engendered of the wild species – Nature has never been as tidy as botanists and gardeners.

'Mme de Graaff' (1887), bred from *N. albescens* by pollen of the bicolor 'Empress', was classed as a white although really milk-white and pale primrose. Self-pollinated seed gave 'White Knight' (1907) a real improvement in vigour and all-round quality. It would be thought dwarf now, but it was taller and larger than the species. Narrow well-formed trumpets with a good flange combined with petals which were reasonably wide and smooth. They were held slightly forward but not so much as in the white species.

By crossing 'King Alfred' with 'Mme de Graaff' the fine 'Mrs E. H. Krelage' (1912) was bred. Although registered as a white trumpet it was always a pale bicolour. Vigour was now firmly established. It was a tall kind of good form, and was still being sold after the Second World War. It was in the garden when I started breeding as a child.

Engleheart had bred a number of good whites but the most exciting development took place when he topped all previous triumphs with his 'Beersheba' (1923). From 'White Knight' crossed by a seedling, it was immediately recognized as way out in front of any other runners. Strong bulbs, healthy dark foliage, and sturdy stems held flowers of amazing size and very distinct character. Long triangular pointed petals were welded at right angles to the trumpet, with no hint of leaning forward. Trumpets were long and narrow but neatly flanged. Above all else, soon after opening, the flowers were a sparkling pure white. It was the first white to gain real recognition from the general public.

Broadly, there were two main types of white trumpets being bred. 'Beersheba' was followed by Guy Wilson's 'Cantatrice' and these typified one type, one having flowers with narrow trumpets and pointed petals. They were closer in character to the original species. Bred in parallel were pale bicolours masquerading as whites, which had widely-flanged trumpets and more rounded petals.

The Brodie's 'Askelon' (1923) was typical of this second persuasion. It marked the beginning of a trend towards larger wide-petalled flowers. Its perianth was a marvel of its age, an ample backcloth lying flat away from a bell-shaped trumpet. It was widely used to breed long cups and trumpets. The Brodie registered 'Courage' in 1933 whilst Guy Wilson introduced his 'Kanchenjunga' in 1934, both of these owning 'Askelon' as father.

12cm-wide 'Kanchenjunga' made the way forward plain enough. The width of its petals was such that three could have done perianth duty for the whole six, and a purist might have said that the trumpet was too wide. This giant's pollen on pale bicolour 'Trostan' gave the even larger 'Broughshane' (1938), named after the small Co. Antrim village where Guy Wilson spent his life. This massive flower was whiter than either parent, and whilst it had a huge trumpet, this was now in better balance. It would grow to 15 centimetres across in Broughshane.

Pollen of the fantastic 'Kanchenjunga' was widely used, and to some considerable effect. On long cup 'Courage' it gave, amongst others, the fine 'Glenshesk' (1950) and the pure white 'Vigil' (1947). This last, with pointed petals and a narrow trumpet neatly flanged, was highly thought of for decades and is still grown. It married the two traditions in white breeding. 'Kanchenjunga' pollen on the white-and-cream long cup 'Guardian' (1942) gave Guy Wilson what he felt was the finest flower he introduced, 'Empress of Ireland' (1952). It certainly set new high standards and, well grown, is still a most formidable show flower and garden plant. Beautiful as it is at all times, I do not think I have ever seen it as miraculous as grown in its Northern Ireland birthplace. Here its 15 centimetres are easily attained, but it is not the size but the quality of its perianths, like perfect, flat snowfields and trumpets which are narrow but finished with a perfect rolled flange, that impresses.

Mating 'Empress of Ireland' with 'Courage' gave 'Queenscourt' (1956), and 'Birthright' (1956). These were whiter still, smooth-textured and of impressively precise form, 'Queenscourt' having more rounded petals than the square rigged 'Birthright'. 'Ulster Queen' (1962) from 'Empress of Ireland' × 'Vigil' is another faultless pure-white flower.

The Wilson line of whites ended with 'Panache' (1962), named in the year of this fine breeder's death. This probably remains the finest white trumpet in cultivation. It is pure white, utterly refined and a wonderful size.

Reversed bicolours

The lives of flower breeders are measured out in doses of excitement and disappointment. Fortunately the first more than cancels out the second. Few things can equal the satisfaction of finding some new flower of exceptional beauty and distinctiveness. When Guy Wilson made the cross 'King of the North' × 'Content' he cannot have known what magic he was to release. When the seedlings bloomed nothing like them had been seen before. One was outstanding. Opening a rich biting lemon with the trumpet somewhat darker, after a few days the trumpet, especially the inside surface, had become paler. The bleaching continued until the trumpet was left virtually pure white, though the petals and the brim of the mouth remained sparkling lemon. 'Spellbinder' (1944) had been born.

'Spellbinder' is now a popular garden plant. It was a pet of Guy's who would persist in showing it in competitive collections even in the knowledge that some conservative judges were prejudiced against it. There is no doubt that it would have made its way with the gardening public for its rich greeny-lemon alone, but by performing tricks it made itself a real favourite. Earliness gained it additional points, and its size and good form added others. It had to be in everyone's collection.

Grant Mitsch in Oregon repeated the cross, but this time instead of sowing relatively few seed, a crop of some 10,000 was sown. Some chance of exploiting the potential of the cross was allowed. A reasonable number of selections were made, and some of these were crossed with the reverse bicolour long cup 'Binkie'. This new generation was mainly of long cups but a useful number measured trumpet proportions.

From the initial cross, the first to take the stage was 'Lunar Sea'. (1954). With flatter, rather narrow petals and a narrower trumpet this was quite distinct from 'Spellbinder'. The reverse was made more quickly, but the colours were paler. 'Entrancement' (1958) was one of the finest of the first series, a tall plant with neat foliage and plenty of tall stems carrying many well-proportioned flowers. Flatter in the petal than 'Spellbinder' and with a more slender trumpet, it was close to 'Spellbinder's' bright colours. 'Honeybird' is thought the better show flower, but it is paler and hardly so effective in the garden.

'Binkie' × ('King of the North' × 'Content') gave many fine things. 'Moonlight Sonata' (1960) was one of the first to be seen, a later flower than some and a decorative one, with wide rich-lemon petals tending to reflex a trifle from widely-flanged trumpets fading to white inside but retaining pale lemon outside. The latest to bloom of these reversed flowers is 'Chiloquin', a perfect small flower, immaculate with its rounded creaseless perianth at right angles to the stocky trumpet that quickly becomes white. Crossed with the strong long cup 'Playboy' it has given some outstanding new flowers in the long cups.

It proved difficult to make further advances along this road, and so a number of other cultivars were brought into play. 'Sun 'n Snow'

(1970) came from a complicated parentage involving pink-crowned flowers from Australia. It is a big yellow, with very broad petals a vibrant lemon-gold behind a noble trumpet that gently turns to nearly pure white, but leaves a kiss of colour on the lip of the flange. Sir William Stern's tough pale yellow 'Handcross' mated with 'Salem' gave the tailored 'Teal' (1976). Triangular broad petals back a flanged and notched trumpet. Petals shine vivid lemon gold, whilst the trumpet quickly changes to pure white and also bestows a narrow white halo to the base of the perianth. 'Daydream' crossed with the giant white 'Empress of Ireland' gave 'Lime Chiffon' (1975), one of those haunting pale flowers I find fascinating, but which like Guy Wilson's 'Moonstruck' do not always please the judges and indeed seem to frighten some of the public. Probably the whispered colours are thought to imply a lack of strength and gardenworthiness. If so the idea is mistaken. 'Lime Chiffon's' large pale emanations float above foliage giving an impression of greenness, with the milky-white petals suffused with this haunting greeny cast. Its trumpets are decorative with generous flanges frilled and goffered.

Miniature and dwarf trumpets

Biggest is not always best, and smaller flowers are easier to place in some of today's gardens. Many small trumpet owe much to *N. cyclamineus*, and these are reviewed in the chapter devoted to its hybrids. They are fortunate in having good constitutions. Some tiny trumpets are bewitching but not the most extrovert of growers. Introducing blood of strong-growing things has the effect of enlarging the flowers and threatening their status as miniatures or dwarfs. Obvious species for producing small flowers are going to be the tiny *N. asturiensis*, *N. cyclamineus*, and the slightly larger *N. minor*, *N. nanus*, *N. obvallaris*, and the little white species. Diminutive size will be supplied by *N. asturiensis*, but it is not always the smartest, the petals falling forwards. One or two old kinds grow well and are useful plants. 'Wee Bee' was grown for a long time before it was registered in 1948. Growing only about 10cm high, it is prolific, with neat little mid-yellow flowers of quite good form, and early.

The future trumpets

What of the future? Can we expect steady advances adding a millimetre to the petal here, firming the substance there by some tiny fraction, and perhaps strengthening the colour by a flicker of a tone? Or shall we see new breakthroughs that will open up new avenues? Some objectives beckon. Bicolour flowers with white petals and orange or red trumpets could be startling; many seedlings already presage the introduction of strongly coloured lemon-petalled flowers with rich pink trumpets; and yellow-and-orange trumpets have ample scope for improvement. Some seedlings of ours have tangerine petals and dark orange trumpets. The introduction of an all-orange trumpet daffodil is still probably some way away – our seedlings are scruffy flowers. However it then suggests the possibility of orange-petalled flowers with white trumpets, or even with coronas of several colours. There would seem to be a real possibility of breeding trumpets completely white but with a rim of colour around the trumpet brims, something that might be pleasing. The possibilities are infinite.

1 *N.* 'Acropolis'. 4W–R. Now one of
the most widely grown of the new
race of doubles bred via the 'Falaise' –
'Gay Time' gateway. Strong
stemmed and producing uniformly
good flowers

2 *N*. 'Bartley'. 6Y-Y. Of the longer-trumpeted cyclamineus cultivars this is one of the most reliable. 'Peeping Tom' is similar but not quite so good and likely to be virused

3 *N*. 'Blue Bird'. 2W-W. Still one of the whitest of all daffodils and a fine garden plant as it produces very heavy crops of flowers and strong bulbs increase quickly and healthily

4 *N.* 'Brer Fox'. 1Y-R. One of the W.
O. Backhouse 'red trumpets' and
thought by him to be his best

5 *N.* 'Brunswick'. 2W-Y. 60 years after
being named by the raiser, P. D.
Williams, still grown in quantity and
making an excellent garden plant that
naturalizes well

6 *N.* 'Chanterelle'. 11Y-Y. One of the most reliable of Jack Gerritsen's split-corona cultivars. A good plant and free bloomer, it attracts attention whether in the garden or cut

7 *N.* 'Charter'. 2Y-W. Has proven to be one of the finest of the lemon kinds in the garden. It is free flowering, blooms are durable and boldly posed, and the bulbs increase quickly

8 *N.* 'Congress'. 11Y-YYO. The
colour–code classification would seem
to be incorrect as it comes with the
corona segments uniform orange, a
vivid shade that fades only a little with
age

9 *N.* 'Emperor'. 1Y-Y and 'Empress'
1W-Y. Two famous cultivars bred
by W. Backhouse before 1869 seen
here growing in a churchyard where
they have been undisturbed since
before the First World War

10 *N.* 'Falstaff'. 2Y-R. A Lionel
Richardson flower and deserving a
very long future as it is not only one of
the strongest-coloured
yellow-and-red flowers but also one
of the earliest. Stems are sturdy

11 *N.* 'February Gold'. 6Y-Y. The most widespread cyclamineus hybrid now grown for some 70 years during which time it has opened approximately 69 times in March. It is still very much worth planting because of its easy character and long-term value as a naturalizing plant

12 *N.* 'Evendine'. 3W-WWY. A most perfectly-formed flower of beguiling crystalline texture opening with a cream edge to the corona but ending uniform white

13 *N.* 'Frolic'. 1W–Y. In an underpopulated class, one of the cleanest bicolours and a good garden plant

14 *N.* 'Golden Ducat'. 4Y–Y. A sport from 'King Alfred' and well used as a cut flower, can be impressive in the garden but needs to be kept out of the worst weather as there is a weak spot in the stem

15 *N.* 'Hawera'. 5Y–Y. Probably 60 years old but almost unbeatable of its kind. A hybrid from *N. triandrus albus* x *N. jonquilla*

16 *N.* 'Ice Follies'. 2W–W. Dutch flower that for several decades has been a leading garden plant, a prodigy of vigour giving huge crops of flowers. The classification code is misleading, the flowers open with primrose-lemon crowns. This colour fades but only old flowers will be completely white

17 *N.* 'Jenny'. 6W-W. Probably the best of the *'Mitylene'* x *N. cyclamineus* seedlings bred by C. F. Coleman. Opening with a cream trumpet the flowers soon become all white

18 *N.* 'Jumblie'. 6Y-O. Alec Gray raised this from a pod of seed from the almost completely sterile 'Cyclataz' bred from the disparate parents, *N. cyclamineus* and *N. tazetta* 'Soleil d'Or'. The three seeds of the pod became 'Jumblie', 'Tête à Tête', and 'Quince'. It would be difficult to think of a more worthwhile podful

19 *N.* 'Kilworth'. 2W-YOO. The cornerstone of the breeding of modern white-and-red flowers. Still a good garden plant and able to naturalize well

20 *N.* 'Lemon Cloud'. 1Y-Y. A large character flower in the garden, often more than six inches (15 centimetres) across

21 *N.* 'Liberty Bells'. 5Y-Y. Still one of
the best of the garden
yellow–triandrus hybrids

22 *N.* 'Minnow'. 8Y-Y. Small tazetta hybrid that opens with pale primrose petals and darker cups, but soon has creamy-white petals

23 *N.* 'Nylon'. 12W-W. The name covers a series of seedlings from the crossing of *N. cantabricus foliosus* and *N. romieuxii*. They can be in bloom from late autumn through until spring

24 *N*. 'Panache'. 1W-W. Probably still
unbeaten as the best white trumpet for
show or for the garden

25 *N. poeticus recurvus*. 10W-GYR. The 'Pheasants Eye Narcissus' is a selection from the wild but, unlike most of these it grows well in cultivation. Characteristics, apart from visual ones, are the delicious perfume and the lateness of its season

26 *N.* 'Romance'. 2W-P. A lively pink combining strong colour, wide petals and an interestingly scalloped crown

27 *N.* 'St Patrick's Day'. 2Y-Y. One of
the best garden daffodils. From 'Ice
Follies' and 'Binkie' it inherits great
strength and freedom of flower. The
cup colour fades with age

28 *N.* 'Sundisc'. 7Y-Y. One of the most
perfect of the little flowers bred by
Alec Gray and a plant of abundant
vigour. It blooms and increases very
quickly

29 *N.* 'She'. 2W-P.   Firm-textured
flower neat in proportions and of
good clear colouring

30 *N.* 'Soldier Brave'.
2Y-O. Medium-sized flower but
of exemplary character with
ramrod stems, smooth thick
parchment texture and vivid
sunproof colours. It blooms late,
after almost all other yellow-reds
have faded away

31 *N.* 'Testament'. 2W-P. A strong
plant and flower rather like the
famous 'Passionale' that is now
being marketed widely through
garden centres and elsewhere

32 *N.* 'Tête à Tête'. 6Y-Y. Now probably the most famous of all dwarf daffodils. Sold by the millions for bowls, pots, window boxes, rock gardens, borders and shrubberies. We have had it successfully naturalized. Welcome for its very early colour and its amazing durability in bloom

33 *N.* 'Thalia'. 5W-W. Dating from around 1916 this kind is still widely grown, an indication of the popularity of many-headed white flowers. The narrow petals and windmill perianth that are anathema to the fancier are found pleasing by many gardeners who enjoy the informality

34 *N.* 'Tripartite'. 11Y-Y. Bred
from 'April Tears' x 'Bacarrat' and,
although classified as a
split-corona, to my mind a
candidate for the almost empty
Division 12 for miscellaneous
daffodils. From 'April Tears' it
inherits blood of *N. jonquilla* and
N. triandrus. It is a splendid
late-flowering cultivar that is free
of bloom and not too large

35 *N.* 'Tudor Minstrel'. 2W-Y. For
decades reckoned the best large cup
of its colouring, and still able to do
well in competition but also
splendid in the garden

36 *N.* 'Tuesday's Child'. 5W–Y. A Blanchard flower, one of the few good bicolour triandrus hybrids and sister seedling to the all–white 'Arish Mell'

37 *N.* 'White Lion'. 4W–WYY. A 'John Eveleyn' seedling, a Dutch flower, and quite one of the most useful of doubles. More pointed petals than most of the new doubles. A prolific, easy plant with young flowers having a buffy suffusion in the yellow segments

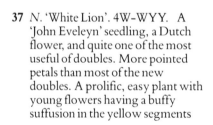

38 *N.* 'Widgeon'. 2Y-PPY. Of the new race of pink-and-yellow flowers 'Widgeon' is one of the best; not only is the form and colour appealing, the plant is very strong, producing large crops of flowers and propagating rapidly

39 *N.* 'Worcester'. 2W-W. The texture of the flower is such that it sparkles as if frosted. The neatly balanced crown opens with a cream edge and looks well then and after its quick change to pure white

40 *N.* 'Unique'. 4W-Y. Probably the best known of the newer white-and-yellow doubles. Can have impressively large flowers. A strong plant

41 *N.* 'Van Sion'. 4Y-Y. Officially 'Telamonius Plenus' and known since the beginning of the 1600s. Nobody knows what *N. pseudonarcissus* 'Telamonius' is supposed to be so it seems best to call an old friend by the name it has borne most frequently through the centuries. Early, faithful, and always welcome. Naturalizes. Seen here in our churchyard, St James, Colwall, Herefordshire

42 Trade Stand. Only a few potential customers can get to a commercial grower's grounds, so the grower takes his flowers to the spring flower shows. Our practice was to take 20 flowers of 100 varieties to the main shows. To keep the Chelsea show stand fresh meant having at least 10,000 flowers in cold store before the show opened

43 Trial Beds. The Royal Horticultural Society gives awards to deserving plants, the main ones being an 'award of merit' or, very much more rarely, a 'first class certificate'. These are given for different uses, the two most important being for garden use and for exhibition. Here is part of a trial at the RHS gardens Wisley where cultivars will be judged for garden merit

44 *N. pseudonarcissus*. The 'Lent Lily' of parts of the British countryside and a variable species that is a playground for botanists. The British forms are delightful plants for naturalizing and die down early enough not to cause too much awkwardness when grass is to be tidied

45 *N. cyclamineus*. A rare Portuguese plant that can have a potent and totally beneficial influence in breeding. Grown in a rather moist, slightly acid soil it can increase well. It is best established from pots of growing bulbs or by fresh seed

46 *N. obvallaris*. A plant known wild only in the countryside outside the Welsh town of Tenby in Pembrokeshire. Much more amenable to cultivation than *N. pseudonarcissus* and therefore a useful early dwarf to plant with shrubs or in grass

47 *N. bulbocodium.* A species that spreads from southern France throughout the Iberian peninsula to Gibraltar and into the Atlas mountains in Morocco. The illustration shows the species growing in the alpine meadow of the RHS gardens at Wisley

48 *N.* 'Mount Hood' 1W-W. Raised in Holland before 1938 this cultivar became the dominant commercial white trumpet and still sustains a strong position as a garden variety. It is best on fertile soils that maintain substantial-sized bulbs and thereby a good flowering record

49 *N. hellenicus*. In cultivation this would appear to be a single clone, the very neat small poeticus flower with wide petals that formed one of the cornerstones of daffodil breeding

50 *N. canaliculatus*. One of the smallest N. tazettas. To get it flowering freely the surprisingly large bulbs need to be well grown in a well–drained spot that gets baked in the summer. Like other tazettas it will not withstand very hard and prolonged frosts

10

Long-cupped daffodils

This is easily the largest division, and it is also the most diverse. Almost every new colour or combination of colours has been seen first here. It could be argued that the proportions of these flowers are the most aesthetically pleasing. Practically, the coronas are of a sufficient size to make their colours effective and still allow the perianths a full role. Every flower in the garden is not going to look directly at the admiring grower. However trumpet and long-cupped daffodils have enough corona to make significant colour contributions when seen from various angles, which is not always the case with the short-cupped ones.

Crossing two short cups can produce mainly long cups; one of the first results of increased vigour is extra length on the corona; and any foreign blood in crosses involving trumpets will often produce a large proportion of long cups. The division is one where the most work is being done, and it is being topped up from crosses involving other divisions.

Breeding aims veer from one objective to another. To start with, diversity and the benefits of hybrid vigour were rewards enough. Then for a long period all strove for better yellow-and-orange kinds, first to improve the amounts and depths of orange and then to make the pigment sunproof. Almost phrenetic interest was shown later as breeders raced to produce good pink cups. White-and-orange flowers followed the same pattern as the yellow-and-oranges, but were somewhat later in making any great progress. Reversed bicolours were treated intensively by Grant Mitsch and by his daughter and son-in-law, the Havens, in Oregon. White long cups marched forward alongside the white trumpets. Now the most changeable frontline positions are those taken by the yellow-and-pinks, and by the heavily pink-painted kinds that approach the elusive red. All yellows, and also white-and-yellow flowers have tended to arrive as byproducts of work aimed in other directions.

Yellow long cups

Some of these all yellows have made the grade as commercial plants, with 'Carlton' a prime example, used in unparalleled quantities as a cut flower as well as a garden plant. These yellows have been in the shadow of the trumpets. The argument may not be fully articulated, but it would seem that if a yellow flower is wanted it may as well be as big as possible, and therefore the trumpets win.

Early development of hybrids made any of improved size and quality a matter for rejoicing and a good number were all yellows, either of a uniform shade or, more often, with yellow petals backing darker cups. 'Sir Watkin' (1884) was one of the first to excite growers, but its origin is obscure. It was grown in Wales for decades as the 'Giant Welsh Daffodil' before being given a regular name and becoming widely grown. From illustrations and text is would seem to have been a large flower for that time, one with relatively wide pointed petals of primrose, and a rather fluted half-length corona a tone or two darker. Sold for decades, it gave way to competition from newer things and must have deteriorated. What I take to be the remnants of this plant are the rather weedy plants with small starry flowers still to be found in gardens today – virus must have taken its toll.

It is difficult to know exactly how growers evaluated the yellows in the years up to 1914. 'Helios' (1912) bred by Engleheart was certainly hailed as an advance in quality. With primrose petals and a darker crown it was seen as a move towards the orange cups, though it is doubtful whether the colour would now be deemed orange. As in other sections it was the work of P. D. Williams that really set the standards. In 1927 he registered a whole series of important kinds including 'St Egwin', 'Crocus', 'Havelock', and 'Carlton'. 'St Egwin' had the smallest cup, but was exceptionally smooth; 'Crocus' was much richer in gold and showed to a greater extent than the others the *N. hispanicus* background, looking like a trumpet (it may have been from 'King Alfred' × 'Fortune'); and 'Havelock' was a well balanced flower of mid yellow, rather richer than 'Carlton' and with more rounded oval petals.

Looking at these kinds in 1927 it would have been a fey person who picked 'Carlton' as destined to be the most important commercial plant. The paler 'Carlton' may have been larger, but only fractionally, and most would have backed 'Havelock' as the winner – certainly this is the one that was showered with awards in Britain and Holland. 'Carlton' however won through to a position of prominence by virtue of its outstanding vigour. Bulbs of massive size and prolificity impressed professional growers, and amateurs were happy to benefit from its strength and free flowering. It is still a remarkable kind, despite the touch of commonness that tends to make fanciers look askance.

P. D. Williams kinds held sway in the thirties. In the forties a number of others came on the scene and managed to hold their place. 'Golden Torch' (1942) from the Brodie had the advantage of looking like a long cup and not a failed trumpet. It stood tall and tailored, with mid-yellow broadly triangular petals held firmly at right angles to the stigma, and the slightly darker crown being a good size with a regularly serrated light flange. The following year saw the début of 'Galway' (1943). It almost crept into the combative lists, without the usual ushering in of Richardson novelties. It may be that it improved as the years passed, for it became the acknowledged premier show kind in its class, despite being a perfect illustration of the difficulty of operating a classification. 99 out of 100 people looking at it would say it was a traditional trumpet daffodil, the 100th would be uncertain. In truth flowers may well measure long-cup proportions before the trumpet grows to its mature length. There is no easy way to deal with such anomalies. 'Galway' remains a fine deep-golden flower of velvety texture. Its strong bulbs make a good garden plant, but it is not one of the quickest to increase and although giving adequate shows of blossom, its yield in the commercial field is hopelessly below that of many lesser flowers.

1949 saw two similar flowers registered: 'Ormeau' from Willie Dunlop in Northern Ireland, and 'St Keverne' from Cornwall as its name suggests, a seedling from Michael Williams, son of P. D. Williams. Both are thick-textured and deep gold, and the coronas are longish slender cups only slightly opened at the mouth. As we have grown it, 'Ormeau' is slighty less tall and is perhaps the darker. 'St Keverne' has a more serrated flange.

Several good yellows came in the fifties, but none really marked a significant change of direction or a very big leap forward. The coming of 'Camelot' (1962) however, did just that. From trumpet 'Kingscourt' by the gold-and-orange long cup 'Ceylon', the resulting flower was large with rounded perianths different from previous yellows, with flat petals which were exceptionally broad. The coronas were large bowls, not all that much short of trumpet length, but flangeless and wide enough to look proper cups, and the colour was mid yellow. 'Camelot' is no mean garden plant, and has been used with effect in breeding.

'Camelot' × 'Daydream' gave good seedlings. 'Amber Castle' (1976), 'Blessing' (1978), 'Cairngorm' (1976) are three intermediates, and their lemon-gold shines out. 'Blessing' remains lemon, but 'Amber Castle' and 'Cairngorm' take on passing shades of amber.

Grant Mitsch crossed 'Golden Torch' with 'Galway' to combine good qualities in 'Butterscotch' (1963), a tall upright plant, more floriferous than 'Galway', but darker toned than 'Golden Torch'. Smooth perianths stand at right angles to the sensibly flanged serrated crowns. 'Butterflower' (1976), from 'Alchemy' × 'Butterscotch', joined the cupped fraternity that look like trumpets. This sizeable one is mid yellow with a copy-book perianth and a narrow trumpet crown. 'Asteroid' (1978) and 'Gold Coin' (1980) both came from 'Ormeau' × 'Butterscotch', and are firm textured, deep coloured flowers. 'Asteroid', with a well-displayed serrated flange looks the part of the traditional trumpet but lacks a millimetre or two; 'Gold Coin' is a firmly-drawn flower, later than many, with a distinct slender corona with only sufficient deckling of the margin to avoid any suspicion of sheered abruptness.

Different approaches were made by mating Guy Wilson's very strong upright 'Playboy' (1944) with the reverse bicolours 'Daydream' and 'Chiloquin'. The seed parent was a tall tough flower, rounded and with a prominent bowl of pale tangerine. It was good sense to mate this amazon with the very perfect but small 'Chiloquin'. The cross gave 'Sunny Thoughts' (1979) for Eileen Frey, daughter to the Mitschs. It is a strong-stemmed, very smooth, thick golden bloom with a frilled crown just a shade darker. 'Playboy' × 'Daydream' gave a fine series including 'Scio' (1969), 'Top Notch' (1970), 'Executive' (1974), 'Imperial' (1975), and 'Symphonete' (1975). 'Top Notch' typifies the series in its firm texture and exact form as well as by having a white halo at the junction of perianth and cup. Petals are a irridescent soft lemon, with the crown darker but often taking on hints of amber in the same fashion as 'Amberglow' (1969), from 'Lunar Sea' × 'Daydream', which glanced at casually might be thought an attractive trumpet. It looks the part, but after a day or so classification scarcely matters as rich shades of glowing buffy amber invade the rich lemon corona. 'Imperial' is strong and distinctive, with a white halo at the bright perianth base. 'Symphonette' is later and is an effective quality lemon flower with rounded petals and a longish, more flared crown.

'Constancy' (1981) is a leading yellow from the medium-sized copy-book lemon 'Scio' by pollen of the large 'Camelot'. Strong stems hold perfectly-arranged tough blooms of rich lemon-gold. Absolute smoothness is demanded of the perianth and neat crown. Its character is not dissimilar to that of Richardson's rich 'Golden Aura' (1969), a tall plant with a very wide flat perianth and a restricted crown, the perianth glistening behind a corona which is a touch closer to breaking the gold-orange barrier.

If progress was to be made in these yellows, fresh blood had to be imported. Lemon reverses did this. Another route was taken when 'Paricutin' was crossed with 'Daydream'. 'Paricutin' (1955) remains one of the strongest-coloured and most striking of orange cups. Its round petals back a wide crater crown of an incandescent orange which almost beggars description. What would result from mating this with the lemon-petalled but white-crowned 'Daydream'? 'Copperfield' (1978) and 'Diploma' (1979) were part of the answer. Both star in a crowd. 'Copperfield' does it best to favour both parents equally by having firm lemon-gold petals and crowns of coppery yellow; in 'Diploma' the pale lemon perianth has a lightly-drawn halo at the base of a lemon cup shading to lips of pale tangerine.

And now for something totally different. Grant Mitsch introduced some flowers that, having opened one colour, then changed as they aged. Dr Throckmorton has worked for many years with flowers such as Mitsch's well-known 'Aircastle' and 'Irish Coffee'; together with a handful of others that appeared to perform similar tricks. All this is very confusing for those interested in exact classification, but a delight for those watching their flowers develop day by day. These cultivars are often referred to as 'toned' flowers.

Most Throckmorton seedlings are small cups, but a number measure long cups. 'Lark' (1979) was a Mitsch flower from 'Irish Coffee' crossed with a short cup reversed bicolour seedling of Richardson's. 'Lark' looks like a short cup and opens uniform pale lemon, but the flared and fluted shallow cup fades to near white with possibly a touch of rim colour left. 'Easter Moon' has given Dr Throckmorton many fine flowers, one of the most imposing of which is 'Raw Silk' (1983), which it gave when mated with 'Irish Coffee'.

'Raw Silk' has smooth rounded perianths of pale yellow surrounding cups which open yellow with a paler eye, but then becomes whiter with age and end close to a reverse bicolour.

Yellow-and-orange/red long cups

Daffodil fanciers have keen eyes. Any hints of buffiness are seen as pink, and rich orange becomes red in their terminology. Early breeders were possessed of great faith – a prerequisite for success. Starting with only the orange of the edge or eye of the poeticus as the apparent source for the envisaged orange trumpets and long cups, hybrid seed was sown. Early generations were mainly narrow petalled with coronas only edged with colour. This poeticus inheritance was seen as the source of colouration.

Breeders were bedevilled by the burning or fading of orange in the sun. Bright flowers, spectacular when newly opened, were reduced to a tragic ruin by the sun's rays. Corona tissue was burnt and left as dry brittle brown waste, something that happens to the rims of poeticus eyes. Others fared a little better as the tissue was unaffected, but the colour faded. It was a war of attrition, and bit by bit the situation was improved. Most breeders resisted the temptation to introduce flowers that burnt, however marvellous they looked. By the late thirties kinds were being marketed with orange colouring that did not burn and did not fade badly.

Orange in daffodils is merely the result of a greater concentration of the pigment governing yellow coloration, carotene. As years passed, seedling selection favoured those with richer colours – ones endowed with greater amounts of carotene, and width of petal expanded. P. D. Williams's 'Killigrew' (1907) was a major advance in quality, size and colour. Engleheart's 'Helios' (1910) was a good free-flowering kind for its time, although not so bright. Breeding progress was slow with these cultivars and was then pushed into the background by the epoch-making 'Fortune' (1923). This was quite simply the largest and best. Well-named 'Fortune', it was originally valued at £500 and many bulbs were distributed at £50 each. Even now, 60 years later, it is grown by the ton and its early blooms harvested for market. Earliness has ensured its value for growers, especially as this precocity is underwritten by a sound constitution. Bold crowns are of tangerine that may seem pale in comparison with modern kinds, but is still bright. Although it was much used in breeding and gave good kinds, few of these were remarkably better.

1927 saw the registration of two novelties destined to improve the section, 'Porthilly' and 'Carbineer'. 'Porthilly' from Williams, was richer than 'Fortune' and later in bloom. With shallow bowl crowns it had petals with a suggestion of backwards tilt. It was a typically healthy Williams plant with blue-green foliage. The second cultivar was bred by a cousin, A. M. Wilson. This was 'Carbineer' which is still grown by the acre. Sturdy and tall with strong leaves, it is tough with golden petals and a crown rich orange at the mouth but shading to a tangerine-gold base. Lionel Richardson said that for many years he always sowed around 1,000 seeds from 'Carbineer', believing it to give good plants and well-coloured tough flowers.

Plantswoman Miss G. Evelyn bred 'Rustom Pasha' in 1930 from 'Hospodar' × a seedling. It was a potent breeding force, unlike any other in being tall, floriferous, and with long egg-shaped petals and goblet crowns opening rather dull and almost green, but quickly becoming a deeper colour than any other.

'Sunproof Orange' (1935) from Guy Wilson was a good gold and orange, indicating by its name the preoccupation of breeders. In the same year Richardson introduced 'Bahram', a wide crowned plant of good contrast, which was an improvement on its father 'Porthilly'. Later came 'Sun Chariot' (1943) from 'Porthilly' × 'Rustom Pasha'.

Although Guy Wilson's name is inextricably linked with the whites, he produced top-ranking flowers in every class of the main divisions. 'Armada' (1939) was clearly unbeatable early in the season. Wide golden petals backed a bold crown of rich orange – a big step forward in the 'Fortune' tradition. As a seedling it had been admired by his friend, the Dutch grower Matthew Zandbergen. During the Second World War Guy managed to get a message through to Matthew after Holland had been overrun – 'Armada' would be a gift to Matthew to help him get going again after the war. And so it came to pass.

Richardson lines of yellow-reds made steady progress. Small but neat 'Narvik' (1940) came from 'Carbineer' × 'Porthilly'. Its strong colours were outshone by 'Ceylon' (1945), a kind very much worth growing today. Sturdy leaves and stems betoken a really tough plant, flowers are held rigidly to make the most of a flat perianth of thick golden petals and goblet cups which open dullish but become fiery orange. With not too many leaves, a neat habit, and with durable blossom, this is excellent in the garden. It was of course used in breeding. 'Vulcan' came from 'Carbineer' × 'Ceylon' looking like a very improved 'Narvik'; and similarly tall and strong but larger-flowered 'Air Marshall' (1953) from 'Carbineer' × 'Malta' has proved itself over the years, being fine with rounded petals and a rather small straight-sided cup of deep orange.

'Falstaff' (1960) is undoubtedly one of the finest of Richardson flowers. Coming from 'Ceylon' by a seedling, it is of similar character to its mother, being tough, sturdy, and even earlier. Flowers are of brilliant gold and deep orange-red, the red being made more effective by the flange of the crown, and the silken texture of the whole bloom. It would be oustanding at any time, and blooming so early it is without peer.

Other breeders had been busy. Willie Dunlop produced a good series, and his 'Craigywarren' (1949) is still grown in quantity. It is from a different mould – golden circles back neat cups of rich orange, usually solid to the base but sometimes shading down to gold. Tall and stately 'Sealing Wax' (1957) from Herbert Barr is a good-sized flower with silken overlapping petals and neat small goblets of dark orange.

American competition was keen. Mitsch brought out a number of early kinds, one of which 'Sacajawea', a 'Fortune' seedling, is very early. His late-flowering 'Paricutin' (1952) from tough 'Klingo' by brilliant short cup 'Ardour' has wide golden petals, but startles with its intense fluorescent orange-red saucer crown. It had to be used in breeding. 'Velvet Robe' (1966) came from 'Playboy' × 'Paricutin', and is a large, late and flamboyant flower in gold and scarlet. From ('Armada' × 'Paricutin') × 'Falstaff' came several fine flowers of which 'Monal' (1977) and 'Toucan' (1979) are two of the better ones. 'Monal' is early and built like 'Falstaff' but larger; 'Toucan' is more informal, and large with a brilliant golden reflexing perianth and a flared crown vibrating with flaming quintessence of orange-red. 'Trogon' (1979) has 'Falstaff' as pollen parent; it has good form in its wide perianth and crown with frilled flanged margin. Glowing gold and vermilion are very telling in strong tall-stemmed flowers. 'Vertex' (1980) has 'Falstaff' as father. Its good sized but neatly tailored golden petals lie flat away from tidy medium-sized cups.

John Lea's flowers are all characterized by their high show quality. Achieving this was his primary aim, and that they might also be good garden plants came as a secondary consideration. His yellow-reds tend to have impressively wide perianths of egg-shaped petals and straight-sided cups of deep contrasting orange.

Concentration on breeding early bright flowers rather left the later ones in the shade. Most yellow-petalled daffodils bloom in the first half of the season. Late yellow petals used to be at a premium, but we now have a number. 'Feeling Lucky' got a First Class Certificate as a garden plant after a trial at the RHS gardens at Wisley. Opening late, it is distinctive. The neat plants have medium-sized blooms of broad petals pointing out from behind a flattish shallow cup with a very unusual scalloped edge. The cups open a greenish-orange but move day by day towards intense vermilion. Taller and with medium-sized and impeccably formed flowers is 'Soldier Brave', which is the last of the yellow-reds with us. When we were growing commercially, the fields towards the end of seasons would be white with one splash of rich gold and orange – 'Soldier Brave'. Firm petals lie flat from a neat crown well flanged and all a solid intense deep orange-red. Gold petals sometimes show the beginning of an orange flush.

Orange-petalled long cups

Every now and again flowers appeared amongst seedlings with yellow petals flushed orange. Some were short cups, but later more were long cups. Dr Lower registered short cup 'John Peel' in 1928, which is smallish but with pinky rouging in its petals. This featured in the background to 'Ambergate' (1950) bred by Denis Milne from a series of seedlings. With wide strong orange bowls it opens with golden petals heavily suffused with tangerine. Sunlight tends to bleach the colour. Guy Wilson's 'Kindled' was neat and made more interesting with a coppery flush in the petals. 'Tawny Lad', bred by Mrs Richardson from a seedling × 'Flamboyant', is one of a number of newer flushed flowers, this one being well formed with an even orange suffusion through the petals. 'Fiery Flame' from 'Vulcan' × 'Firecracker' has golden petals shimmering with a copper-orange cast reflecting the strong colour of the neat serrated cup. 'Caracas' from 'Firecracker' × 'Spelter', with large vermilion goblets, has pointed petals of tangerine, a shade that appears to increase in intensity. 'Red Hot' hails from Australasia; it is medium sized and of show form, and is flushed an even orange.

It is surely only a matter of time before we have petals concolourous with the coronas. Whether we need an all-red daffodil is however debatable – somehow it seems out of character for our spring flower. Extrovert red tulips are acceptable, but daffodils are surely quieter, more introverted charmers.

White-and-orange/red long cups

With as long a history as the yellow-reds, these have lagged behind, probably because the brightest of the white-and-reds were closer to the poets, and were often short cups. They were also more beset with the problem of colour fading or burning. Engleheart had produced a sensational kind by crossing the little white trumpet *N. abscissus* with solid red-eyed *N. poeticus poetarum*. The resulting 'Will Scarlett' received a First Class Certificate in spring 1898. Some breeders, looking back, may have felt it would have been better issued with a government health warning, suggesting that breeders used the flower at their peril. Its wide crown of flaming orange it could pass to its seedlings, but it also gave them its very informal perianth. P. D. Williams would not have had it on his land. Other breeders were tempted, notably the Backhouses. Perhaps this was just as well because they flowered an important 'Will Scarlett' seedling – 'Hades' (1925).

'Hades' just made long-cup size and so may have been showing the restraining and purifying influence of better poeticus ancestors than *N. p. poetarum*. Milk-white petals were stained at their bases by the strength of the red pigment of the small puckered cup, easily the darkest colour to have been seen then. This pigment cried out to be used, and the almost inspired red cross was made by placing 'Hades' pollen on the white-and-primrose 'White Sentinel' with its do-gooding background of 'Beacon', 'Princess Mary', and *N. poeticus hellenicus*. 'Kilworth' (1938) was the result. Late, large, deep orange-red and cream, with wide petals and quality enough to show the way forward, it still remains a fine flower, and can be grown to almost rival its famous progeny.

Another white-and-red was registered the same year. This was 'Arbar' from the thick 'Monaco' by the neat short cup 'Forfar'. 'Arbar' was totally dissimilar to 'Kilworth', with a firm smooth perianth backing a flat cup of medium orange. It is strong stemmed and tall. Crossing 'Kilworth' by 'Arbar' was done on a larger scale than had been the Waterford pattern, but this certainly paid off as there was a welter of fine things to be picked out of the seedlings, mostly long cups but with some belonging to division three. In one stroke the character of the white-and-red class was changed.

One of the first of the series to be introduced was 'Avenger' (1957), and this remains one of the best. Whilst not as large as some it is still a reasonable size and has an immaculate white perianth with flared and fluted cups of deep solid vermilion. 'Rameses' is a 10cm flower with a beautifully overlapping sparkling perianth and a restricted cup of deep red colour. The cup may be finished with a serrated flange. 'Don Carlos' (1962) is larger, with a very fine perianth of wide petals, and has a wide large crown of uniform dark orange-red. 'Orion' (1959) and 'Victory' (1961) are a couple of showy ones with large bowl crowns, whilst 'Anthea' rings the changes by haming very large flowers with splendid perianths and flared crowns of orange that shade down to golden centres.

Other fine flowers from the same cross include 'Ancona' and 'Artillery' (Div 3); 'George Leak', 'Hotspur' and 'Kilmurry' (Div 3); 'Lorenzo', 'Mikado', 'Nantucket', 'Norvak', 'Parsifal', and 'Parthia' (Div 3); 'Privateer', 'Ringleader', and 'Rockall' (Div 3); and 'Royal Regiment', and 'Toreador' (Div 3).

It takes a while, perhaps three or four seasons, to get bulbs from the opposite hemisphere to reveal their full potential. 'Landmark' is now an old favourite, being most welcome for its early flowers. The 'Kilworth' progeny flowers belong very definitely to the second half of the season, and 'Landmark' (1963) is very much on its own when it opens as the first of the white-and-orange ones, attractive with its disc-crown of bright tangerine. 'Masquerade' (1955) is another New Zealand cultivar that looks good here, with overlapping perianths and bowls of glowing scarlet.

All-white long cups

Early-bred white cups were pretty little things, but often not the hardiest of plants so that they flaunted their prettiness for a few brief seasons and then tended to fade away. Many breeders worked with these, but the main contribution was that of Guy Wilson who set himself the highest of standards. Relatively early on he brought out 'Slemish' (1930), named after the Co. Antrim hill he could see from his windows and where, according to legend, St Patrick herded sheep. It was a fine white, with the perianth set square from a bold trumpet crown in such a firm manner that it is no surprise to know that the pollen parent was 'Beersheba'. All is satiny white.

A procession of fine things followed. 'Truth' (1936) was a sure-textured flower with a bold crown less trumpety than that of 'Slemish'. 'Zero' (1935) was stocky with large flowers with extraordinary long pointed petals and flanged trumpet crowns, all snow white. 'Ave' (1935) came from 'Truth' × 'Slemish' and is a model white long cup, faultless in its even perianth and crown finished with a neat rolled flange. The unadulterated purity of its flowers is a delight.

'Knowehead' (1954) and 'Glendermott' (1957) marked a further advance in strength and size, with firm pure-white flowers showing a certain allegiance to the trumpets. The corona of 'Knowehead' could make it qualify as a trumpet if it were not for the tremendous width of the perianth. 'Glendermott' from 'Truth' had the huge trumpet 'Broughshane' as pollen parent, and it inherits some of its vigour.

Whilst increase of size and refinement was happening on the trumpet flank of the class, the other flank against the short cups was undergoing changes. 'Easter Moon' (1954) was a triumph, with thick firm creaseless petals. Its cups are neat puckered goblets which start with a touch of cream but soon become white, though always showing green from the perianth tube in the base of the cup. Its quality means it has been much used in whites, and also in the toned flowers of the 'Throckmortonii'.

Other breeders did not ignore the whites. Richardson bred a number including 'Early Mist' (1953), a tall plant with early blooms with good petals and trumpet crowns. John Lea crossed Wilson's 'Ave' with Richardson's 'Early Mist' to produce 'Canisp' (1960), a flower that won him many awards and prizes. Judges were captivated by the satin-smooth finish and the vivid whiteness, and perhaps they were also intrigued by the coronas which may be just lightly opened at the mouth, but can have a rolled-flange finish that adds extra sparkle to a highly groomed flower. Fred Board was a strong advocate of 'Easter Moon', and bred 'Broomhill' from it by pollen of 'Knowehead'. It inherited 'Easter Moon's' waxen smooth quality and is a snow-white show flower that has won top prizes all over the world. Board's 'Glenside' came from 'Easter Moon' by the small but perfect 'Pigeon'. Its frosty whiteness is enlivened by a touch of green in the base of the narrow crown. Assessing the quality of whiteness is a matter of comparison. One of the most vivid flowers we grow is 'Blue Bird' (1969), a rather late flower with thick oval petals and a bowl crown that seems to have shadows of blue, the snowy whiteness is so bright. 'Inverpolly' (1980) and 'Ben Hee' (1964) are also runners in the whiter-than-white stakes, both bred from 'Easter Moon' × 'Omeath'. They are high-quality show flowers, immaculately groomed and pristine. Strong-growing 'Worcester' has a wide, sparkling perianth and wide-bowl crown, opening cream but soon becoming white.

White-and-yellow long cups

After a lifetime growing daffodils it still surprises me that the white-and-yellow flowers are not more popular. The colour combination is fresh and spring-like, and the two-tone bicolouring echoes the much-loved wild daffodil of parts of the English and Scottish countryside. Certainly when totting up the number of bulbs of different types that have been sold we have always found these to be low in the charts. It is not as if there were not many fine kinds of this colouring, and as plants there are none better; their low scoring in the popularity polls is one of life's little mysteries.

Some of the finest of this class were bred by P. D. Williams and, amazingly after so many years, there are still some kinds that are widely grown and worth planting in the garden. 'Polindra' (1927), with pure white thick-textured petals and neat primrose goblet cups is still to be found. 'Tunis' (1927) was another Williams flower, this time with a flanged crown of pale yellow but painted with hints of buff, especially around the mouth. Both were strong plants and had a long period in catalogues, and in America they were not only welcomed as garden plants but they were seen as important breeders. Frank Reinelt used 'Tunis' very extensively, whilst 'Polindra' features in a selection of Grant Mitsch's and Murray Evan's breeding. 'Niphetos' (1927) was a third Williams flower that was recognized as important for breeding. Good white perianths backed a trumpet crown of palish primrose. 'Niphetos' was extensively used for raising whites, but was also crossed with red cups to give flowers like 'Fermoy' (1938), which itself features in the pedigree of many fine modern red and whites.

Nearly 60 years after its registration, 'Brunswick' (1931) is still grown by the ton in Britain. It is used as a cut flower as well as in the bulb trade. Despite all the many fine flowers that have come along in the past 50 or so years, I would still recommend planting 'Brunswick' in the garden where a white-and-lemon flower is needed. It is a fine strong bulb for naturalizing in grass or between shrubs, is not too prone to splitting, and is able to stand and deliver ample crops of flowers year after year without being lifted. Its petals are roughly triangular, and the crowns have flanged serrated mouths and, starting lemon, fade in the centre to a greyish base with white above and with the lemon retained around the mouth. Blue-green foliage with white and lemon makes a very pleasing spring picture.

Two other flowers from way back are still talked of, and their influence in breeding honoured. These are Engleheart's 'Mitylene'

(1923) and 'White Sentinel' (1926). They were siblings from 'Beacon' × a seedling. They were very smooth flowers with pointed wide satiny petals and crowns of primrose. It was a good day's work when Engleheart made the cross that produced these two flowers, since they formed a pivot which enabled breeders to move forward on a broad field. Not only were other white-and-yellow flowers bred from them, but they helped in the betterment of the whites, were used to improve the red cups, and surprisingly became important founder members of the pink breeding club. Open pollinated seed of 'White Sentinel' gave 'My Love' (1948), a tall imposing flower of such good quality that it is still winning prizes four decades later. Its wide oval petals are made out of pure white satin, and the not-too-large primrose crown is gently flanged to give just the right balance.

Another pivotal breeding flower arrived in the form of 'Green Island' (1938). It was bred from the good Dutch flower 'Gracious' (1931), a tall white-and-pale-yellow flower, by pollen of 'Seraglio' a round, pale yellow-petalled one with a shallow crown banded with tangerine. 'Seraglio' had come from two yellow-petalled flowers, the smaller rimmed 'Mozart', son of 'Princess Mary', by pollen of 'Gallipoli', a 'Will Scarlett' seedling – altogether a mixed and potent brew! 'Green Island' inherited the wide rounded petals of 'Seraglio', but they were pure white, and the bowl crown, a compromise in size between the parents, was broadly banded lemon around the brim but pale lemonade or white within. It was a plant bursting with energy. Another strong plant, 'Tudor Minstrel' (1948) arrived a decade later. It is widely grown today for flowers which are often easily 13 centimetres across with wide petals behind bowls of deep egg-yoke yellow, a colour spilt onto the base of the petals. This flower has a neck problem, a tendency to look downwards when young. Crossing 'Green Island' with 'Tudor Minstrel' gave the more upright 'Irish Minstrel' (1958), a flower favouring its father in form and colour. This, by open-pollinated seed, engendered 'Irish Mist', still one of the best fully-coloured bicolours of this section. The America 'Festivity' registered as long ago as 1954 was clearly a rival to 'Tudor Minstrel' which at the time was making all the running. Its colour and quality were at least as good: thick firm flat petals and its fractionally less-flared crown ensured a very correct show form, and its stems were taller and the whole flower more boldly posed. It won on points but although a strong, healthy bulb, it has proved a slow and steady rather than a spectacular increaser.

Nearly every type of flower got crossed with 'Green Island'. One mating was seen as a very good bet by almost every breeder, issue from 'Green Island' crossed with the Division Three 'Chinese White' would have all the blood to produce quality flowers, and so it proved. They came in various guises. There were short and long cups, some were all-whites, others were bicolours, and a few started playing tricks by opening with white petals but ending up coloured. There are a few crosses that mark watersheds in breeding: the 'King of the North' × 'Content', and 'Kilworth' × 'Arbar' crosses were two, and this 'Green Island' × 'Chinese White' coupling was a third. Fine flowers came from amateur and professionals alike. Richardson's 'Pontresina' (1958) was an early entry that has stayed the course and is still one of the finest products, with a perfectly rounded pure-white perianth encircling an almost flat crown of pale primrose neatly serrated. Grant Mitsch completed the cross with a generous number of seeds. Some of the best seedlings were all white like the small cup 'Silken Sails', one of the loveliest of all-whites, but there were impressive large cups with some yellow painting. 'Oratorio' (1959) and 'Bit o' Gold' (1965) are two impressive ones, 'Bit o' Gold' having the flatter perianth and a shallower corona. Very wide circles of snow white echo the shape of the almost disc-like cup which, opening pale lemon, fades to near pure white but with a ruffled ribbon of bright lemon–gold retained.

'Oratorio' is a bulb and flower of great vigour, the extraordinarily wide petals almost falling over themselves to make a strong white sphere around the bold crown of pale lemonade shading to shining lemon as a band at the margin. It has given some interesting seedlings. 'Yellowthroat' (1975) was the result of mating with the strong pink 'Accent'. Its perianth is all-white orthodoxy, but the large crown opens orange-yellow and fades to ivory cream except in the deep-honey base.

Buff-coloured cups are nothing new. 'Penvose' (1927) was a Williams entry with tough thick upright blue leaves, and stems with boldly-posed flowers which had triangular petals and a flanged trumpet crown opening yellow but quickly becoming an interesting warm, tawny, amber buff. These colours arrived in seedling beds where the aim had been to produce pink cups, yellow cups, and white seedlings. From self-fertilized seed of the large white trumpet 'Broughshane' came 'Careysville' (1958). It has a very ample good white perianth behind a large trumpety crown of warm biscuity buff made all the more attractive by the much-rolled-back edge.

White-and-pink long cups

The story of the breeding of the pink-corona daffodils is a fascinating one, concerning a worldwide endeavour with results beyond all the apparently idle dreams of early breeders. There is no record of anyone setting out to breed pinks before the first ones arrived fortuitously. Admittedly the first ones to show the beginnings of the colour usually had only pale fleeting suggestions rather than firmly painted facts. Faith was needed in the eye of the beholder, but then faith is part of the stock-in-trade of daffodil breeders. Fleeting fawny flushes were enough to start everyone on concentrated and prolonged breeding work.

Pink colour seems to have appeared as the result of two influences, the genetic material donated by the *N. poeticus* ancestors, genes governing the pigmentation of their red-rimmed eyes, and the genetic input which came originally from the little wild white species, the *N. moschatus* forms then called *N. abscissus* and *N. alpestris*. Hints of the possible derivation of this later genetic donation was seen, with hindsight, in the browny-pink colour of the dying tissue of the trumpet flowers as they faded away. The rimmed-eyed poets were on the whole flowers with grand perianths, while the little trumpet species were nodding flowers with petals which tended to fall forward towards trumpets shaped like drainpipes. As breeders got to work it seemed as if there was a considerable amount of linkage between genetic material governing colour and that influencing flower form. As new flowers bloomed in the seedling beds, the best-formed ones would have pink confined to an edge around the corona lip, while the flowers showing good flushes of pink all down the corona were likely to have wretched floppy petals and to be peering shyly downwards. Inheritance, as usual, was a mixed blessing.

Poeticus influence was transmitted through such flowers as 'Princess Mary' (1884) that I imagine came from *N. poeticus hellenicus* and a yellow or bicolour trumpet kind. 'Princess Mary' crossed with a poeticus gave Engleheart 'Beacon' (1897), a yellow flower with red in the cup. In 'Beacon' he had a flower with the magic touch, and its seedlings transcended the parents. It seemed able to add smoothness to almost any breeding alliance. Crossed with a seedling it gave Engleheart the two fine white-and-primrose flowers 'Mitylene' and 'White Sentinel' that for a long time formed one of the main base lines for pink breeding. 'Princess Mary' was parent to 'Mozart' which, mated with 'Gallipoli', gave 'Seraglio', the pollen parent of 'Green

Island'. This last has given a number of pink-crowned flowers, but the most important was 'Rose Caprice', useful in strengthening the constitutions of modern pinks. 'Gallipoli' had 'Will Scarlett' as one parent so it was thereby contributing both the rather disastrous perianth influence of *N. poeticus poetarum* but also possibly the benefit of solid cup-colouring. The other parent of 'Will Scarlett' was a white trumpet species and so in this instance the two strands of pink inheritance came together early.

Poeticus blood was strengthened via Engleheart's poet 'Dactyl' (1923), which gave Guy Wilson a lovely little white flower with a green eye, 'Cushlake' (1934). This in its turn was a parent to 'Interim' a very decorative tall flower with reflexed petals and a crown of citron banded bright pink. Many 'Interim' seedlings came with cups uniformly bright pink. One of these was 'Irish Rose' (1953), probably one of the parents of 'Passionale'.

Whilst the breeders were getting excited about their little flushes, and were working away trying to strengthen colour and improve quality, gardeners were unimpressed – until the introduction of 'Mrs R. O. Backhouse' (1923). Fanciers are inclined to look askance at this flower nowadays and to curse it for its ability to pass on a very indifferent perianth to some of its descendants. However, it really was a remarkable advance. The young flowers had reasonably smooth white petals, but unhappily these soon curled to become very windmilly just as the originally chrome-yellow trumpet crown became strongly suffused with rich rosy pink. The public however was convinced – there was such a thing as a pink daffodil. For decades catalogues of wholesalers and more popular retailers listed 'Mrs R. O. Backhouse' as 'The Pink Daffodil'. The purist breeders tended to fight shy of using it too heavily, but more adventurous spirits were willing to throw away a lot of dross in order to treasure one or two good things. Mitsch produced 'Radiation' (1954) from it, and this was a very pleasant smooth flower of good form with a silky perianth and a trumpet crown of pleasing pink.

The masterplan in the pink breeding was to combine the quality of the poeticus inheritance with good solid colour influenced by the trumpet background. On the whole it was a long war of attrition against the degrading factors, while trying to combine the best of the two strains. Against this trend a useful bit of line breeding resulted in pinks where the colouring may have been governed by recessive factors. Open, probably self-pollinated, seed from 'White Sentinel' gave 'Rose of Tralee' (1937), with a fine perianth backing a chaste trumpet crown nicely flushed rose pink throughout its length. 'Rose of Tralee' selfed gave 'Salmon Trout' (1948), still a very fine flower with an excellent wide smooth perianth and large, flanged crown opening yellow but soon becoming a very rich solid pink.

'Passionale' (1956) came from 'Rose of Tralee' probably crossed with 'Irish Rose', although it just could have been selfed. 'Passionale' is an exceptional kind. Its flowers are very freely produced and are all of satiny snow quality with widely triangular petals held flat away from neat flanged crowns of pure dog-rose pink. Its bulbs are prodigiously vigorous. It has won prizes all over the world as a show flower and as a garden plant. Commercial growers have been happy to grow it as it is obviously the sort of plant that the gardener wants – floriferous, easy, and reliable. It is now grown by the ton.

'Evening' (1935) was a smallish plant with flat pointed perianths and long straight-sided trumpet crowns all in white. However it did give pink seedlings, of which 'Lisbreen' and 'Wild Rose' were two. Bright little 'Wild Rose' (1939) had a relatively small cup, but it was the brightest, darkest pink of its day. Despite its small size, it just had to be used in breeding. Richardson crossed it with 'Rose Caprice' to try to get larger stronger plants and flowers of richer colouring. 'Debutante' (1956) was a bright one combining good qualities from both parents, and this was used in breeding even better things. 'Rose of Tralee' × 'Lisbreen' gave 'Rosewell' which, when crossed with 'Salmon Trout', gave some excellent plants such as 'Marietta' and 'Rhinemaiden'.

'Green Island' influence, via 'Rose Caprice', helped to produce a whole new range of strong plants and large bold flowers. 'Salome' (1958) is now grown in large quantities in Britain and Holland, and comes from 'Salmon Trout' × 'Rose Caprice'. 'Rose Royale' (1958) has 'Salmon Trout' as father and is still reckoned one of the best show flowers yet seen. Perfect pure-white perianths enhance the neatly modelled opened crowns of unadulterated rose-pink. Size and quality here combine in a strong flower and plant. 'Infatuation' (1954) was a strongly-coloured flower of high quality from 'Glenshane' × 'Waterville' that in its turn gave some of today's top pinks. 'Fair Prospect' (1962), from 'Infatuation' × 'Debutante', joins superb quality with rich colour, the pink enlivened by a touch of green in the base of the crown. 'Romance' caused great excitement when first shown. Coming from 'Rose Caprice' × 'Infatuation' (1959), it remains a distinct and outstanding flower. A heavy-substanced pure-white perianth generously surrounds a cup that is unusually but neatly lobed by cuts two thirds of its depth. The colour is a rich dark pink just a little paler in the base.

Before they devoted themselves exclusively to lilies, the Oregon Bulb Farms had taken a real interest in breeding daffodils as well. Some of their seedlings have become widely grown, being chosen perhaps for garden rather than show qualities. Amongst others, they produced two pinks that were to prove useful in breeding. 'Mabel Taylor' (1955) was an upright rimmed pink rather like 'Interim' but without the reflexed perianth; 'Carita' (1958) was instantly eye-catching with a very wide, flared, rosy crown, too wide for the purist but wanted by everyone else.

Grant Mitsch and the Havens have persevered with pink-crowned kinds to such an effect that many of the latest seedlings are now being described as red, so deep is the colour. An important early success was bred from 'Mabel Tayor' × 'Green Island'. 'Precedent' (1961) is a tall strong plant with bold flowers of definite rounded form, and with a shallow crown broadly ribboned with apricot pink. Another flower was introduced the same year. This was 'Accent' (1961), from 'Interim' × 'Interlude'. It marked a big step forward in the depth of colour, with a longish crown of a reddish pink blended from a deep rose and salmon. Colour contrast was noticed first, but almost as quickly the smooth quality registered. Whilst not ignoring the possibilities inheritent in other cultivars, Grant Mitsch made the foundation of his breeding stock the cultivars 'Accent', 'Precedent', 'Carita' and their progeny, especially 'Cool Flame' and 'Tangent'.

'Cool Flame' (1969), from 'Precedent' × 'Accent', marked a further step towards the red-corona daffodil. 'Accent' had been strong but this flower with thick smooth white petals has a shorter cup which is heavily fluted and a dramatic dark pinky red. Introduced in the same year was 'Tangent' (1969), from 'Green Island' × 'Accent'. This is a tall immaculate flower with white alabaster petals and neat cups of dark pink but a little lighter towards the centre. Other very fine things came from the 'Precedent' × 'Accent' mating. 'Elirose' (1973), 'Ruby Throat' (1973) and 'High Repute' (1975) were three outstanding ones. 'Elirose' comes before many other pinks, and is a bold decorative flower with large singing pink crowns made all the more obvious by the reflexing of the heavy-calibre white perianths. 'High Repute' has taken its parent 'Precedent' for its model, but is even larger, with wider rounded petals which make a flat background to a shallow saucer of solid salmony pink. 'Rubythroat' is in the 'Cool Flame' mould but larger, wider petalled, and starting life with a greater depth of contrast between the white and the rich rosy red.

Other flowers were bred from 'Precedent' × 'Carita', some startling both in form and colour. 'Plover' (1976) is given a surprised look by its somewhat shot-back perianth – and certainly it surprises with its fluted saucer centre of salmony pink. 'Confection' (1974) and 'Lilac Delight' (1975) look exciting, the first with very wide crowns of rich pink shades, and the second with good perianths and saucer crowns of salmon pink with more than just a hint of lilac. For those who enjoy flamboyant daffodils a third one from this parentage, 'Sentinel' (1974) will prove irresistible. This is tall and large with good round perianths that are almost lost behind an almost ridiculously widespun plate of salmon and rich-pink colouring.

New generations of seedlings show advances on the parents. From 'Romance' × 'Cool Flame' came 'Culmination' (1982), combining the qualities of both parents, but with perhaps a more even set of flowers than either. The colour of the crowns is a rich deep coral pink. 'Refrain' (1983) is making its way as one of the top exhibition flowers and is tall, strong, and beautifully coloured. From the high-grade parentage ('Accent' × 'Rose Caprice') × 'Cool Flame' came 'Magician' (1982). This has tended to put all former dark pinks in the shade. It has wide thick white perianths, but the flared bowl is beyond any definition of pink – the pigment intensity has resulted in a deep orange-tinged red.

Yellow-and-pink large cups

Battle is engaged now a broad front in breeding. In one spot the activity will be a matter of steadily entrenching and consolidating previous successes; in another spot there are rapid advances being made; and in one or two areas a new breakthrough enables a whole new front to be engaged. Yellow-petalled pink cups are one such new front, one of total mobility. They were first bred in Australia and New Zealand, and a number of fine kinds are well established there. A few have turned up in British breeding, but the main influx of new types is coming from the Mitsch-Havens seedling beds.

Yellow and pink is not always a happy combination. There are dahlias of these two colours, and they are not on the whole my favourites amongst this flamboyant lot. Most yellow-and-pink daffodils are painted in muted tones, with the yellows tending to be of the lemony persuasion rather than brassy golds. Perhaps this is the reason that the colour combination seems an acceptable one – the slight astringency of the lemon helps to avoid a too sickly feel. The same applies to the pleasant 'Pastel Pink' (1964) from David Bell in New Zealand. We have a number of these flowers from the southern hemisphere, in varying shades of lemon and pink. They look well in the garden, and are quite delightful cut.

One of the first of the Mitsch flowers of this genre was 'Milestone' (1971). Pointed petals of soft primrose-lemon back a somewhat frilled longish crown well flushed with apricot-pink that is darker at the mouth. 'Memento' (1981) and 'Lorikeet' (1979) are yellow-petalled 'Rima' derivatives, but both are trumpet kinds. 'Widgeon' (1976), coming from open-pollinated 'Daydream' seed, typifies the type of flower that can be bred. This is a marvellous plant with lots of large flowers of excellent form. The petals make a widely overlapping soft lemon perianth, whilst the gently flared, quite large crown is basically the same colour but develops a lovely soft shell-pink colour. It grows and increases quickly.

White-and-pink 'Leonaine' has yellow-petalled ancestors, and it will give seedlings with yellow. Mitsch introduced 'Bookmark' (1978) from 'Leonaine' × 'Daydream', and this has proved another good grower and an excellent flower. Its ironed perianths are deepish lemon with a leaning towards buffiness, and its well balanced crowns are suffused a salmony pink and are made decorative with a frilled edge. The hint of buff in the perianth suggests the possibility of all-pink daffodils sometime in the future. 'Sugar Maple' (1979) comes from the same parentage. Rich lemon perianths of fine quality back bold crowns that develop to have a whitish base, but are painted most of their length with a rich amalgam of apricot and salmon-pink especially deep at the mouth. 'Irresistible' (1982) is from the next generation of seedlings, coming from 'Milestone' × 'Sugar Maple'. The perianth is of very good strong substance, but coloured pale shades of biscuity lemon. The open crown is buffy on the outside but very much more pink inside.

Reverse bicolour flowers of trumpet and large-cup proportions often show hints of pinky apricot colouring. We had one seedling the crown of which we decided could only be described as brown. Yellow-petalled pinks arrive by other routes. 'Leonaine' is one gateway, but most would seem to trace their colour back through such flowers as 'Green Island' to 'Seraglio' and relations. Pink-crowned 'Rose-Caprice', a 'Green Island' seedling, can give flowers with yellow perianths. 'New World' (1984) is one with lemonade-shaded petals and an attractively flanged and ruffled crown of similar colour but flushed with salmony pink.

Reverse bicolour long cups

An enthusiast in Tasmania, daunted by the high prices of many novelties, wrote to Guy Wilson in Northern Ireland to ask if he would consider sending out some seed. To Guy Wilson there could only be one response to such a request, and a selection was sent and duly planted. After five years there appeared amongst the resulting flowering plants a pleasing lemon–petalled flower with a bold, slightly darker crown. Looking at it a few days later the grower was excited to notice that the flower had changed – whilst the perianth remained lemon, the crown had faded to a paler shade and eventually ended up almost pure white. This was the first flower of the cultivar that was registered as 'Binkie' in 1938. Bulbs were sent to Britain and from there it went all over the world, the sole representative of a new type of daffodil for which the class 'Reversed Bicolour' had to be made. 'Binkie' is still widely grown and is worth its place. It is sturdy with well-formed flowers that last well. It makes a useful garden plant for naturalizing, the bulbs being strong and persistent bloomers if planted fairly deep.

For some time 'Binkie' was the sole representative of its new class. Grant Mitsch changed that. He involved it in his lemon breeding programme. As seed parent to his 'King of the North' × 'Content' seedlings, 'Binkie' soon produced a wonderful range of flowers. 'Bethany' (1958) was followed by 'Daydream' in 1960. They were clearly advances, similar flowers with very wide, completely flat petals and bold trumpet crowns. 'Bethany' opens a day or so earlier, and 'Daydream' is half a tone darker in its vibrant dark lemon. Both organize their coronas to pass to white. 'Daydream' increases rather more quickly and has become the standard against which all following kinds are measured as show flowers. It remains an outstanding contender itself, and must have by far the greatest number of show honours of any of this class.

From this same cross came a number of taller flowers. 'Limeade' (1962), 'Halolight' (1960), 'Nazareth' (1958) and 'Charter' (1964) were four. They are characterized by having flat perianths standing at right angles to the coronas which are narrower than those of 'Daydream'. In the garden they look quite stunning. 'Charter' opens earliest and is still going strong after later flowers have opened and show signs of fading away. It has won all the major awards for show and for garden use, and is looked upon as one of the very best garden plants. The bulbs grow well, the plants are excellent, and the many flowers are boldly posed so that their long life is fully exploited. Like the others it opens with coronas a shade or so darker than the mid-lemon petals, but it speedily becomes a reverse bicolour, quicker than 'Binkie' and many others, and is soon shining lemon and white.

To increase the genetic variability of the class, crosses were made with flowers that were not reverses but could possibly contribute useful characteristics. Tough yellow 'Butterscotch' was involved, as well as 'Playboy'. 'Playboy' crossed with 'Daydream' gave a number of good seedlings, of which 'Green Gold' (1976) was one of the most successful. It is a strong, sturdy plant with lots of flowers, all out of an immaculate mould. Wide rather pointed petals back a slender crown neatly expanded at the brim. Sharp deep intense lemon permeates the gold to such an extent that it gives a really 'greenish' cast to the flower. The crown fades to a paler colouring. From open-pollinated seed of this 'Playboy' × 'Daydream' cross came some well-contrasted flowers of which 'Glisten' (1982) is a most effective one, with trumpet-shaped crowns that quickly bleach to white but leave a fluorescent deep-lemon perianth.

Eyes are sometimes deceived by actual measurements, and what looks like a trumpet may just fail to measure correct proportions. This may matter to the show fanatic, but to the gardener of normal mental equilibrium it is of little or no consequence. 'Scholar' (1977) from 'Bethany' × 'Butterscotch' is one of these borderline cases. It may be called 'Scholar', but it has little to learn in the matter of correct form and colour. The trumpet crown is finished with a neat roll and fades to near white. 'Taffy' (1977) is one of a number of flowers that not only have some buffiness showing in the flared crowns, but have it suffusing the petals too. 'Water Music' (1976) comes from the same parents, 'Nazareth' × 'Butterscotch'. As might be guessed from this parentage, this is a tall strong flower of splendid form and pose. It is a cool pale flower with an ironed, pointed perianth amply backing a slender crown that gently pales day by day, and eventually becomes almost pure white.

'Aircastle', the lovely small-cup kind with a disc-like cup, has given several fine reverse bicolours. 'Dotteral' (1976) came from 'Daydream' pollen. Mr Mitsch had declared the object of this extensive cross to have been the production of small-cupped reverse bicolours. The majority of the seedlings were too large and vigorous to fit into this category, but there were some lovely flowers neverthe-less. 'Dotteral' has the rounded perianth of its mother, the lemon petals tending to have a little incurved edge but still being most pleasing. The deep bowl soon becomes white but with a pencilled rim of colour. 'Shearwater' from 'Aircastle' × 'Homage' is one of the crosses that has not involved the usual reverse ancestors. It is a large, rounded flower with a white perianth that soon becomes a beige lemon. A small, shallow primrose cup becomes white with a residual lemon rim. 'Lark', which comes from the small-cupped 'Irish Coffee' by another small-cupped seedling, has the look of a small cup. Opening pale lemon, the shallow cup quite soon becomes white. It is a smooth, rounded flower unlike the majority of this class. 'Parody' (1983) comes from the more obvious orthodox parentage 'Daydream' × 'Binkie', and is in the same colour range as 'Binkie', but it has a longer crown and the reflexing petals ape the cyclamineus hybrids.

Another interesting group of hybrids has evolved by using reverse bicolours with *N. jonquilla* and, more particularly, with the fertile jonquil hybrid 'Quick Step'. These plants could have a considerable future as they are of a pleasing size, not too large for modern gardens; they grow easily and increase quickly; and they are floriferous and attractive. Progeny of this breeding has been allocated either to the jonquilla division where two or more heads are deemed better than one, or to the long cups when single headed. All classifications must have some areas of artificiality. I cannot look at flowers like 'Cloud Nine' (1964), 'Misty Meadow' (1981), or 'Ptarmigan' (1976) without thinking of them as jonquils. These are all intermediate-sized plants and flowers, very substantially smaller than the other reversed flowers and wonderful garden plants either in the border or a larger rock garden. They are healthy bulbs with rapid rates of increase. The first two came from 'Quick Step' × 'Daydream'. 'Cloud Nine' is a dandy flower with pointed flat petals and neat goblet cups. All is a rich shining lemon gold, but the cups become pure white. Arriving towards the end of the flowering season, they are very freely produced and look quite enchanting.

There is a shadow of doubt about the father of 'Misty Meadow' which was raised from open-pollinated 'Quick Step' seed, but it certainly looks as if pollen of 'Daydream' made its way by insect, wind, or unrecorded brushstroke. It has an excellent lemon perianth and a flared, pure-white cup. 'Ptarmigan' came from 'Daydream'. The pollen parent is registered as *N. jonquilla*, which may be correct, but although the flower is only of modest size there is little else to back this parental claim. It has a perfect deep lemon-gold perianth and a showy crown of very decorative frilled and lobed form in white, with a lemon smile lingering around the edges.

The past few decades have seen the consolidation of this class and a substantial vote of approval from the general public. These flowers are much sought after, and their future seems very secure. Some interesting ones are bound to arrive that combine a yellow, or yellow-and-white, perianth with a crown that may have several colours, pinks and oranges as well as whites and lemons. The buff to be seen in some petals raises the possibility of orange or pink-petalled flowers with paler coronas. Other flowers with the outside corona tending to be a different shade to the inside suggest all sorts of interesting and subtle colour zones to stretch further the minds of classifiers.

11

Short-cupped daffodils

Short-cupped cultivars are closer to the poeticus ancestry than the long-cupped, and this has brought both blessings and drawbacks. In the beginning the better petal shape, the smoother texture, and surer substance all told in favour of the blood. Possible drawbacks were the late flowering season and, more importantly, the tendency of any red colour to burn or fade fast in the sunlight. Also, for a few generations the shape of the bulb often left a lot to be desired, being frequently very necky and rough, and the plants lacked some of the robust extrovert nature of many of their long-cupped relations, and were inclined to be less happy about being out of the ground.

Over the generations the bulbs and plants increased in vigour, but this often produced a paradoxical situation in which breeders succeeded so well in improving the vigour of the plants that the flowers tended to put on extra length to their coronas. The extra vigour and tissue of a good seedling goes almost straight to the corona, and this is one reason for this division being less populated.

Other reasons for smaller numbers of short cups are not hard to find. Short cups are defined as those with flowers with coronas not more than one-third the length of the perianth segments. It would seem obvious that the odds are stacked heavily in favour of the long cups numerically, since their cups can be one third to within a whisper of full trumpet length. Maybe it is less obvious that the short cups lack sales potential in a couple of ways. Firstly, they lose out by being late into the field with their flowers, since earlier blossom is going to catch the eye of the gardener first. For most gardeners the earlier flower is the more important anyway, and of course the earlier flowers are easier for growers to exhibit to a flower-hungry public. Secondly, quite simply the larger cups have a much larger acreage of flowers with which to beguile the onlooker, and large cups of orange are going to look more impressive than small cups of the same shade.

In the last decade or so there has been an influx of new varieties into this divison, due almost entirely to the work of one amateur breeder. Dr Throckmorton in America has taken those flowers that change perianth and corona colour after opening to be his specialized field, and has produced a stream of very high-quality flowers. Whilst some of these have infiltrated their way into the large-cup category, often whilst still looking like Division 3 flowers, the majority of his seedlings are clearly short cups.

Some of the first flowers of small-cupped proportions would look very weedy nowadays. 'Barrii Conspicuus', bred by Backhouse of York, won a First Class Certificate in 1886, and was for years a leading kind. Writing in 1910 the Rev. Joseph Jacob descibes it as 'the most popular Narcissus in commerce.' It had primrose petals and a yellow cup edged with orange. Some of these early kinds can be found in the pedigrees of today's flowers. Engleheart's 'White Lady' (1898) sometimes features in this way. I can remember it growing in grass in Northern Ireland, a pretty little white-petalled flower with a small puckered cup of lemon. Undoubtedly the most important of these early flowers was Engleheart's 'Beacon' (1897), with palish-yellow petals and a small cup rimmed orange. It was still to be found growing in the stocks of Guy Wilson in the early 1950s. Though quite a small thing as I saw it then, it had the ability to produce very much larger flowers by its seed or pollen, and the smooth quality of these seedlings was quite exceptional.

Yellow-petalled short cups

These may be sorted out into three groups: those showing orange or red colouring, the yellow-petalled bred before the toned flowers, and the newer toned flowers. Most of the red cups were attractive but dogged by their inability to shun the heat of the sun. 'Birma' (1960) is a pleasing smooth flower with golden petals slighty swept back from a neat dark orange-red cup, but alas the cup burns whilst you look at it. Other red cups are more interesting. 'Altruist' looks like a poeticus in form and satiny quality. It has a nearly flat small cup of dark scarlet, but the petals are a pinky rouged shade making it a most attractive flower, especially when young since its petal colour fades. 'Sabine Hay' (1970) is somewhat taller, a little larger, and much richer in the pinky tangerine of its perianth around a neat dark cup. This colour too eventually fades, but these flowers must point towards things to come. More traditional is a small, very late Australian flower called 'Oakwood' which is normally a uniform mid-yellow, but can have a rim of orange in some seasons. It may be useful for breeding late yellow-petalled flowers, of which we have still only a few.

Richardson's 'Lemonade' (1959) was for some time almost the only serious contender in show classes for yellow short cups. It was a rounded pale-coloured flower, but perhaps not the most reliable of the genus.

The toned flowers, the ones opening one colour and assuming others afterwards, are really most exciting. After all, no flower remains exactly as it first opens, and it makes life more interesting if flowers grow and change in character. This series started in earnest with Mitsch's 'Aircastle' (1958), 'Beige Beauty' (1960), 'Irish Coffee' (1967), and 'Old Satin' (1967). They came from 'Green Island' × 'Chinese White'. These are all high-quality flowers, 'Aircastle', possibly the largest and smoothest of a very smooth lot, being twice best flower at the London Daffodil Show. Its petals are widely-overlapping circles that open sparkling white behind a flat disc cup of palest primrose with a slightly darker rim. After a few days the petals take on soft lemon-beige shading so that it spends at least half its life with coloured petals. 'Beige Beauty' does a similar trick, the very shallow saucer cup fading sometimes so that the flower can end up close to a reverse bicolour. Its petals are a fraction less wide. 'Old Satin' performs similarly by changing colour and sometimes becoming a reverse bicolour before ending its days. It opens looking like 'Aircastle' with its wider circular petals, but is of rather firmer substance. 'Irish Coffee' is delicious. Smooth ivory petals surround a shallow cup of primrose-edged tangerine, but the perianth soon becomes quite richly suffused with lemon, whilst the cup fades to white but perhaps retaining some colour around its rim.

Dr Throckmorton has been introducing toned flowers from 1974 onwards via the Mitsch-Havens catalogue. 'Easter Moon' × 'Irish Coffee' produced a number of early successes. 'The Benson' (1975) is a kind that changes less than most, and the firm circular perianth is a soft yellow, whilst the shallow cup opens and remains a darker yellow. 'Raw Silk' (1974) has large quality blooms. Its wide perianth is a pale primrose, and the neat cup opens yellow with a pale centre but whitens as it ages, so that the flower is virtually a reverse bicolour for much of its long life. 'Late Snow', (1975) from 'Old Satin' × the old, very white, tiny-cupped 'Bryher', has much of 'Bryher's' sparkling white in a very much firmer, broad perianth, whilst the small cup is centred with a telling dash of green with shaded beige and white above.

'Marque' (1974), from 'Old Satin' × 'Russet', is a strong grower with a perianth that opens near pure white but begins a process of darkening yellow, whilst the cup has a red rim that shades down first to orange and then to a golden eye somewhat shaded green. 'Russet' (1947) was a Guy Wilson small cup with a red centre and golden petals with a glistening sheen that suggested orange like a reflection of the cup colour. 'Russet' × 'Altruist' gave 'Centre Ville' (1976) which has a buffy, fawny perianth with the same glistening crystalline reflections of the deep red of the small cup.

A number of other flowers were brought into the breeding stud. Pink-rimmed small cup 'Gossamer' was used. Its pollen on 'Aircastle' gave 'First Formal' (1974) which looks, when opening, like a lovely flower of 'Aircastle' but with a pink rim. The perianth is a sparkling white but the flat corona has subtle shades rather like some shell colours – the pink later gives way to a rich gold, and the greenish eye becomes a little less obvious. 'Lalique' (1977) comes from the reverse cross and opens with a snow-white perianth and a yellow-cup but they then change dress with the cup ending nearly pure white whilst the perianth becomes steadily more yellow.

The most obvious step forward in breeding with these toned flowers would have been the stirring up of the genetic potential of the 'Aircastle', 'Old Satin', and 'Irish Coffee' cultivars, and this was duly done. 'Irish Coffee' × 'Aircastle' gave Dr Throckmorton 'Stinger' (1980), a most lovely quality flower with firm broad perianths of pale yellow and neat little cups of yellow usually edged paler. Every flower is of first-rate quality. Turning the parentage round the opposite way gave a number of fine flowers of which 'Earthlight' (1977) is one of the finest, a very perfectly organized circular flower of beige-yellow, but with slightly more yellow in the pale cup though this has a pale throat. 'Suave' (1976) is a smaller flower, opening with a firm white perianth that becomes yellow, and with a shallow cup that starts an interesting opalescent blue-grey but becomes yellow. 'Johnnie Walker' (1977) is a shining overall-yellow flower with a perfect rounded perianth and neat cup.

The rouge-petalled 'Altruist' was used as pollen on 'Old Satin' to give a number of interesting quality flowers. 'Star Trek' (1976) has a rather startled appearance with thick white petals tilted slightly back and a small green-centred cup which is yellow with a pencilled rim of red; 'On Edge' (1977) has a pale whispered-yellow perianth and a green-centred cup with a scarlet edge; 'Star Wish' (1977) is a rather fuller flower than sister 'Star Trek', with rounded petals gently reflexed from a sizeable flat cup of green-shaded lemon edged with a contrasting waved edge of red – the whole sparkles with crystalline quality; and 'State Fair' (1980) is a nice round flower with a fine yellow-toned perianth and a flattish, wide cup of various zones, with a green eye which gives way to yellow that is narrowly-edged red.

Grant Mitsch did not ignore these toned flowers after introducing the first ones. His 'Lyrebird' (1977), from 'Irish Coffee' crossed with a small-cupped reversed bicolour Richardson seedling, is a true reverse small cup. Pale lemon petals reflex slightly from a shallow fluted crown that opens lemon but soon turns to nearly snow white with an eye shaded as if with a grey pencil. 'Surfbird' (1981) came from 'Aircastle' × 'Homage', the pollen parent being a strong white kind capable of throwing fine coloured seedlings. 'Surfbird' starts with a firm white perianth that becomes a fawny yellow later, and the neat cup, opening lemon, pales just a little with age.

White-petalled small cups with coloured cups

White-and-yellow small cups are relatively scarce, red-cupped ones are much more numerous, and there is a goodly number of fine rim-eyed kinds. Quality has always been high in types that are close to the poeticus, and some of the red-rimmed flowers look like poets with a touch of magic added. 'Merlin' (1956) has long held a honoured place in most collections, a polished jewel. Faultless pure white perianths surround flat eyes of pale citron immaculately edged with dark red. It came from self-fertilized seed of the solid red-eyed 'Mahmoud'. Now 'Merlin' has given a few good seedlings. 'Scarlet Thread' is one with a double-triangle perianth shimmering behind a wide yellow flat corona of yellow-rimmed scarlet made more interesting with a green eye. Rather in the same medium-sized mould is 'Whitbourne' with thick white petals and eyes of green, yellow, and red. 'Dress Circle' is larger than 'Merlin' and maybe a day or two earlier, but has the same quality and colour.

Quite different is 'Kimmeridge', one of the most successful of all show flowers and larger than most of these rimmed types, with thick ivory petals held completely flat and a cup that is a pale citron but edged with pinky orange. This colour is stronger at the edge and shades away, sometimes quickly to leave a narrow rim but on occasions merging more gently into the very pale yellow. However this is one of those flowers grown by exhibitors but few others, since the colour fades without protection. 'Audubon' (1965) has a snowy perianth with a shallow cup opening pale citron with a bright rose-pink edge. The yellow fades with age.

There are a number of yellow-cupped kinds, often with green eyes that are particularly bewitching in the garden or cut. 'Green Hills' (1960) is a tall, very late, largish one with thick petals and neat cups of green-edged bright lemon. 'Grace Note' (1966), from 'Cushendall' × 'Cantabile', is another end-of-the-season flower, small with frosty white petals and a tiny eye of green with a frill of citron. 'Lemon Tree' (1980), from open-pollinated 'Cushendall', has mother's rounded perianth all sparkling white around a small frilled cup of lemon-centred green. Some years it will add just a touch of orange lipstick around the edge.

Other white-and-yellow flowers are in a different category, being larger and often with rimmed edges. Some are virtually pure-white flowers but have just an edge of cream or pale yellow. 'Syracuse' (1958) and 'Silken Sails' (1964) are two 'Green Island' × 'Chinese White' seedlings that many would think of as all-whites. They are rounded flowers with shallow cups opening cream but becoming almost completely white with only a hint of colour on their brims. 'Silken Sails' is a very large sparkling flower, one of the loveliest of the many fine kinds to come from this breeding. Another newer flower with delicate colouring is 'Evendine' (1985), a seedling from 'Pontresina' selfed. It has a faultless perianth of wide smooth sparkling petals behind a wide flat corona opening with a suggestion of cream, but with a brim of soft yellow. It fades to nearly pure white but a smile remains to play around the lips.

'Limey Circle' (1980), from 'Carnmoon' × 'Green Island', is a heavy-calibre flower of lovely form, whose white petals back a frilled white cup ribboned with lime yellow. 'Eminent' (1963), although a much older flower, is an excellent free-flowering plant with even crops of sparkling flowers. Rounded petals lean back just that degree or so to give added point to the saucer bowls of lemonade-shaded rich lemon at the brims.

White-and-red flowers look dramatic, blood on snow. Most early-bred types were hopelessly stricken by sunlight. As late as 1946 flowers were being introduced that looked quite splendid at shows, the blooms having been carefully protected, but which were a travesty in the garden. 'Professor Einstein' (1946) must have caught many a customer's eye at a show with its wide flat centres of brilliant scarlet, but a day in the sun soon puts paid to such brilliance. One of the first flowers to show any real resistance to the sun was 'Limerick' (1938), a neat flower with good pointed white petals and neat cups of deep orange-red. 'Mahmoud' (1937), with ivory petals and a small red cup centred with green looked like an extra-good poeticus. 'Matapan' (1941) was more rounded and more vivid, with the contrast of a snowfield with a flat ruby centre. 'Woodland Beauty' (1964) came from 'Mahmoud' × 'Matapan', – and is a larger flower than either with a sparkling white perianth and dark red, flat eye. 'Snow Gem' (1957) is rather in the same field. 'Irish Splendour' (1962) from Willie Dunlop outdid his previous fine red-and-whites by being larger and of lovely quality and vivid colour. Its flowers are often over 12 centimetres across and spread a pure white satin around a small cup of crimson. The brilliance is better than that of the best poeticus, but the size dismisses all thoughts of poets.

Size of flower is a dominant factor in breeding. Some of the smaller flowers are wonderful, but they are being lost behind the new introductions that have often stemmed from the famous 'Kilworth' × 'Arbar' production line that produced so many large cups. Some of the seedlings failed to make large-cup proportions. They were on the whole larger flowers than previous small cups, and were perhaps of a slightly different character – the white of the petal could have an undertow of cream, or the substance and texture were perhaps a little less frostily crystalline than the best of the previous kinds. However it is difficult to be critical of flowers like 'Rockall' (1955), 'Privateer' (1958), and 'Artillery' (1961), all with splendid perianths and bright coronas. Attempts were made to marry the strong-growing features of this series with the older more poeticus types. 'Cherry Spot' (1978) came from 'Artillery' × 'Avenger', with a pointed perianth and brilliant cup. 'Doctor Hugh' (1975) was from 'Mahmoud' × 'Don Carlos', and has proved a successful amalgam of the perfect shape and quality of the mother with the size and vigour of the father. The petals are a shining white, and the wide cup is flaming vermilion but with a green eye. 'Lucky Star' (1973) is from 'Irish Splendour' × 'Orion' and, as may be imagined, is a large flower. A circle of glistening white surrounds a small cup of scarlet red. In a somewhat different vein is 'Cherry Bounce' (1975), a flower from the pink-rimmed 'Gossamer' × 'Aircastle'. Initial snow-white perianths back small cups of a pinky cherry red, and petals take on a shadow of beige as they age.

All-white small cups

This is not a huge gathering, but what it may lack in quantity is more than made up for by the quality. Some small ones have good breeding with quality to spare. Guy Wilson produced his two seedlings, 'Cushendall' (1931) and 'Frigid' (1935), from a couple of Engleheart flowers, 'Emerald Eye' (1913) by pollen of the poet 'Dactyl' (1923). 'Cushendall' is circular with milk-white petals and a green cup edged with cream. 'Frigid' is frosty white, pointed petalled, and with a small cup centred dark green. Both are late flowers, and 'Frigid' particularly so. 'Dallas' (1948) is also a 'Cushendall' seedling, but much whiter. Its medium-sized flowers glisten like snow in the sunshine and the small flat cups are centred with green. These small flowers were diploids.

All the modern flowers are tetraploid and considerably stronger plants. The foundation of this new breeding was laid by the crossing of a tough, thick-textured flower called 'Rinsey' (1934) that had *N. poeticus hellenicus* as grandparent with the curious flower called 'Silver Plane' (1927), with thin white petals and a disc-like corona of lemon. A series of lovely flowers resulted, of which the most famous was 'Chinese White' (1937). Far larger than anything that had been grown of this type hitherto, it produced large circles of beautifully smooth, pure-white round petals and a corona, spun out like a plate, which was virtually pure-white and beautifully fluted.

The mating of 'Chinese White' with the large cup 'Green Island' was undertaken both ways, and was one of those pivotal bits of breeding like the 'Kilworth' × 'Arbar', or 'King of the North' × 'Content' series. One of the first of this progeny to be registered was 'Sacramento' (1949), a well-rounded, thick-textured smooth flower with a small frilled cup of milk white. It starts life with a touch of dark green deep in the centre. From the reverse cross, 'Green Island' × 'Chinese White', came a different character. This was 'Verona' (1958), a faultless exhibition flower that is still winning prizes. It wins by virtue of the sparkling petals that lie so completely flat and creaseless behind a corona that is spun flat against the perianth, but with attractive fluting. This centrepiece opens with a touch of rich cream but soon becomes white. Several other outstanding flowers of the same breeding followed. 'Dream Castle' in 1963 was taller than 'Verona' by over 10 centimetres, a huge round snowy-white moon with a small white saucer. 'April Clouds' came in 1966, another tall round white flower of lovely silken quality.

One of the most generous flowering kinds is 'Wings of Song' (1964) which was bred from 'Chinese White' by a seedling, one of whose parents was 'Sylvia O'Neill', a sibling of 'Chinese White'. Wide but pointed petals form a double-triangle perianth with just a suspicion of reflexing from the white saucer corona. 'Cool Crystal' (1966) is still a very sought-after bulb as its flowers are rounded and lovely like those of its 'Chinese White' mother, but with a slight reflex and a corona which is a shallow saucer crown. In it good size and quality are allied to purity of colour and a strong plant. 'White Tie' (1978) is a spin-off of the toned flower-breeding programme, a seedling from 'Aircastle' × 'Irish Coffee'. The perfection of its rounded form is linked with a sparkling, crystalline, pure-white perianth and a fluted, flat corona that opens with highlights of gold but soon becomes as pure as driven snow.

12

Double daffodils

Many gardeners dismiss double daffodils. They maintain that the description is tantamount to a contradiction in terms – the idea of a double daffodil is unthinkable, the whole point of this flower is its unique single form, and to abandon the form in imitation of a carnation, a camellia, or a dahlia, is a perversion. This is a viewpoint with which I can be sympathetic. Once I too was a rabid anti-double man. It was not only aesthetics that made the double division seem a second-rate assorted collection of monstrosities – they were damned also for their poor garden record, their unreliability, the failure of some to open their flowers properly, and their tendency to bow low over the ground, sometimes even touching it, because their stems were overburdened.

Doubles are mutants in which the sexual parts, the stigma and anthers, have been transmuted into extra petaloids. This happens very rarely either in the wild or under cultivation. Records from the 1500s onwards show that doubled forms were highly valued and carefully propagated. Some of the smaller of these do have real charm and, being smaller, are often less vulnerable to wind and rain. Double jonquils and some double trumpets became great favourites: 'Queen Anne's Double Jonquil', 'Queen Anne's Double Daffodil', and 'Van Sion' are three that are still grown and which have been treasured for centuries.

Perhaps we can adopt an attitude of mind that views the doubles as interesting, useful, and beautiful flowers, even if they are recognized primarily as flowers and only secondarily as daffodils. Some of the older kinds may have weaknesses in the garden, but others either outside or as cut flowers may have the advantage of being colourful for a longer period than their single counterparts, their extra petals helping them to fly the flag longer.

In the past new doubles have arisen as mutants, sports that have appeared in stocks of normal singles. 'Golden Ducat' was found amongst 'King Alfred', 'Dick Wilden' popped up amongst 'Carlton', and the double tazetta 'Cheerfulness' was found amongst 'Elvira'. This last is fortunate in having stems adequate for the flowerheads, but the two large yellows illustrate clearly the likely weakness of doubles arising as sports. Whilst both 'King Alfred' and 'Carlton' as single flowers have stems of perfectly sufficient strength, in their double manifestations the extra weight discovers a weak spot a third or half-way down the stem. The result is that many, if not all, fold over in times of wind and rain. Moreover the large heads can retain significant amounts of rain which add significantly to their weight and make them even more vulnerable.

Breeding new doubles has presented problems. If all the sexual parts of the flowers have been changed into petaloids, it is more than just difficult to know where to start. Some kinds like 'Queen Anne's Double Daffodil' make a complete job of using every molecule in forming their pale stars, but some doubles, whilst usually doing a whole-hearted conversion, may have weaker flowers in which the remnants of stamens are to be found fused on petal segments. Sometimes bits of stigma and even ovary are to be found. It was found that by using this pollen on another single flower, or by harvesting the odd seed that the incompletely doubled flower produced, there was a possibility of producing at least a proportion of doubled flowers amongst the seedlings – doubling was an inherited characteristic. 'Van Sion' pollen was used to give one or two doubles at the Oregon Bulb Farms.

Most modern doubles trace their pedigree to one particular variety. Through this narrow gateway came the magnificent modern legion. In 1934 Lionel Richardson noticed a flower head of the old double 'Mary Copeland' that appeared to be producing a seedpod. Two seeds were sown and of these the survivor was a poor weedy plant, but one that produced white-and-orange flowers that were doubled but not so completely as to do away with all the stamens and stigmas. This was 'Falaise' (1945). It may have been the result of self-pollinated 'Mary Copeland', or could have been the result of accidental pollination from a nearby poeticus. I am inclined to think it was self-pollinated, but if a nearby poet was involved its name is not recorded, although certainly the poet 'Smyrna' is inclined to give doubled flowers amongst its seedlings.

'Falaise' was mated with various single flowers and produced a number of good doubles of which perhaps the outstanding one was 'Gay Time' (1952). This is a splendid late flower with many milk-white petals making a pleasant rounded flower. Smaller red segments nestle between the white ones. A proportion of the flowers have complete stigmas and so it was an easy matter to produce a further generation, amongst which were a significant number of doubles. Almost every type of standard flower was offered to the seed parent 'Gay Time'. The most important factor in this breeding programme was that the stems of these new doubles were strengthened. A new race of flowers had been born – they may not look like daffodils but they are pleasing, and they are not damned by congenital weaknesses.

Yellow-petalled doubles

In the beginning, or very nearly so, there was 'Van Sion', the early double yellow which generations of gardeners have enjoyed. It is a Falstaffian character of obvious good nature, its golden blossoms either confining their doubling to the trumpets or, more probably, belching forth into wide laughing flowers. Slightly two-toned, the darker, richer-textured segments derived from the trumpet enliven the whole. Parkinson tells how the Fleming, Van Sion, who was living in London, owned the first bulbs in Britain and flowered them in 1620. Bulbs passed to a florist, George Wilmer, whose name also became associated with it until Haworth gave it the tedious name '*telamonius plenus*', by which it is officially registered. On this occasion officialdom is snubbed, and 'Van Sion' remains the commonly accepted name – unless it is just called 'that early double one'.

Several early doubles arising from the mixed breeding of trumpet and poeticus kinds, at that time commonly called 'incomparabilis', had been treasured for many years before breeding got underway in earnest towards the end of the 1880s. 'Butter and Eggs' may be the same flower that was also known as 'Golden Phoenix' and 'Yellow Phoenix'. It is rather difficult to tell, since the naming of garden plants was not so carefully controlled then. Phoenixs were arising all over. 'Primrose Phoenix' was registered in 1902, and 'Orange Phoenix' is still in use as a name although it is a supposed synonym of 'Eggs and Bacon', a singularly unpoetic name for a pleasing-enough pointed-petalled flower. 'Inglescombe' (1914) is a pale primrose carnation-like flower with a tall weak stem and 'Camellia' (1930), a sport from

'Emperor', is an evenly formed larger flower of similar colour but not really strong enough in the stem.

In its favour 'Golden Ducat' has size, a neat layered construction, and rich mid-gold colour. Grown where the stems are not subject to undue strain it can be impressive. The same may be said of the 'Carlton' sport 'Dick Wilden' with large blooms of pale and deeper primrose. 'Papua' (1961) was one of the first new yellow doubles, this one from 'Falaise' × the yellow trumpet 'Kingscourt'. It is a round full flower of bright golden yellow. The backing petals are rounded and broad, and the inner ones too are predominantly broad, although there are smaller ones interleaved. 'Gay Time' × 'Daydream' gave some excellent seedlings. 'Elixir' (1977) is a strong plant and flower. Looking full and precisely arranged, the blooms are in fact made up of smaller numbers of segments than some, but this is no drawback and may be thought a definite advantage by many. Very wide perianths of deep golden lemon surround inner petals of the same shade and some of pale tangerine towards the centre. 'Discovery' is a similarly rounded flower of deep lemon with, in the centre, some petals rather more orange than those of its sister. 'Affable' (1978) is of similar character but the colouring is distinct, the main segments having a distinct buffy suffusion, a reflection of the tangerine of the little ruffled centrepieces.

Yellow and orange are popular carnival colours for the spring festival. 'Orange Phoenix' did duty before such as 'Texas' from Mrs Backhouse arrived in 1928. There are many gardeners who may wish that it had never arrived. When seen then at shows, is great mop heads of informal gold and tangerine looked exciting, and untold tons must have sold since, but it can be one of the most annoying of all daffodils. Great fat buds arise looking full of promise, but all too often anticipation proves to be the best part, and they fail to deliver the flowers, not opening properly and often being stillborn so that all one looks at is dried wasted tissue. Modern kinds are reliable. One that has been bulked up to provide stock for gardens is 'Tahiti' (1956), bred from 'Falaise' × 'Ceylon'. It is a rounded flower with alternate inner layers of gold and orange-red. 'Enterprise' (1958) was an Oregon Bulb Farms introduction. It is a large flower with intermingled gold and tangerine parts, the centre ones tending to push forward rather than lie back. 'Grebe' (1979) came from a yellow-and-red seedling by pollen of 'Enterprise'. This is a splendid cultivar, very full with many overlapping rounded bright yellow petals, and with rich orange ribboning worked in between the centre segments. 'Takahe' (1980) is probably a sibling. It is from ('Playboy' × ('Klingo' × 'Ardour')) × 'Enterprise'. Large, very full, and bright, it has perhaps a greater quantity of the orange segments.

White-petalled doubles

All-white doubles range from the small double poets masquerading as carnations, to the large modern kinds several times as large. Oldest, and by far the latest of all the family to bloom, is an old favourite, *Narcissus poeticus* 'Flora Pleno', sometimes known as the 'Gardenia-flowered Narcissus', but more often simply as 'Double White'. There is no mistaking it for anything but a double poeticus, for the firm white petals have the right smooth texture and the scent is a pervasive guarantee. Deep in amongst the white segments can be found tiny flashes of red and yellow, the remnants of the eye. It is a plant that likes to be left alone. Deep planting in a cool spot will suit it best – planting where it may be subjected to extremes of temperature and possible drought will encourage it to react by aborting its flowers, and the stems will arise with only papery tissue to signal their original flowering intent. 'Rose of May' is only a few days earlier, but is a more compact, rounded, double white carnation. Newer flowers of this genre are the 'Cushendall' seedlings raised by Grant Mitsch and introduced in 1973, 'Alabaster' and 'Adoration'. This last is an amusing little plant with firm white flowers of its mother's modest size, sometimes virtually single but often with a little posy of petals placed in the centre. 'Alabaster' is another flower doing a swansong for the season, this with little pure-white flowers of lightweight structure on wiry pickable stems.

Mr W. F. M. Copeland, who started breeding daffodils in the closing years of the last century and died in 1953, introduced a series of doubles. His white-and-red 'Mary Copeland' is still grown in quantity. 'Mrs William Copeland' was introduced in 1930, and I rate this a very useful garden plant. It has really quite large white flowers with pointed petals, making it immediately different from the modern doubles. Growing on sturdy stems it looks very attractive naturalized, very much more at home and natural than the modern more dandified show-bench miracles.

First of the new breed to make an impression, and still highly regarded, is 'Candida' (1956) from 'Falaise' × the fine white large cup 'Petsamo'. With wide circular background petals, the centre is neatly filled with white and pale cream segments in an uncrowded manner.

This pattern of white and pale cream is repeated in several of this type, 'Gay Symphony' (1973) and 'Gay Song' (1968) were bred from 'Gay Time' × white trumpet 'Brussels'. 'Gay Song' is a huge flower unusual in being of uniform white throughout the wide back petals and the neatly arranged inner ones. 'Gay Symphony' is just as impressive in size and quality, but the inner petals of the very full flower are painted a delicate lemon-primrose.

Fully coloured white-and-yellow flowers are quite numerous. 'White Lion' (1949) bred from 'Mary Copeland' × 'John Evelyn' is one of the most successful types as a leading commercial cut flower. Its broad white petals back a inner arrangement of white and orange-tinged buffy ones, but these coloured segments fade to primrose quickly.

Newer kinds stemming from 'Falaise' and 'Gay Time' include the late-blooming 'Westward' (1962) with large clean white and bright lemon-gold flowers, and 'Hope' (1971), perhaps the most vividly white-petalled of the doubles with bright lemon-gold neatly inter-mingled segments. The one with the best show record, and no mean performer in the garden, is 'Unique' (1961), a very large rounded flower with thick white petals and segments. Its rather ruffled smaller inner segments are a bright yellow. 'Duet' (1980) arose as a sport of 'Golden Castle' and is a less full double than many, with inner segments an amber shade before fading.

White-and-red doubles follow a line from 'Mary Copeland', which is still widely grown and capable of a good performance with lots of medium-sized cream flowers with small red pieces nestling in the centre, the whole living in a cloud of perfume. 'Gay Time' (1952) is late and quite large, with thick-textured cream petals and smaller orange-red ones tucked into the centre. Lesser blooms with full stigmas will give a mass of seed.

Other 'Falaise' seedlings include 'Acropolis', 'Monterrico' (1962), 'Centrepiece' (1974), and 'Outer Space' (1974). 'Acropolis', with 'Limerick' as its other parent, is still one of the very finest show and garden flowers of this class. Large flowers are composed of wide snowy petals all satin smooth, with the inner, smaller ones neatly arranged between small bright red ones. The colour holds better than many. 'Montericco' has 'Arbar' as father, and is a large imposing white with the centre interspersed with rich orange segments. 'Centrepiece' and 'Outer Space' have 'Roimond' as pollen parent. Both are good-sized flowers of milk-white and orange-red, 'Outer Space' being taller and larger. Amongst the present leaders is 'Gay

Challenger' (1962) from 'Gay Time' × 'Arbar'. This is a large well-dressed one in pure white and bright, rich orange. Stiff stems hold the blooms boldly and safely.

At one time there were no pink doubles, and there was a worldwide race to produce the first one. Now there are brilliant kinds in Australia, New Zealand, America, and Britain. 'Pink Cloud' (1942) was probably the first to be introduced, a seedling from Oregon Bulb Farms. It is a medium-sized flower with a passable perianth and a centre rather like 'Van Sion' but opening buffy and becoming pink. 'Pink Chiffon' (1963) was rather tidier. 'Tropic Isle' (1976) and 'Replete' are both from 'Pink Chiffon' × 'Accent'. They are full doubles with plenty of rich pink colouring. 'Tropic Isle' has a firm background of two layers of white petals, but the full centre is crowded with rich pink ruffled segments that outdo the white ones that poke through. 'Samantha' and 'Pink Champagne' came from the pink large cup 'Marietta' crossed by the double 'Irani'. They are both good rounded flowers. Salmony-pink segments catch the eye in 'Samantha', 'Pink Champagne' is somewhat larger and with thick broad petals and neatly interspersed rosy-pink segments. 'Pink Pageant' has an immaculate perianth followed by an often unbroken ring of pink, and then neatly arranged petaloids of white and rich pink. The rich colouring is most impressive. 'Pink Paradise' from the same breeding, ('Falaise' × 'Debutante') × 'Polonaise', confounds one by being even better, the whiter being whiter and the pink more rosy and without admixture of orange or gold.

Many-headed doubles

For decades 'Cheerfulness' (1923), the sport from the tazetta 'Elvira', was very popular with several heads of white and cream and a pleasing scent. It was almost without rival. When it sported 'Yellow Cheerfulness' (1938) they went together in tandem, a horticultural success story. 'Bridal Crown' (1953) arrived to challenge their supremacy with larger flowers and an earlier flowering time. Later this was challenged by the considerably bigger 'Winston Churchill' with several impressive white round doubled flowers with intermingled bright amber-gold segments.

There are obviously other possibilities amongst these doubles. 'White Marvel', the sport of the triandrus 'Tresamble', may suggest some possibilities with its flowers similar to its parent's but with the nodding cups filled with feathers.

Miniature doubles

Our 'Lent Lily' has produced doubles in its time, but they remain rare. Like other double forms of the wildings, such as the doubled form of the white trumpet *N. moschatus*, they persist rather than flourish. They are prisoners of their heredity – their progenitors were plants that depend on seed rather than bulb division for increase and so the doubles are left trapped. *N. pumilus (N minor)* is a small yellow trumpet that would seem to be the origin of one or two curious doubles, of which the most successful is 'Rip Van Winkle'. Growing less than 15 centimetres high the flowers are composed of many narrow primrose-and-gold segments, the outer ones often striped green. The flowers are large for such a small plant, and inevitably they arch low over the ground even if they do not embrace it.

Queen Anne is twice-honoured with her double jonquil and double daffodil, (and it is Queen Anne of Austria that is commemorated). 'Queen Anne's Double Jonquil' is obviously a jonquil, the foliage and scent proclaim it, but what is less clear is which jonquil produced it. It would seem to have been a smallish jonquil hybrid. The flower is rounded with petals arranged more or less like a carnation, and they are big for the 15 to 20 centimetre stem. 'Pencrebar', a very similar plant, was found growing in Cornwall. Seeing the two growing side by side still makes it difficult to note any significant differences. The suspicion lingers that they may be one and the same, or that one stock has arisen with some very, very minor mutations from the parent stock.

The double *N. jonquilla plenus* is an interesting plant. Small golden balls replace the normal stars, and it has stems usually content with one to three flowers unlike the single which can often have more than half a dozen.

'Queen Anne's Double Daffodil' is a totally distinct plant with the officially registered name *'Eystettensis'*, but is also known as *'capax plenus'*. *'Capax'* was a name used in the past in conjunction with *triandrus* forms. It looks to have a certain amount of *N. triandrus* feeling, and presumably it arose as a mutation from a natural hybrid between *N. triandrus* and a *N. pseudonarcissus* form or another trumpet kind. As we grow it now, the plant is not one of the most robust. It makes about 20 centimetres in height, and has flattened foliage and pale straw-coloured flowers in the form of a six-pointed star. Layers of petals are laid one after another in shrinking lengths until nothing is left. No remnants of the corona or sexual parts are to be found. It has been known since before 1601, and has intrigued growers ever since.

13

Triandrus daffodils

Triandrus hybrids are classified as those in which the characteristics of *Narcissus triandrus* are predominant, which seems very close to the definition of an archdeacon as being one who performs archdeaconal duties – circular to the point of strangulation. *N. triandrus* is characterized by small size, narrow, usually more-or-less rounded foliage, round flowering stems, more than one flower to a stem, a hanging pose, reflexed narrow petals, and a strong dependence on seed for increase. First-generation hybrids between species forms and cultivars of the first three divisions usually feature intermediate size, dark-green polished foliage, more or less rounded stems, pendant or semi-pendant flowers, petals swept back to a lesser or greater degree, unflanged coronas, and smooth rounded snub-nosed bulbs with offsets that divide cleanly. These hybrids appear more vulnerable than many others to virus, or at least they show the symptoms and effects more clearly. Whilst they are reasonable plants, the best of the first-generation ones are the result of the mating of the species with the stronger hybrids. Most of the triandrus hybrids are sterile, or nearly sterile. The few fertile ones are allowing the breeding of stronger healthier plants, but the danger is that there may be a dilution of the graceful triandrus character. This is based on the multi-headed habit, the pendant pose, the reflexing petals, and the rather lightweight silken texture.

The first hybrids to be noted were the wild progeny of *N. triandrus* and *N. pseudonarcissus*. These attractive plants were given the name *N. johnstonii*, but were better known as 'Queen of Spain' and 'King of Spain'. Under these names they were introduced into our gardens. With long stove-pipe coronas and swept back petals, and standing around the height of the 'Lent Lily', they make a distinctive picture in pale primrose-sulphur shades. A few gardens still retain bulbs of these plants which were originally imported towards the end of the last century, and topped up in the earlier years of this one. As they are such distinctive and sought-after plants, they make natural candidates for artificial increase by bulb chipping or tissue culture.

Most of the early triandrus bred in cultivation are white flowers, the better ones being derived from the large wild white plant formerly known as *N. triandrus loiseleurii* (*N. t. calathinus*). Most have long since disappeared, though in one or two favoured gardens some naturalized ones persist. This is unusual as these plants are not renowned for lasting in a naturalized state. 'Thalia', with starry white reflexed petals and large goblet cups, has been a standard commercial kind offered since 1916. However stocks are now universally virused. Later-introduced cultivars are not in a much better state. 'Tresamble' (1930) with smoother wider petals and cups of cream is a pleasing flower, but probably virused.

These are a limited number of newer types. Grant Mitsch raised a fine series from 'Easter Moon' × *N. triandrus albus*. 'Saberwing' (1977) was the first to be introduced. Normally twin-flowered, each bloom is pure white with a rounded flat perianth and a bowl crown with a dash of green in the very centre. 'Longspur' (1979) has its perianths at a slight tilt and the goblet cups semi-pendant. Still the most outstanding white triandrus is 'Arish Mell' (1961), registered at that time by the father-and-son Blanchard team. This flower typifies all that is best in the triandrus breeding. It has several heads on a stem – three is usual and five possible; it has a good pendant pose with a sensible but not fanatical reflex to the perianth; its wide petals are made more telling by being pointed; the colour is snow white; and it has a finespun silky texture.

Other white triandrus are of rather a different type but no less attractive. They begin to pose problems of classification as they have been bred from the fertile jonquil hybrid 'Quick Step' by pollen of *N. triandrus albus*. Raisers always have first say as to which division they believe their seedlings owe the greater allegiance. First to be introduced was 'Petral' (1974). It has slender wiry stems some 30 centimetres or so high but not giving an impression of height. Stems carry three to six, or even more milk-white flowers with neat little creamy cups reminiscent of their triandrus parent, and hanging. Petals reflex gently and are long ovals which overlap for half their length. In all it is a most pleasing, late-flowering dainty plant, quite correctly listed as a triandrus, but benefiting hugely from the jonquil parentage that helps the bulbs to increase far more rapidly than is the case with most slowcoach triandrus types. 'Silverton' is easily as free of flower, but the blooms are smaller and even better formed with broader very even reflexing perianths. The plant is dwarfer at about 25 centimetres and the flowers smaller, but the gently reflexing perianths are proportionately wider and are very evenly balanced. 'Ivory Gull' (1982) betokens its colour and is similar to 'Petral' in size and freedom of bloom, but the coronas are somewhat longer, breakfast cups rather than coffee ones. Three to six flowers are hung from each stem, and after a bulb has been in the ground for a season or so these stems are prolific. 'Silver Bells' (1964) was from a strong seedling of 'Daisy Schaffer × 'Polindra' by pollen of *N. triandrus albus.* It is a robust kind with somewhat overlarge flaring coronas, but it is like the smaller bright yellow 'Honey Bells' in that it will set seed.

Bicolour triandrus are still relatively scarce. 'Silver Bells' gave a number of seedlings from its open-pollinated seed. Of these 'Lapwing' (1976) is a kind that is usually content to have one bloom to a stem but may be twin-flowered with flat white perianths and bells of pale lemon. 'Kite' (1972) is something altogether different. It is from a poeticus, possibly old 'Horace' by pollen of *N. triandrus albus,* and the only other cultivar it may resemble is 'Dawn', an old kind from Engleheart dating back to 1907. This had long, fly-away wings of white and a corona spun flat as a coin, and shining bright lemon. 'Kite' stands taller at well over 30 centimetres high, with somewhat informal pointed, reflexed petals and wide crowns of yellow not quite so flat as 'Dawn' and a little deeper coloured around the brim. Still the outstanding bicolour flower of this class is 'Tuesday's Child', a sister to the white 'Arish Mell'. It normally has two flowers to a stem, but three slightly smaller ones are possible, or a biggish singleton. Very good white perianths reflex gently from neat cups of lemon. It is a good strong plant.

Yellow triandrus have been bred from the golden-yellow *N. triandrus concolor.* We have had several series of pleasing seedlings, but they tended to be rather taller than we would have wished. Most yellows in commerce are the result of white triandrus forms crossed with long-cupped coloured hybrids. 'Liberty Bells' (1950) is the most widely available yellow triandrus but, as is common with triandrus bulked up for mass sales, virus is prevalent. Good stems carry three long-cupped flowers with swept-back petals all in a shining rich lemon. 'Stint' is altogether newer, bred from a yellow-and-orange seedling by triandrus pollen. Heads of luminous flowers, two or three to a stem, are lemon in the petals but darker in the cups. 'Chipper' (1972) stands only 25 to 30cm high with a usual complement of three pale, typical triandrus flowers, ivory-white in their long, narrow, pointing perianths and lemon in the crowns. *N. triandrus albus* as pollen parent seems to have dominated the 'Polindra' × 'Tunis' seedling mother.

For some while there were bulbs distributed as *N. triandrus aurantiacus* which were particularly deep-coloured forms of the full yellow *N. concolor*, (*N. t. concolor*). Used as pollen parent it gave Grant Mitsch some useful seedlings. 'Piculet' (1969) from (Bahram × Ardour) × *N. t. aurantiacus* is a small hybrid with uniform yellow flowers, with circular petals slightly turned back from wide saucers. One or two small flowers hang from 25 centimetre stems. 'Honey Guide' (1982) is still small, though a little larger and taller than the last. It comes from 'Quick Step' × *N. t. aurantiacus*. It is admired for its very free-flowering habit, many having up to five nodding flowers each. Pale lemon reflexed petals achieve a telling proportional balance with the neat goblet cups. The seed parent can be thanked for a good constitution and a rapid rate of increase.

Crossbreeding triandrus with jonquils makes good sense. Jonquil hybrids are almost uniformly splendid doers, and the blending of triandrus grace with the charm and strength of *N. jonquilla* or one of its relatives is a magic brew – results are bewitching. 'April Tears' (1939) was Alec Gray's offering from *N. jonquilla* × *N. triandrus*, a delightful fairy flower with slightly sloping stems of 15 to 23 centimetres carrying two or three bells with longish reflexed petals all in shining lemon. 'Hawera' (1938) is from the same parents and is somewhat stronger and larger overall, but still a dainty plant usually about 23 centimetres high with stems carrying two to six flowers. Neat, rather shallow cups are a pale creamy-primrose fading a little with age, whilst the long reflexed petals are shining lemon. 'Fairy Chimes' (1977) from Mitsch is a third *N. jonquilla* × *N. triandrus* hybrid like 'April Tears', but taller and a shade lighter. From three to six smooth flowers hang from each of the wiry 25 to 35 centimetre-high stems. As with the others, once the bulbs get going they produce a thicket of flowering stems. At present it is 'Hawera' that the large-scale growers have picked to bulk up, and this is the one most generally available.

More than one breeder has made crosses in the hope of achieving a pink-cupped triandrus. When the seedlings have flowered they have been either white, or white-and-yellow. Pink that looks pink has been an elusive prize. Mitsch achieved it with 'Akepa' (1980) by using the dark pink 'Accent' as mother to *N. triandrus albus* pollen. The result is a dainty, not too large 30 centimetre-high plant with stems normally having a couple of smartly-dressed flowers. Milk-white petals, quite well rounded but with the inner ones somewhat more pointed, are held flat or may just reflex a trifle, and the sharply-cut cups are a good solid soft pink.

There remains much to be done with these flowers: red-and-oranges would give variety and some rimmed cups could be very attractive. The major considerations however remain producing healthy plants that increase well, and ensuring that the species character is not completely submerged.

14

Cyclamineus daffodils

It would be difficult to point to another species that has had such a totally beneficial influence on breeding as *N. cyclamineus*, and which has such a great deal still to contribute. Future developments could mean the popularity of this division moving even further ahead, and it would not be too outrageous to suggest that, in garden terms, this could at some point become the most popular division. It has a lot in its favour.

Firstly, the flowers have character – the extreme reflexed perianth of the species usually becomes a swept-back recurving one in the seedlings, and this is an immediately attractive pose, giving quite the opposite impression from those flowers where the petals tend to lean lazily forward; secondly, the plants are healthy with bulbs that increase well; thirdly, they start blooming early and, with modern cultivars, now cover at least two-thirds of the season. Not only this, but the flowers of these cyclamineus hybrids are possessed of large quantities of the amazing vitality of the species, something that enables them to hold their flowers in good order for many weeks, often in the worst of the spring weather; and fourthly, the size of the plants and flowers is very much more manageable in smaller modern gardens and even public displays than the larger hybrids. They are in scale, and can be grown between small or large shrubs, and also in the rock garden and island beds, although here clumps of large ones may look incongruous and could cause a certain amount of anxiety as their foliage begins to die back after flowering. Lesser amounts of leaves of some makes this problem almost nonexistent, and these hybrids are leading naturalizing kinds.

To improve strength and disease resistance, the use of *N. triandrus* in breeding necessitates the use of the strongest of partners in mating, since back crossing to the species may provide interesting and attractive flowers but is fraught with the attendant risks of less robust growth. With *N. cyclamineus* there is not the slightest risk of diminishing the strength of progeny by back crossing or by maintaining and using a fund of breeding material close to the species – the progeny are going to be excellent garden plants. For this reason it should be possible to keep the character of the division intact much more easily. It means also that there should be a possibility of having a wide range of colours and forms in plants that vary from really quite large ones like 'Bartley' and 'Peeping Tom' down to pygmies not much bigger than the species itself.

Adaptability is one of the happy features of the division. It would have been a bold person who foretold the future of Alec Gray's seedlings 'Tête à Tête' and 'Jumblie' when they first appeared. Who would have foreseen them being sold each year in its millions, to appear as pot plants in shopping centres throughout western Europe, to be used naturalized in grass, and to peep at passers-by from untold numbers of windowboxes, as well as being such popular characters in the garden proper at the front of the border, between shrubs, or in rock garden beds? Success however brings problems. When the demand for a bulb is this strong it appears to become easier for some large-scale growers to overlook the signs of virus disease. It is a pity the disease does not show up as a signal on the dry bulbs, but some big commercial growers take the attitude that a bulb is a bulb is a bulb, especially when there is a queue of keen customers.

Unlike most triandrus and jonquil cultivars, there is very little difficulty breeding from the hybrids, and almost none have an insuperable sterility barrier.

Yellow is a bright cheerful colour after the winter. The first cyclamineus hybrids to be bred and the first to bloom are golden and really do successful battle with the winter, foreshortening its stay, 'February Gold' (1923) is one example, sometimes able to live up to its name but certainly present in March with plenty of 25 centimetre-high blossom. This is a marvellous garden plant, one of the most successful of all daffodils for naturalizing, and plentiful enough not to be too expensive to use in this way. Long crowns, and petals just tilted back a bit, make it look wide-awake. It is very free of bloom, with almost every bit of bulb trying to do its duty. Its blossom is very durable, and the bulbs increase at a very satisfactory rate. 'March Sunshine' introduced the same year has a smaller, more restricted crown, and narrower reflexed petals.

'Peeping Tom' (1948) was all the rage for a while, and little wonder as the flowers seemed to be almost everlasting. However virus took its toll. 'Bartley' (1934) is similar with long tube-like trumpets with neat saw-edged flanges and blown-back petals. It stands some 30 to 38 centimetres high and, opening early, lasts for weeks. Newer is 'Radical' (1980), a vastly improved flower of this same long-trumpeted form. Much greater width of petal with a smoother richer texture make this a joy. It opens with golden flowers on sturdy 23-centimetre stems but they grow taller as the flowers mature. Quite different is 'Alliance Party' (1980), a pert mid-yellow flower with stiff petals curved back from a straight-sided, half-length corona that is held horizontally rather than at an angle towards the ground like many. 'Barlow' has earliness to commend it as well as good form and a rich gold colour. Little 'Mite' is a pleasing small, first-generation hybrid. From open-pollinated seed it gave the taller, 30-centimetre high, 'Bushtit' (1961), a distinct flower with a chaste crown and slender petals making a flat long-pointed star which remains flat while outside but reflexes if picked, a curious habit. In its turn, by self-pollinated seed, this gave 'Catbird' a larger flower, taller at 38 centimetres or so, a third-generation hybrid in soft yellow but still faithful to family traditions in its slightly reflexed perianth and trumpet-like crown made a touch unusual by the prominence of the stigma which sometimes pokes beyond the corona.

'Rapture' is a real cyclamineus character from 'Nazareth' × *N. cyclamineus*. It is a 30-centimetre high startled shooting-star of a flower with a long narrow trumpet almost chopped off at the mouth, and with long petals pushed backwards in the airstream. It glows bright lemon, and lasts for ages.

One of the big jumps forward in this division was taken by the mating of the long-cupped 'Mitylene' with cyclamineus. A litter of fine things resulted. Three have become very well known and are grown in significant quantities: 'Charity May' (1948), 'Dove Wings' (1949), and 'Jenny' (1943). 'Charity May' is a uniform soft yellow, a flower of model form. Wide petals arc backwards to make an excellent perianth and to emphasize the bold crown that is a very telling bell shape with a broad flange. It will grow well in many situations. Some of the best we have grown were clumps that had been naturalized in rough grass for a few years and treated with long doses of absolute neglect.

White-and-yellow hybrids are attractive and range from the small-crowned well-contrasted bright yellow-and-white 'Jack Snipe' (1951), to kinds like 'Jenny' that open bicolour but end their life more or less pure white. 'Dove Wings' is intermediate with oval petals recurving from a longish crown of creamy yellow. 'Jenny' has a touch more character with longer pointed petals swept gracefully back and with downward-looking trumpet crowns that start primrose but are soon within half a hint of pure white. Both open in early mid-season. 'Joybell' (1969) came from seed collected from 'Jenny' and looks like its parent with its sharply-pointed reflexing perianth of wider petals. The chaste primrose crown is finished with an attractive rolled-back lip. It stands six centimetres or so taller at around 35 centimetres. From the bicolour trumpet 'Trousseau' crossed with 'Dove Wings' came the chubby 'Titania', a very smooth one with a tilted perianth and crown of creamy primrose. 'Ibis' is different again, a smaller plant with very neat flowers, the long oval petals reflexing well from a trumpet of lemon-primrose.

Pure white cyclamineus have arrived by various routes. 'Ocean Breeze' (1981) came from 'Titania' × *N. cyclamineus* and reduces the size of 'Titania' down to that of 'Ibis', tall at 30 centimetres and looking very much like a white version of this kind. It has the same clean-cut firm perianth in white with a long trumpet crown that is soft primrose before becoming white. 'Frostkist' was from open-pollinated 'Charity May' and has its looks but is larger and is all in white. One of the goals of breeders has been the raising of pink-crowned cyclamineus hybrids, now successfully done. Things do not always go according to plan. Crossing a seedling with a long pink pedigree, ('Mabel Taylor' × 'Interim') × 'Rima', with cyclamineus pollen brought forth the hoped-for pink 'Carib' (1980), but also the white 'Cazique' (1982). True, this last starts life as a white- and pale-lemon flower, but it soon becomes a faultless white. Faultless indeed describes its exquisite texture and form. Gently reflexed polished petals help to show off the trumpet crown with its finish and perfect balance. It has length enough to make its cyclamineus character obvious, and its substance is such that the flowers last exceptionally. Another all-white flower came from dazzling 'Stainless' crossed by the pink cyclamineus 'Foundling'. This is 'Elwing', a pet with swept-back petals but with an unusually short cup.

Pink-crowned 'Carib' is now only one of the many pink-crowned dainty flowers, but it stands out by virtue of its excellent form with strongly reflexed milk-white petals and a flanged trumpet of rich peachy pink but brighter still inside. From open-pollinated seed of one of the 'Mitylene' × cyclamineus seedlings arrived 'Cotinga' (1977), a look-alike to 'Dove Wings' except that the crown colour is an unusual apricot-pink especially rich at the mouth.

'Foundling' was the seedling that started much of the activity in the pink cyclamineus. As its name suggests, the parentage is unknown and it is just the appearance of the plant and flower that makes this division the obvious home for this sturdy industrious little bulb. Broad white petals curve back from a short wide cup of deep pink. It is rather late but, apart from the perianth and the size of the blooms, the habit of the plant, with somewhat sloping stems, betokens *N. cyclamineus* lurking somewhere in its ancestry. Brian Duncan's sister seedlings 'Lavender Lass' and 'Lilac Charm' from 'Roseworthy' × (R562 × 'Rose Caprice') are sought after as much for their beautiful form as for their intriguing colourings. 'Lilac Charm' is a quite modestly sized plant with flowers of delightful shape, with the sparkling white, pointed petals swept back from a well-flanged trumpet which is a rich fast shade of lilac pink with just a touch of green in the base. 'Lavender Lass' is a little heavier and looks more fully drawn. Perianths are slightly tilted back and, like some of these flowers, become noticeably more so if cut and placed in water. The lip of the mouth may be touched with a rim of rich gold that in other flowers might be called pale tangerine. Both are flowers of satiny refinement. 'Delta Wings' is thought by Brian Duncan to be from 'Interim' × 'Joybell'. One may wonder whether this is not one of those which by sheer size are growing out of the cyclamineus division, but the flowers look charming in the garden. Slimline petals reflex gently from a chaste cylindrical corona lightly opened and serrated at the brim. The corona colour is a luminous rich pink. 'Snoopie', from 'Lilac Charm' by a pink seedling, is a large, quite late flower with very white recurving petals and a long goblet of bright rose.

Perhaps pride of place historically for cyclamineus hybrids showing orange colouring goes to the little P. D. Williams flower 'Beryl' (1907), presumably the result of mating the species with a poeticus type. It is a distinctive small plant with lots of flower stems held out at oblique angles so that the flowers hang like lanterns, with longish yellow petals sweeping back in a curve from small golden cups shaded orange, especially at the rims. The petals fade to pale cream in the sun but they always look attractive and, being so free of flower, they make distinctive little plants to grow in odd corners and between shrubs.

Modern flowers in bright colouring started with kinds like 'Satellite' (1963) from 'Rouge' × *N. cyclamineus*. It is a good little plant increasing rapidly and having lots of swept-back pointed golden petals and quite long crowns of tangerine. An odd bulb I had left by a hedge was dug up after only a few sessons to give over 70 reasonably-sized bits to plant. 'Kitten' (1962) is a pleasing flower with long oval petals of gold winging back from a wide shallow fluted crown of rich tangerine. It is much later than the early 'Satellite'. Still one of the best of this class is 'Andalusia' (1961), a flower that has a very full quota of cyclamineus character. Its golden petals are not only dramatically recurved, but the segments are long and pointed in the shape that emphasizes the species contribution. The crown is long and slender and a very attractive orange.

Grant Mitsch bred a neat series from a yellow-red seedling crossed with the species. The seed parent was from ('Market Merry' × 'Carbineer') × 'Armada'. First to be introduced was 'Jetfire' in 1969, followed by 'Shimmer' in 1978 and 'Soft Touch' in 1983. 'Shimmer' is first to open, with gold or old-gold, broad, oval petals flexed back from a bright orange straight-sided crown. 'Jetfire' opens a few days later but is still amongst the very first to start the season, with lots of sturdy-stemmed bright gold-and-orange blooms. The petals are amply broad, though a little narrower than those of 'Shimmer', whilst the tangerine crown gains strength after the flower opens. Secondary smaller flowers extend the season. 'Soft Touch' is a neat flower not unlike 'Shimmer', but it opens quite a bit later. 'Vulcan' × *N. cyclamineus* gave 'Chaffinch' (1981), a very free-flowering flower taller than many with rich-coloured flowers, golden sharply reflexed petals, and full rather open trumpet crowns of a richer shade hinting at orange. It is a generous character, giving lots of flowers and a satisfying rate of bulb increase.

Commercial and garden success can be claimed for 'Tête à Tête' (1949) and 'Jumblie' (1952). They are a testament to the work of Alec Gray who raised them together with 'Quince' (1953) from a single pod of seed harvested from the curious little hunch-backed hybrid 'Cyclataz' (1923). This was bred from *N. cyclamineus* by pollen of the yellow-and-orange tazetta, 'Soleil d'Or'. It had one or two drooping flowers of yellow and orange hanging from 15-centimetre stems, the petals pointing heavenwards. It was never the most extrovert of plants, quite unlike its three seedlings which have proved prodigious in their ability to increase. 'Quince' has the widest large crowns, and is a soft all-yellow flower. The other two are gold and tangerine. 'Tête à Tête' has made all the initial running, and has received universal acclaim for the longevity of its blossom and its ease of culture. Flowers appear on short stems perhaps only seven centimetres or so high very early in the year, and it is probably the first daffodil to open in most gardens. Carrying one, two, or more rarely three flowers to a stem, these are opened to have the petals at right angles to the longish crown or at a very slight backwards angle. As the days pass the stems lengthen and, depending on their position, they may extend to about 25 centimetres or so. We have frequently had clumps in bloom for eight weeks. 'Jumblie' differs in having rather longer coronas and having the petals very much more reflexed – in fact nearly continuing the line of the corona backwards. These three siblings are likely to be moved into Division 12, for miscellaneous daffodils.

15

Jonquil daffodils

Whilst the cyclamineus division depends on the input of a single species and the triandrus on a smaller, tightly-related group, the jonquils can be the offspring of a number of quite disparate species. Of course *N. jonquilla* itself has up until now been the prime source of genetic material and is a very potent force. It is possible this could change as there are some obvious very good species whose beneficial influence has scarcely yet been tried.

Jonquil hybrids have been with us for a long time. By the sixteenth century they were being grown in the Netherlands and Britain as well as elsewhere. Most of these were the natural hybrids between *N. jonquilla* and forms of *N. pseudonarcissus* lumped together under the appropriate name *N. odorus*. They were good garden plants and enjoyed centuries of popularity, particularly thanks to their perfume. In cultivation they gave rise to double mutants and to slight colour variations. *N. jonquilla* was not over-restrained in the wild, and other alliances produced cousins for the *N. odorus* clan. Mating with *N. poeticus* conceived the plants known as *N. gracilis* and *N. tenuior*. Even more daring was the choice of *N. tazetta* as a partner, occasioning the tallish hybrid, not inappropriately christened *N. intermedius*. All these hybrids have had a long history in cultivation and, alas and alack, one of the concomitants of such a life is the risk of virus. Old stocks are likely to be infected and so weakened. However bulbs could be cleaned by meristem culture, or similar plants might be raised from repeating the crosses and cloning the best of the resultant progeny.

N. odorus covers a series of plants. Clones propagated in the Netherlands include their *N. odorus*, a 25-centimetre-high plant with typical dark shiny leaves and heads of two or three golden flowers with small cups and reasonable perianths. Whenever we have bought bulbs of *N. odorus rugulosus* or *N. odorus rugulosus maximus*, the same plants have been supplied. It could be that there were two different plants in the past, and that the better of the two has survived by unnatural selection in the commercial world. *N. o. rugulosus* is rather taller than *N. odorus*, maybe 30 centimetres high, with wider petals and coronas attractively scalloped. 'Orange Queen' is an old gold or tangerine-flushed kind with several heads but not of such smooth texture. It stands 25 centimetres high.

N. tenuior and *N. gracilis*, which are assumed to have *N. poeticus* as parent, are pretty little things. The usual performance from *N. tenuior* is a couple of pale primrose flowers on stems up to 20 centimetres tall, with rounded petals held well back from a shallow saucer half a shade deeper. Its colour fades to a cream. It is the lack of stature that prompts the niggling feeling that maybe *N. jonquilla* itself is not the parent, but that responsibility lies with a smaller relative. Normally one would expect a taller plant from the mating of *N. jonquilla* with even the shortest-stemmed *N. poeticus*, something closer to *N. gracilis* which, with flowers around five centimetres across, is larger and several centimetres taller. It is one of the latest to bloom, opening with the poets and starting a creamy yellow with darker neat cups, but fading somewhat. These hybrids have become scarce but do suggest that a worthwhile series of late-flowering rather larger yellows could be bred from the use of a good poeticus cultivar with a fertile jonquil like 'Quickstep'.

Scent is a dominant characteristic of first-generation jonquils. 'Trevithian' (1927) is grown as a perfume factory as well as the manufacturer of 51-centimetre-tall multi-headed stems of rounded golden flowers. Smooth texture, good form, and vigour have aided its popularity. It is this robust, quick-increasing habit that is a leading feature of the jonquils. They flourish exceedingly well until virus strikes and begins to take its toll. Some relatively old plants are still regarded highly by show enthusiasts. 'Sweetness' and 'Sweet Pepper' were both registered in 1939, and although the bright yellow-and-orange 'Sweet Pepper' now has quite a number of modern challengers, 'Sweetness' is an all-yellow kind grown by every serious exhibitor. It is somewhat unusual in normally producing only a single perky flower to each firm stem but, as there are plenty of stems, this is of no matter in the garden. Modest-sized flowers are of thick velvety substance, very flat with their pointed golden petals, and precise with glowing goblets with brims scalloped in a restrained manner.

At present it remains true that a good cultivar belonging to any division outside the first four stands a better chance of a longer life in show and garden limelight than occupants of the more crowded divisions, where breeding ferment ensures a rapid turnover of 'stars'. It is not merely the lower level of breeding activity that protects the cultivars of the 'lesser' divisions: any challenging newcomer should still retain the characteristics of the division's parent species, a restraining influence that means that the parameters only permit a circumscribed ability-range of contenders. Even if all offspring of species resulting from mating with flowers of the first three divisions were sterile, there would still be a steady improvement due to the input of these improving big-division flowers. Novelty blood in the species divisions is important so that casualties to virus are more than made good.

Such considerations apply particularly to the jonquils, which are at present clearly the most diverse of the divisions outside the first four, and have the potential with their various constituent species to be even more diverse in the future. Without considering any other factor except colour, they are by far the most varied. Standard yellows such as 'Trevithian' and 'Sweetness' are joined by different types. Smaller is 'Quail' (1974), a deep golden-yellow prolific kind from 'Daydream', neat and thick-textured, and with trumpety crowns. 'Gazelle' (1972) from 'Aircastle' is naturally totally different, with several flowers on tall wiry stems having rounded, pale lemon correctly-flat perianths, and lemon cups that become white but keep a honeyed throat. 'Flycatcher' (1974) is less tall at over 30 centimetres with lots of stems, the stronger ones carrying graceful twin blooms. The seed parent is an orange-and-yellow 'Playboy' × 'Firecracker' seedling, whilst the pollen parent is the diminutive *N. juncifolius*. Dainty graceful mid-yellow flowers have wide cups of a darker shade. 'Stratosphere' (1968) is not badly named. It inherits from 'Narvik' a tall stem that reaches heavenwards to a height of 61 centimetres. One, two or three top-quality rounded golden flowers have small cups of half a shade deeper.

'Buffawn' (1977) indicates possible avenues for breeding. It is a sturdy tough plant, stockier in build and character than most, with two or three largish blooms. Petals are buffy primrose and the crowns deeper. Perhaps it has lost some of the grace of the species, but it certainly retains the fragrance.

Yellow-and-orange jonquils seem a natural extension from the wild species, their strong colour and fragrance marrying well. 'Suzy' (1954) was bred some time before by P. D. Williams and introduced by

Matthew Zandbergen. It proved capable of ridiculous feats of self propagation. It increased almost faster than the strong demand for its services as a show and garden flower. Its stems have one to three or occasionally, four blooms. Each is large, with widely-pointed petals of gold, and broad saucers of glowing solid orange. It is a late mid-season kind. Quite one of the earliest jonquils is the smallish but very free-flowering 'Pet Finch' (1975). Flocks of flowers arrive early, and others open later so that they have a considerable season. Single round flowers in gold and tangerine sit on a forest of stems. 'Bunting' (1965) is more formal with thick smooth perianths and deep orange cups. 'Triller' (1979), from the rich-coloured 'Vulcan', has inherited much of 'Vulcan's' colour. This is not immediately obvious, since on opening golden perianths are accompanied by neat crowns just a hint deeper, but as days pass the corona deepens to a rich orange-red. Quantities of stems each carry one or two persistent blooms.

To my mind the most spellbinding jonquils in a division of bewitching flowers are those that have bred from the lemon long cups such as 'Binkie' and 'Daydream'. Many become reverse bicolours, somehow an even more magical colour pattern than ever in these smaller flowers of perky, dainty size and posture. Mating with 'Binkie' produced 'Dickcisell' (1964), a vigorous doer with lots of stems normally bearing two or three alert, pointed-petalled florets of bright lemon-gold, the flared cups quickly becoming white in a most vivid contrast. 'Pipet' (1965), from the same batch, is another out-standing grower with an abundance of blooms. Slightly paler, but still a shining rich lemon, the blooms quickly become reversed, the base of the pointed petals and the fluted goblets then being nearly snow white. Stocks are now sufficient for it to feature in showcases in shops.

'Daydream' × *N. jonquilla* was the next major cross and, amongst others, this gave 'Canary' (1978) and 'Hillstar' (1979). They are dissimilar, 'Canary' with long oval petals forming a starry lemon perianth but with a white halo at the junction with the neat longish corona which becomes ivory white, and 'Hillstar' with petals that open glowing lemon but lose half their colouring, their bottom halves being a wide white zone around the flared ivory crowns that become pure white at their edges, but shade to buffy lemon in the centre. Average stems have two or three blooms.

This progression led to the use of the very fertile jonquil hybrid 'Quick Step'. This by pollen of 'Daydream' gave the second-generation hybrids 'Songster' (1972), 'Step Forward' (1972), 'High Note' (1974), 'Cloud Nine' (1974), and 'New Day' (1975). 'Cloud

Nine' is registered as a long cup because it gives single flowers to a stem, but its dancing, dandy character would seem to mean it belongs with its jonquil siblings. Pointed flat perianths glow deep golden-lemon behind long goblets that bleach completely. It is delightful in the garden or picked. 'Songster' too has been classed as a long cup. Its corona can be suffused with amber. 'Step Forward' may have up to three blooms to a stem, all being perfectly groomed. Golden petals back primrose crowns that become white. 'High Note' is not dissimilar, with widespread deep-lemon perianths and large flared crowns that whiten quickly. One of the pleasing features of this series is the rapid increase of the healthy shiny bulbs. 'New Day' is as free as the rest, an intriguing character with lemon-gold rounded perianths and a white halo behind bold lemon cups which, after becoming white, surprise with a flush of biscuity buff.

'Oryx' (1969) and 'Avocet' (1983) are cast in a different mould. 'Oryx', from 'Aircastle' × *N. jonquilla*, is a dainty kind with two or three rounded flowers showing 'Aircastle's influence in their shape and in the creamy lemon shades, the little cups fading close to snow white whilst the perianth is gaining a shade or two. The bulbs are diligent increasers. 'Avocet' from a 'Green Island' × 'Chinese White' relative of 'Aircastle' is a robust daffodil usually with three round flowers on 51-centimetre stems. Petals and saucer crowns are white with only a hint of yellow, and so this kind leads naturally to the consideration of the relatively few white jonquils.

'Nancegollan' (1937) was a P. D. Williams flower with plenty of white-petalled blooms with longish goblet crowns of cream. It was virtually alone till 'Pueblo' from 'Binkie' × *N. jonquilla* arrived in 1966, a creamy white medium-sized flower. 'Dainty Miss' (1967) from a 'Rubra' × 'Coverack Perfection' seedling has the brilliant white little species, *N. watierii*, as pollen parent. Standing just over 30 centimetres high, it is a pretty little thing with flat petals and almost flat saucer crowns. 'Eland' (1969) from 'Aircastle' is closer to 'Avocet' with two or three rounded flowers which open in white and pale lemon but become uniform white after a day or so. It is very generous with blossom, 'Curlew' (1973) from the white long cup 'Killaloe' is distinct, with good white perianths and long crowns of ivory. 'Snow Storm' (1984) from 'Dithynia' is a free-growing and free-flowering plant with one or two well groomed flowers of white and cream when new, which soon become an unsullied white.

There are a few white-and-yellow jonquils. 'Pretty Miss' (1974) came from the old P. D. Williams white-and-lemon 'Polindra' and has a decent inheritance from this cultivar in its clean-cut pointed form, firm substance, and clean colours. The buds look yellowish but the flowers develop to a good white-and-primrose arrangement, perky and strong. 'Fruit Cup' (1979) is a delightful dwarf with 30 centimetre-high stems bearing one or two flowers. It is from 'Green Island' × *N. juncifolius* with wide, white petals. The three outer ones would be wide enough to do the whole perianth duty. The neat cups are primrose. 'Desert Bells' (1984) has the intriguing pedigree of 'Quick Step' × *N. juncifolius*. With *N. jonquilla* as grandparent and *N. juncifolius* as father it has two different doses of jonquility. Some 25 to 30 centimetres high, its generosity in blossom borders on profligacy. Two or three little flowers on each stem open with nicely rounded petals flat or just a shade tilted backwards. The opening statement is yellow, but the flowers then adopt a predominantly white dress although the neat cups remain lemon. In early days a clump will have a pleasing mix of new yellow and older white-and-yellow blossom.

Pink-cupped jonquils are not a new revelation. 'Cherie' was registered in 1935. Opening yellowish like many jonquils that end with white petals, it quickly transforms itself into clean-cut flowers of white and rosy pink. There is probably no virus-free stock left, but other plants have come along with this colouring. Although not brilliantly pink, 'Quick Step' (1969) has proved an extremely important little plant. Most previous jonquils were sterile or very nearly so, but this late-flowering prodigy proves extremely fertile by pollen or seed. With the bright 'Wild Rose' as one parent, it produces three or so nodding heads of white and cream which sometimes has a flush of pink. It is a small plant standing only about 30–38 centimetres high. 'Quick Step' seems happy to mate with any type of flower, and historically it could prove one of the most important cultivars to be raised in the past 50 years.

'Bell Song' (1971), from a ('Wild Rose' × 'Interim') seedling × *N. jonquilla*, is a more immediately attractive garden plant of similar stature to 'Quick Step'. Its extraordinary free-flowering habit makes a group look a fascinating picture of gracefully-hung flowers of perhaps three to each stem. Well formed perianths tilt back slightly and open a buff-primrose that may contain the beginnings of a hint of pink, but then fade to ivory. The cups open pink and remain bright into old age. It suggests the possibility of all-pink flowers. 'Pink Angel' (1981) is a sibling but with two or three milk-white flowers with each cup centred green and finished with a smartly painted, deep-pink margin. 'Punchline' (1982) represents the next generation and widens the genetic pool by being from 'Quick Step' × 'Silken Sails'. It is a larger plant than the ones just named. Two or three sizeable rounded blooms top a 26 to 50-centimetre stem with interesting buff-suffused milky petals and almost disc-like crowns of amber-rimmed pink.

Really small jonquils are engaging little creatures. They are often of perfect show form, and are probably the fastest-increasing of all daffodils.

Alec Gray did a wonderful job in breeding and rescuing all sorts of tiny daffodils. His 'Bobbysoxer' (1949) has one or two relatively large rounded primrose flowers with almost flat crowns shaded orange on 20-centimetre stems. 'Bebop' (1949) is smoother and very rounded, an all-yellow dandy. 'Sun Disc' (1948) is a tremendously vigorous plant throwing up large numbers of stems about 18 centimetres high with completely circular flowers with flat crowns – quite one of the most perfect of all daffodils. 'Sundial' (1955) is another jewel-like bloom, a fraction smaller, but often with two blooms to 15-centimetre stem, the flat eyes centred with a tiny touch of green.

'Pixie', 'Pixie's Sister' and 'Chit Chat' were all free-flowering progeny of *N. juncifolius* × *N. jonquilla*, golden yellow multi-headed sweet-scented miniatures that would be tall at 25 centimetres. We have abandoned our stocks as virused, but they are mentioned here as some growers may have clean stock, and even if all are blighted it is well worth repeating the cross. They are engaging elfin things.

N. watierii has not been properly harnessed in breeding programmes. Alec Gray introduced one or two lovely seedlings, rather surprising some recipients of his 'Xit' by sending out at least two different clones under this name. Both we have grown are lovely. The better known is a startled, pure white little flower with a flat corona. It is described as little, but it is large for its few centimetres of stem. The second clone has coronas of primrose. 'Demure' with 18 to 20-centimetre stems has flowers with white petals and pale pink crowns. Obviously there are many possibilities awaiting.

16

Poeticus daffodils

To the florist these are the true narcissi. To the man or woman in the street, as opposed to the one in the garden, these flowers are 'Pheasant's Eyes', though by a gardeners' consensus this common name is now the rightful property of *N. poeticus recurvus* only. To the commercial grower these are plants of modest economic importance, but to gardeners the poeticus are especially dear. Delight is taken in their perfection of form and a sense of nostalgia may be felt when viewing them – here is the familiar face of an old garden friend which has been grown for centuries, and whose appearance each year marks the end of another flowering season. Frustration hovers however because, lovely as they are, the gardener has all too little choice, and there really are not sufficient bulbs to satisfy the potential demand.

For long enough the classification definition of a poeticus was quite simply, 'distinguishing characteristics; characteristics of *N. poeticus* group without admixture of any other group.' Such a restrictive definition meant that the genetic pool was confined to the closely related wild plants and their interbred derivatives, and the breeder had little or no room for manoeuvre. It was the only division with such a 'pure blood' provisor. To bring the poeticus in line with the other divisions, the classification was then reworded, becoming 'distinguishing characters; characteristics of the *N. poeticus* group predominant.' This made things a little easier, but did not change practical procedures dramatically as the character of a poeticus was seen as a very stylized and precise one. The current definition reads '... characteristics of the *N. poeticus* group without admixture of any other,' meaning that blood of other types may be present, but not if this involves mixing foreign characteristics. Poeticus petals must be white. Coronas must be small flat discs, or very small shallow cups. Corona colour must be solid red or include at least a rim of red. However nothing is forever, not even the law as laid down by the classification subcommittee of the RHS Daffodil Committee. Future interpretations of poeticus could be envisaged as including flowers without red in the corona, and ones with petals showing some colour. We shall see.

Wild poeticus blooming in groups high up in the European mountains, or maybe covering wide stretches of hillsides in the late spring or early summer, are sights that have excited the awe of many travellers. During the last century enthusiasts dug up bulbs to try to bring them back home as living souvenirs of foreign parts. Here was a problem – like some wines they travelled badly. Generally, *N. poeticus* does not like being lifted, and resents all disturbance. It is happiest where its bulbs luxuriate in almost constant moisture below ground, often very deeply ensconced, and happy to spread their territory by casting their seed around. Regimes of annual or biennial lifting dictated by commercial bulb production were anathema. Most imported bulbs made the choice and died – they may have done so quickly or by a more heart-rending slow but inexorable decline.

Even modern cultivars are best left growing undisturbed and, when lifting is essential, replanting should be almost immediate. All the group are somewhat vulnerable to the depredations of virus as they are in full growth later than most daffodils, at a time when aphids and other insectiverous virus carriers are more active.

It is unlikely that any of *N. poeticus poetarum* as used by Engleheart and others now still exists in cultivation. This and other forms that were important in the early days have faded from the scene. On the other hand a couple of wildlings, *N. p. recurvus* and *N. p. hellenicus*, proved noteably free of the poeticus death-wish.

Pheasant's Eye Narcissus, *N. poeticus recurvus*, responded magnificently to propagation in Holland, and became one of the widest-grown of daffodils. It is remembered by generations as the little sweet-scented late flower that grew in granny's garden, and granny remembers it in her granny's garden too. Although used in breeding it was really completely swamped by the more dramatic, solid red-eyed *N. poeticus poetarum* which was used widely, despite its second or third-rate perianth, and also by one of the real founder members of the modern daffodil family, *N. p. hellenicus*, (*N. p. verus*). Though a small flower, its perfection of form and its exceptional quality made it very much worth trying, and breeders soon found it a completely beneficial and a most potent influence. It grew well even if it was not so commercially exploited as a bulb as the 'Pheasant's Eye'. One other wildling was used extensively earlier in the century as a cut flower as well as in the garden: this was N. *p. ornatus*, a typical rim-eyed poet with a flattish perianth and opening before N. *p. recurvus*.

Engleheart worked with all types of daffodils and never lost his interest in the poets. Early successes were 'Horace' (1907) and 'Sarchedon' (1913). 'Horace' was a rimmed one that was grown by the million up until the outbreak of the Second World War. British government regulations demanded that land be used for food production and ornamental horticulture was cut back almost to vanishing point. Tons of bulbs of 'Horace' and others were tipped down the cliffs of Cornwall or were otherwise disposed of. The changed economic conditions of post-war Europe did not encourage any major attempt to re-establish 'Horace' or any similar plant.

1923 saw the introduction of Engleheart's 'Dactyl', a fine smooth thick-textured flower with sparkling pointed petals and a yellow eye edged red. There are still some commercial stocks. This was a parent of Guy Wilson's 'Shanach', a slightly larger and more rounded flower. These rimmed flowers appeared to be easier to breed than those with solid red eyes like the Brodie's magnificent 'Smyrna' (1927). This was tall, a rounded flower large for a poet and with a relatively wide flat eye of rich scarlet. This same year saw the registration of 'Actaea' by G. Lubbe and Son from Holland. It illustrates the relative lack of breeding and meagre possibility of advance that this cultivar should have dominated the commercial poets for so long and that, after a First Class Certificate awarded in Haarlem in 1923, it should have been judged worthy of an award of garden merit as late as 1950 after a trial at Wisley. It has been very popular, and is much larger than most with wide white rounded petals and small yellow cups well banded with dark red. Gardeners enjoy the mid-season flowers, and delight in its scent. Fanciers, rather more governed by show values, looked at it somewhat askance at first, and murmurings about its possible parentage were heard – was it really 'without admixture'? Tainted blood was suspected. Gardeners were right to enjoy it for itself.

A. M. Wilson provided two fine poets, 'Felindre' (1930), a large flower with wide yellow-disc eyes narrowly edged red, and 'Milan' (1932), a tall immaculate flower, rounded, boldly posed, and with neat yellow eyes encircled orange-red. Guy Wilson's 'Cantabile' was introduced the same year. A seedling from 'Dactyl' it is a jewel-like flower with thick rounded petals and a green eye thinly ribboned red.

The green fades to yellow in the sun, but young cut flowers preserve the colour. Two years before Engleheart had registered 'Sea Green', a slightly larger flower with a fractionally wider eye, the red rim giving way to a little yellow around a green centre. Like all poets the colour is fleeting in the sunshine.

One or two of today's breeders have made forays in this division. Mitsch produced 'Quetzal' from 'Cantabile' × 'Cushendall', the pollen parent being the short-cupped green-eyed Guy Wilson flower from 'Emerald Eye' × 'Dactyl'. Thus 'Quetzal' is three-quarters poet, and looks like a more solid 'Cantabile'. 'Quetzal' by pollen of 'Smyrna' gave Mitsch a series of cultivars. Three were launched in 1977. 'Angel Eyes' was the strongest and most free flowering, round, white, and with small eyes of green, yellow, and red; 'Bon Bon' is one of the scarcer red-eyed beauties; and 'Tart' is similarly red eyed, a very bright small flower. 'Emerald' and 'Suspense' followed in 1980 from the same parentage. 'Emerald' sparkles white around a wide green eye pencil-edged orange-red. 'Suspense' is perhaps a little taller and has the eye green-centred but surrounded with a yellow zone before the red edge.

Most poet seedlings are attractive – it is difficult to breed a rank outsider. Brian Duncan has fostered a nice series from 'Milan' × 'Cantabile'. 'Lyric' is a better groomed 'Milan' with its yellow eye red-edged. 'Webster' (1982) is a tall strong flower of vivid colour, and like 'Campion' it makes virtue of necessity by giving prominence to the cochet points of the rounded petals, the clasps that had held the buds locked. 'Thackeray' is a wide-awake flower with broad sparkling perianths leaning back a little on the breeze, and so throwing extra emphasis on the large target centres of ringed green, citron, and orange that are held flat against the perianth.

So we are almost ready to turn from a division short on numbers but long on beauty. Anyone who takes to breeding should sow a few seeds of the poets, as an obeisance to a main founder species of the whole modern family, an insurance against the poets' complete submersion in the tide of modern breeding, and a very sure way of knowing that at least some of the seedlings are going to be quality flowers.

17

Tazetta daffodils

It is a mistake not to have an estate somewhere with a Mediterranean climate where the tazettas would be more at home than they are in cooler parts. Though some may manage in sheltered spots in cooler climes, the family is basically a Mediterranean one. They like to feel the sun on their backs. Some of the hybrids with poeticus and other divisions and cultivars of other divisions, boast a more hardy sinew and can grow outside through normal winters in slightly less warm countries.

Breeding work has been centred in Britain and places with similar climates, and this has led to the tazettas being poorly dealt with in breeding terms. There is a lack of a French, Spanish, or Italian Daffodil Society whose members could vie with each other to better the tazettas that grow so easily around them.

Another problem confronts the breeder. Most hybrid tazettas are sterile, or nearly so. Their differing chromosome count, a basic ten count rather than the standard seven, does not help matters. However, there is at least one gateway open: the cultivar 'Matador' is fertile by seed or pollen. All is not lost.

Most early work with tazettas was undertaken in the south western peninsula of Britain or in the Netherlands. Poverty threatened the lives of the inhabitants of the Scilly Isles off the coast of Cornwall in the last century, and disaster was narrowly averted by the pioneer work done by Augustus Smith, the then Lord Proprietor of the Scillies, and by T. A. Dorrien-Smith, both of whom encouraged the islanders to grow daffodils, especially the tazetta types. Augustus Smith had dispatched a trial box of flowers to Covent Garden in 1870 and got a return of £1. It was the beginning. Dorrien-Smith garnered all types of tazettas to test and flowers of these and other precocious types went to London and other major markets. The favoured climate (frost was unknown) ensured early blooms just at the time of year when the city dwellers were crying out for living colour. Good returns were obtained. Nowadays tourism is seen as the main support of the island's economy, but there are still plenty of bulbs grown.

'Paperwhite' (*N. papyraceus*), 'Scilly White', 'Compressus', 'Grand Monarque', and 'Grand Primo Citroniere' were white or white-and-creamy yellow varieties. These were either wild plants, probably collected years ago and grown on in Holland, or types that had arisen under cultivation there in the dim and distant past. Most important came to be 'Grand Soleil d'Or', usually demoted in a nomenclative sense to plain 'Soleil d'Or' or the market traders' 'Sols'. This marvellous plant with many heads of glowing gold and orange is a joy to see and intoxicating to smell. It is only recently that we have realised afresh what a fine plant it is. Over the many years of culture stocks had accumulated a cocktail-mix of viruses that steadily depleted their strength. The plant became a wretched, beggarly parody of its real self. Now the true character has been revealed through a controlled programme of meristem culture to rid the tissue of virus and then bulking up by chipping. What a very worthwhile operation!

Early hybridizing used such tazettas as 'Grand Monarch', 'Grand Primo Citroniere', and 'Gloriosus' with *N. poeticus ornatus* as seed parent. 'Elvira' (1904), the kind that sported the double 'Cheerfulness', was one of the results. White-and-yellow 'Laurens Koster' (1906) was another.

'Scarlet Gem' (1910) is still with us, being fairly widely grown, and is a pleasing kind with several rounded primrose-gold flowers each centred by an almost flat corona of bright tangerine. In 1916 'Silver Chimes' arrived, the result we are told of the mating of 'Grand Monarque' with *N. triandrus loiseleurii*. It had a long career in the show limelight, being reckoned almost unbeatable in its class with its many satiny rounded heads of white and pale cream. Virus eventually brought it to its knees, but cleaned stock would still find a ready sale.

'Glorious' (1923) was bred by J. C. Williams, cousin to P. D. Williams. With three or so sizeable rounded blooms of white and dark red, it looked impressive and had a good run for a few decades. Rather different is 'Cragford' (1930), a cream-and-orange hybrid of such energetic precocity that bulbs shoot up bouquets of blossom in a few weeks, almost like jack-in-the-boxes. I have seen it growing and blooming in a border at the end of September. 'Cragford' can be used for pot or bowl culture, and may be timed for Christmas easily. It is tidier than many, with rather shorter stocky pale foliage. 'Geranium', also introduced in 1930, is still popular for growing in pots as well as in the garden, but this is a late kind opening in the second half of April. Its rather fleshy stems and leaves are tidy and the flowers are larger than many, with perhaps three of four circles of white centred by glowing orange saucers.

Relatively few new kinds have been introduced over the past decades. 'Avalanche', named in 1955, has been grown since early this century, and is of unknown origin. It is a very fine traditional tazetta, a strong plant that can have well over a dozen well-formed white-and-cream florets on tall sturdy stems. It is now making a name for itself as a show flower. 'Golden Dawn' (1958), from the Oregon Bulb Farm, was welcome with bright yellow petals and flat discs of vivid orange. 'Matador' (1958) was hardly as bright, but it proved fertile and so is a most important cultivar.

Possibilities abound in this division if the sterility barrier can be purposefully broken and a range of multi-headed hybrids raised. An early straw in the wind was provided by 'Martha Washington' (1948) with two or three heads any one of which could have done duty for a Division 2 or 3 flower, with its broad white petals and ample saucer orange crowns. 'Sir Winston Churchill', a doubled white-and-amber-kind, looks like 'Cheerfulness's dream of greater glory – its florets are two or three times the size. The range of modern cultivars of the first three divisions that one could marry to the tazettas makes the possible improvements and increased diversity limitless. In years to come the multi-headed may be the norm, two, three or four heads being better than one.

The work done by Miss Fry in breeding new tazettas, basically for the cut-flower trade in south western Britain has resulted in some 60 clones being taken over by the growers there to multiply, test, and market. Some of these are likely to be important cut flowers as well as possibly pot plants and garden plants for warmer climes. Recently the growers of the Scillies have entered a five-year contract with the Ministry of Agriculture Advice Service to carry on the research into these tazetta hybrids. The breeding programme started at Rosewarne in 1969, with the first two clones passing into island ownership in 1982. The 60 clones were bought in 1988.

The main parent of these new tazettas has been an early form of 'Soleil d'Or' known as 'Autumn Sol', a kind that often blooms as early as October. This was crossed with the paler but early 'Newton',

'French Sol', and *N. tazetta aureus*. Others later involved in the breeding were 'Gloriosus', 'Grand Monarque', 'Avalanche', and even 'Paper White', all with the idea of extending the range of flower colours and season.

'Matador' × *N. jonquilla* gave some fascinating hybrids in America, both sweet-scented and multi-headed. 'Falconet' (1979) is neat with good pointed petals in gold, and flared lightly scalloped coronas in bright orange. Three to five florets on a 46-centimetre stem make a real picture. Sister 'Hoopoe' (1979) has two to five slightly larger florets to a stem, round golden petals and bright orange cups sitting in the epicentre of a perfume explosion.

Small tazettas are scarce. *N. canaliculatus* is a shy blooming species with white-and-rich amber 25-millimetre flowers on stems only 15 centimetres high. 'Pango' (1949) stands about 20 centimetres with two or three quite large white-and-cream flowers. 'Minnow' (1962) is floriferous with perhaps five small white-and-cream flowers on a slender stem. Depending on its position it may be 20 to 30 centimetres high, taller than the flower size would lead one to expect.

Division 12 is for all daffodils not falling into any of the other 11. Elitist or a dustbin? In the nature of things it is not overcrowded – a crowd would suggest the need for new divisions. Two very attractive hybrids have been housed here. They are the result of crossing the tazetta 'Matador' with *N. cyclamineus*. 'Bittern' (1982) stands some 25 to 30 centimetres high with stems bearing two or three unusual blooms, long crimped cups of orange-red and bright yellow perianths held well back. 'Dovekie' (1982) has pale lemon petals and richer yellow crowns nicely lobed and crimped. Lesser stems will have a single flower, but others can have up to four. They are nicely formed and arranged. Happily it is free both of bloom and increase.

We are just at the beginning of the road. All sorts of excitements lie in the future. After all we have only been playing for about 150 years.

18

Split-corona daffodils

Once in a very long while a mutation occurs that causes a major change of behaviour or appearance. Splitting the corona into six lobes that then do not project but lie flat on the perianth transforms the character of the flower – some would say that the deviation destroys it. One such mutation was spotted by Jaap Gerritsen amongst his father's seedlings in 1929. This started him on over 50 years of work trying to improve and diversify flowers with split coronas.

There is within most gardeners an uneasy dichotomy: a love of established plants true to traditional values, and a hunger for novelty, a taste for unusual new things. Confronted with this new range of flowers, daffodil fanciers tended to mine unexpectedly inventive seams of pejorative judgement. Flower arrangers, however, frequently waxed lyrical about the dramatic beauty of the 'material'. Controversy has died down, and the flowers are now accepted. Some few love them passionately, whilst others find them useful, and others acknowledge their existence.

There is now a wide colour range of split coronas – the form of the flower means that the corona pigment dominates. In most cultivars and numbered seedlings awaiting introduction, the six lobes of the corona lie flat over the petals and cover them all except for rounded tips that act as a frame to the surrealistic picture. Some are traditional daffodil yellow, one of the best known of these being 'Baccarat'. This is a tough pug-faced rich golden flower with the flat corona lobes and petals all the same rich shade. Somewhat newer is 'Chanterelle', much in the same mould but with the petals half a shade paler than the centre. It is somewhat smoother.

Most of the yellow-and-white 'splits' are palish flowers. 'Valdrome' is a large one with wide white petals almost completely obscured by pale cream lobes which are pressed hard back and have throats a shade or two darker. 'Gamay' is another big one, its white petals almost lost behind frilled lobes of lemon. 'Cassata' opens white-petalled with the split corona laid hard back in tones of pale primrose which fades steadily to creamy milk white. Only the tips of 'Mistral's' petals are seen peeping from behind its flattened corona of primrose. None of these paler flowers flaunt their unorthodox daffodil behaviour too obviously. 'Pearlax' is smooth and rather similar but with more pointed petals and the corona segments having hints of pink. There are at present many pink-centred ones being grown on under number. Grant Mitsch produced his 'Phantom' in 1975, with white petals behind a widely pressed-back centre of rosy pink.

Some of the orange-centred 'splits' are really rather gaudy, but not without considerable impact. 'Oloron' is a newish one with cream petals lost behind a ruffled orange centre with touchs of gold on the edges, the colours of a ripe juicy orange. 'Tricollet' is more unusual in having a wide milk-white perianth that is more obvious as the corona is now reduced to a small orange centre from which three, not six, similarly-coloured blades project over the perianth. The impression given is that three must have been cut away, an unusual effect. 'Congress' is brilliant in gold and vibrant scarlet.

We have a number of these split coronas growing in our garden, so we are not of the violently 'anti' party, but they are not our top favourites. However even those who are not at all happy with them should be careful about dismissing them completely. They may provide useful breeding material. One very attractive cultivar was bred with 'Baccarat' and the *N. jonquilla* × *N. triandrus* hybrid, 'April Tears' as parents. Such divergent partners might have produced almost anything, but 'Tripartite' is a pleasing plant and flower. At around 38 centimetres it is not too big or too tall. It has foliage similar to that of jonquil hybrids, and its flowers are semi-pendant and very late. The colour is a lovely golden lemon. The stems carry one, two, or three blooms with pointed, slightly fly-away petals and a flattened corona with lobes between half and three-quarters as long as the petals. The whole thing is dainty and, with the petals not being fully covered but playing a full role, the balance of the blooms is pleasing. As the plant increases rapidly and the bloom is freely produced 'Tripartite' should be popular in years to come. It is already a useful prize-winner, but it is as a garden plant and a cut flower from the garden that it is going to make its greatest contribution.

The breeding of new split-corona kinds is going on apace, and they are becoming steadily more reliable as plants.

19

Hybridizing

There is no point in sowing just any seed, and an equally mistaken move could be to rush into a high production plan – there are going to be batches of seedlings from one to five years old to be housed and looked after. Even when seedlings bloom it is rare for the five-year-olds to be scrapped completely. Some few may not have flowered, and others you may be doubtful about scrapping, feeling it safer to give them one more chance. Highly organized persons may see every flower in the fifth year and be able to mark and lift the most promising ones and discard the rest, but for one reason or another the whole or part of the planting will really need looking over a second time, so making the sixth year the clearance one. There is a powerful incentive to attempt to grow your seedlings strongly in order to achieve a high percentage bloom in the fourth year, in which case you can certainly make the fifth the time of the last judgement.

Wisdom may prevail and demand the restriction of endeavours to limited but clear objectives – it is best to be master of a programme well within the limits of your space, time, and energy. Selecting seedlings can be the most difficult part of the programme, albeit the most enjoyable. One should be ruthless. Only the significantly better or distinct flowers should be numbered and kept. Certainly adopt the idea that all are going to be discarded except the chosen few, rather than the other way around. Selected seedlings then enter a life of continual assessment: only after critical comparison with the very best should there by any question of giving a seedling a name and registering it. Experience suggests waiting a few seasons, since a maiden bloom may prove disappointing the following year. Cultivars do vary in performance season by season, and usually seedlings improve in their first few seasons.

If it is decided that a seedling is worth registering a name is needed that has not been used before, and which is not likely to be confused with another – not all that easy as over 20,000 names have already been recorded. The registration authority for daffodils is the RHS. After obtaining the registration form from the International Narcissus Registrar, RHS Offices, Vincent Square, London SW1P 2PE it needs filling in with the chosen name and probably an alternative one, as well as the particulars of the flower. The registrar will inform you if the name is acceptable and, if so, a modest registration fee has to be paid, and the new daffodil is officially named. US raisers normally submit their registrations to the American Daffodil Society (ADS) Registration Chairman who then forwards them to the RHS.

Really distinct novelties will be noticed by other growers and exhibitors, and you may be asked for bulbs. Professional growers may be interested, but they have to look to the long-term future of the cultivar – listing an extra kind involves a commitment of money and energy that must seem worthwhile. If the hobby pays that is fine, and most of today's businesses grew from hobby status. You may however decide it is best just to swop bulbs and forget the profit motive.

Practical points

Crossbreeding techiques are simple: pollen is transferred from the chosen father and applied to the stigma of the proposed mother. Most stigmas are held well clear of the anthers, and it is an easy matter to get the stigma covered when it is moist and receptive – two or three days after opening is usually the best time, since they are normally receptive then and you will probably arrive before some passing insect. These pollen-bearing busybodies are no great bother early in the season, but can be more of a nuisance later when their numbers increase. Flowers seem to take the pollen more readily when it is not too cold. It is not usually thought worthwhile to remove the anthers of a flower to be pollinated. They may set seed to their own pollen and a few will do so in large quantities. This is exceptional behaviour, and most are disinclined to set seed to their own pollen.

Poeticus and some short-cupped kinds may have their stigmas nestling between bursting anthers. With these kinds it is sensible to nip out the anthers just as the buds open, thus preventing the pollinating brush or instrument getting contaminated with this pollen as well as stopping it spilling onto the stigma. Tweezers will manage the job. When any difficulty is encountered, it is best to get hold of the anther with the tweezers and, instead of immediately pulling forwards, move a little inwards to the flower's centre before removing the anther – filaments holding the anthers are broken by the reverse movement.

Sometimes pollen is needed for use on a later flower. It may be stored for a matter of several weeks if kept dry and cool. Anthers are detached young and allowed to dry out in something like a clean, open plastic pill box. These are best labelled both on the side and the lid. When the fresh anthers have burst and dried, the lid can be fastened and the boxes stored in the refrigerator out of the way. Pill boxes can be bought very cheaply. If pollen is to be stored for months it may be wise to ensure the elimination of any moisture by enclosing some deliquescent chemical such as calcium chloride in a twist of tissue.

Pollen can be applied to the stigmas by the tip of a finger, by thrusting forward a twister-held anther, or by using the traditional small watercolour brush. If the stigma seems a little reluctant to take pollen it may be moistened, ideally with a glucose solution, but more likely a mouth-moistened finger.

Clear permanent labelling is important from the time of pollinating onwards. Pollinated blooms can have a tie put around their neck. Alternatively, plastic labels may be inserted in the ground. These are semi-permanent and may stay with the plants and seeds when harvested in June, with less chance of mistakes occuring. Using a reliable waterproof pen or pencil, the cross needs marking with the seed parent first and then the pollen one, e.g. Empress of Ireland × Candyfloss when 'Candyfloss' is the pollen parent. We adopt a shorthand for some long names, Empress of Ireland becoming EOI. At one time we thought of giving all stocks their computer codes and using these on labels, but on reflection it was thought wiser to use the full names because numbers and initials are very easy to muddle.

The details of raising seed is dealt with in another chapter. Here it is worth emphasizing that the greatest proportional increases in weight and size are going to be achieved when the little seedlings are in their first two years and are easily managed close together. Concentrating on growing the seedlings especially well in these early stages may well save a whole year waiting for the flowers.

Choosing parents

Articles in the annual publications of the Daffodil Society, the RHS 'Daffodils', the American Daffodil Society Journal, and breeders' catalogues contain a wealth of information. Advice is freely given by fellow enthusiasts. You read and listen and decide what seems appropriate to your schemes.

It may be worth looking first to the divisions which have been least worked. Here there is huge scope for raising new types by taking the best of the crowded first three divisions and crossing them with certain species or kinds close to the species such as *N. cyclamineus*, *N. triandrus*, *N. jonquilla* and other jonquil species. These may be expected to give something different from the jostling multitude of the first three divisions. These highly-bred divisions need not be ignored however – you may hit the jackpot with a cross that provides something quite superlative and beats all comers.

As the breeding stock improves in quality so the odds move more in your favour. It is a mistake to think that because you have paid an extortionate amount for a bulb it will necessarily give better seedlings than an older and much cheaper cultivar. By looking at the parentages of the best modern types one can spot that certain names tend to appear frequently, and they are often cultivars of quite modest value. Some kinds seem to have a much greater ability to pass certain qualities or combinations of qualities to a significant number of their seedlings, whilst another wonderful flower may tend to have disappointing children.

Basic planning could mean choosing the cheaper of the known good parents to use as seed parents with new promising kinds as pollen parents. Astronomical numbers of pollen grains are produced by a single flower, so very many blooms may be parent to the pollen of one flower. If the right seed parents are sitting in the garden it is possible to obtain pollen of exalted kinds, maybe even new seedlings, merely by asking at a show. Professional and amateur growers are almost always exceedingly generous with pollen.

Triandrus, jonquil, cyclamineus, split corona, poeticus, and tazetta divisions have had relatively little breeding attention. Much could be done with them without promoting a programme covering huge acreages. A lot could be done restricting work to the species *N. triandrus*, *N. jonquilla*, and *N. cyclamineus* and crossing these both ways with the best of the first three divisions. As *N. cyclamineus* blooms so early its pollen will need storing. On the other hand *N. jonquilla* is one of the last to open, and so a potful of these may be forced to get earlier pollen.

It is worth looking to the first-generation hybrids of the species as although many may prove sterile, quite a number will be partially fertile, and one that is normally obstinately sterile can suddenly prove capable of fertile seed or pollen. Statistically, the pollen is bound to prove the most likely bet – each flower will have thousands of times more pollen grains than egg cells, and a huge number of these can be placed on the stigmas of known fertile cultivars so that if only one or two grains are viable these have their chance. Triandrus hybrids are the most difficult; most cyclamineus ones are at least partially fertile; and, whilst some jonquils are infertile, some will set an occasional seed. Jonquil 'Quickstep' is one of the most fertile of all daffodils.

No flowers are more wide open to exploitation than the tazettas. Much could be achieved without venturing beyond the first generation from the species, there is such a multitude of high-quality flowers of all colours and forms waiting to be allied with the tazettas. A galaxy of multi-headed kinds is waiting to be born. 'Matador', the fertile tazetta hybrid, could be the cornerstone to the building of a new race. *N. tazetta* itself is somewhat tender, but this need not deter the breeder, since most of the hybrids are perfectly hardy in most daffodil-growing districts. The challenge to produce even hardier ones is a part of the duel with chance and nature.

Many points could be launching sites for exciting exploration, and starts have been made with some. 'Matador' × *N. jonquilla*, and 'Matador' × *N. cyclamineus* have given lovely things. 'Frou-Frou' is an example of a cross that could have been dismissed as impossible, 'Frigid' × 'Silver Chimes'. 'Frigid' rarely sets seed, and 'Silver Chimes', from a *N. tazetta* crossed with *N. triandrus*, would have been expected to be infertile.

Most multi-headed types have short cups. Maybe some pleasing and unusual novelties could have long crowns.

Colour is the first characteristic to be noticed and, although there is a wide range of colours at present, some cultivars indicate future new pigmentations, and some may suggest novel combinations of colours. Pink breeding is moving rapidly towards deeper and deeper shades, and red is being approached by this route rather than by the intensification of traditional oranges. By taking some of the pinks showing lilac or lilac tints, it is not difficult to envisage a range in which this colour is intensified and becomes established fact. Leading trumpets of all colours are all-nigh perfect flowers. It would be interesting to find how they looked with a rim of some other colour around their trumpet brims – 'Empress of Ireland' with a ribbon of pink or orange could be jolly.

Some reverse bicolours suggest other possibilities. They often develop a halo of white at the base of deep-yellow perianths. Tri-coloured flowers, or even four or five-coloured ones, do not seem extravagant promises. Petal colours could be yellow or orange giving way to a white base; coronas could be pink-banded orange with a green base.

Back-crossing outstanding new seedlings to their parents is done all too infrequently. This should be almost standard procedure, since it could release recessive characteristics.

Miniature and dwarf kinds

Interest in smaller types is intense and they represent a field whose exploitation has only just begun. The emphasis on these smaller kinds is going to increase as gardens become smaller and plants in scale with them are desired. Colours in miniature are still limited: there are only a few showing good orange, and there are intermediate-sized pinks but scarcely one good dwarf. 'Tête à Tête's' popularity shows the demand for good dwarf kinds. Small is beautiful, and diversity in smallness must be even better.

N. rupicola, *N. watieri*, *N. asturiensis*, *N. cyclamineus*, and *N. triandrus* are only a few of the obvious small ones to begin working with. Could the autumn-blooming species throw some exciting material into the genetic melting pot?

Traditional breeding

Few coming to daffodil breeding are going to ignore the main divisions despite what has been written above, and it would be a shame if it were so. Hobbies are not to be pursued in a mental strait-jacket. Flowers of trumpet, long and short-cupped divisions, and the doubles, are often so bewitching that there is no resisting the temptation to try to further gild the lily/daffodil.

Looking at the pattern of breeding to date may suggest the way forward. The cultivar review chapters have borne this in mind, and here a look can be taken at a few lines that have proved successful.

Trumpets are the most traditional of daffodils and have been treated as such by breeders. Their history has been one of more or less gradual improvement rather than by quantum leaps. Only two real departures from the norm have taken place. Firstly, the birth of reverse bicolours was a real change of direction. Although the public welcomes these unusual new flowers, and their first raiser Guy Wilson wholeheartedly backed them, judges were not at first so keen. Guy Wilson would include his 'Spellbinder' in groups at shows, perhaps Engleheart Cup entries, even though he knew that by doing so he might be losing points in the eyes of some judges. Secondly the introduction of 'red' trumpets was a triumph, though a foreseeable one.

White trumpets perhaps illustrate the kind of muddled line breeding that has brought these and other types to their present fine state. Nearly all new whites have 'Empress of Ireland' in their pedigree. It was a real advance in its time and can still be used in breeding with the knowledge that its influence is beneficial. A glance at the pedigree of 'Queenscourt' shows the influence of yellow trumpets in strengthening the weaker constitutions of the early whites. 'King Alfred' appears behind the parentage of three of the four grandparents and I believe 'Naxos' shows *N. hispanicus* influence clearly, so that in all probability all four grandparents have this species in their blood.

When looking at the pedigrees, the parentage of any cultivar can be found by looking at its number; this doubled gives the mother, and the following number gives the father. Where a parent appears more than once its ancestry may only be printed once.

PEDIGREE OF 'QUEENSCOURT'

1st generation
1 'Queenscourt'

2nd generation
2 'Courage' × 3 'Empress of Ireland'

3rd generation
4 seedling × 5 'Askelon'   6 'Guardian' × 7 'Kanchenjunga'

4th generation
| 8 ? | 10 seedling | 12 'Niphetos' | 14 seedling |
| × 9 'Naxos' | × 11 'Nevis' | × 13 'Trostan' | × 15 'Askelon' |

5th generation
20 'Weardale Perfection'   28 'Conqueror'
× 21 'Duke of Bedford'   × 29 'White Knight'

22 'King of the North'   26 'King Alfred'   30 seedling
× 23 seedling   × 27 'Askelon'   × 31 'Nevis'

6th
generation

40 *abscissus*   58 'Mme de Graaff'
× 41 ?   × 59 'Mme de Graaff'
44 'King Alfred'   52 *hispanicus*   60 'Weardale
× 45 'Glory of Noordwijk'   × 53 ?   Perfection'
                                54 seedling   × 61 'Duke of
                                × 'Nevis   Bedford'
                                                    62 'King of the
                                                    North'
                                                    × 63 seedling.

Looking at a trumpet kind in which breeding has been predominantly
for yellow shows how the smoothing influence of the whites has been
used to give extra polish to the golden metal. Behind the reverse
bicolour 'Gin and Lime' can be traced the development of straight
yellows on the 'Goldcourt' side. 'Moonstruck' was sister seedling to
'Spellbinder'.

PEDIGREE OF 'GIN AND LIME'

1st
generation

1 'Gin and Lime'

2nd
generation

2 'Goldcourt'   ×   3 'Moonstruck'

3rd
generation

4 'Crocus' × 5 'Cromarty'   6 'King of the North' × 7 'Content'

4th
generation

10 'Hebron'   12 'King Alfred'   14 'Lord Antrim'
  × 11 ?   × 13 'Glory of   × 15 'Beersheba'
                              Noordwijk'

5th
generation

20 'White Emperor'	24 *hispanicus*	28 'Lord Roberts'
× 21 'King Alfred'	× 25 ?	× 29 'King Alfred'
	26 'Mme de Graaff'	30 'White Knight'
	× 27 'Victoria'	× 31 seedling

6th
generation

		56 'Monarch'
		× 57 ?
42 *hispanicus*	52 'Empress'	58 *hispanicus*
× 43 ?	× 53 *albescens*	× 59 ?
		60 'Mme de Graaff'

7th
generation

104 *bicolor*
× 105 *pseudonarcissus*

The long cups derive their character from the melding of the qualities of the founding trumpet and poeticus species, and thereafter to their further refinement and expansion. In the breeding of 'Amber Castle', 'Blessing', and 'Cairngorm' it is 'Binkie' that is the unknown factor. This was raised from mixed seed sent to Tasmania by Guy Wilson. Guesses hazarded about its parentage could feature 'Beersheba' and a kind with a smaller corona, something of the 'St Egwin' mould. It seems conceivable that there was triandrus blood in the background somewhere.

PEDIGREE OF 'AMBER CASTLE', 'BLESSING' AND 'CAIRNGORM'

1st
generation
1 'Amber Castle', 'Blessing', 'Cairngorm'

2nd
generation

2 'Camelot'	×	3 'Daydream'

3rd generation

4 'Kingscourt' × 5 'Ceylon'   6 'Binkie' × 7 seedling

4th generation

8 'Royalist'	10 'Marksman'	12 ?	14 'King of the
× 9 'Crocus'	× 11 'Diolite'		North'
			× 15 'Content'

5th generation

16 'Cleopatra'	20 'Hospodar'	28 'King Alfred'
× 17 'Broadford'	× 21 seedling	× 29 'Glory of Nordwijk'
18 'King Alfred'	22 'Hospodar'	30 'Lord Antrim'
× 19 'Fortune'?	× 23 seedling	× 31 'Beersheba'

6th generation

32 'Monarch'	40 'Firebrand'	56 'Empress'
× 33 ?	× 41 'King Alfred'	× 57 ?
34 'King Alfred'		58 'Mme de Graaff'
× 35 'Lord Roberts'		× 59 'Victoria'
36 *hispanicus*	44 'Firebrand'	60 'Lord Roberts'
× 37 ?	× 45 'King Alfred'	× 61 'King Alfred'
38 'M. J. Berkley'		62 'White Knight'
× 39 'King Alfred'		× 63 seedling

7th generation

64 'Empress'		116 'Empress'
× 65 *albescens*		× 117 *albescens*
68 *hispanicus*		
× 69 ?		
	88 'Princess Mary'	120 'Monarch'
	× 89 *poeticus*	× 121 ?
	radiiflorus	124 'Mme de Graaff'
		× 125 'Mme de Graaff'

8th generation

176 seedling		232 'Empress'
× 177 *poeticus*		× 233 *albescens*
hellenicus		

Long-cupped white-and-reds are still dominated by the 'Kilworth' ×
'Arbar' mating that produced such a wealth of talent. Some of the
kinds named from this cross are listed here.

**1st
generation**

1 'Ancona'	'Eribol'	'Mikado'	'Parthia'
'Anthea'	'George Leak'	'Nantucket'	'Ringleader'
'Artillery'	'Glowing Ember'	'Norval'	'Rockall'
'Avenger'	'Hotspur'	'Orion'	'Royal Regiment'
'Don Carlos'	'Lorenzo'	'Parsifal'	'Toreador'
			'Victory'

**2nd
generation**

2 'Kilworth'   ×   3 'Arbar'

**3rd
generation**

4 'White Sentinel' × 5 'Hades'   6 'Monaco' × 7 'Forfar'

**4th
generation**

8 'Beacon'	10 'Will Scarlett'	12 ?	14 seedling
× 9 seedling	× 11 ?	× 13 ?	× 15 'Sunstar'

**5th
generation**

16 'Princess Mary'	20 *abscissus*		28 'Beacon'
× 17 *poeticus*	× 21 *poeticus*		× 29 'Fortune'
	poetarum		

The breeding of pinks shows the influence of both the small white
trumpet species and the poeticus kinds. Two pink pedigrees are given,
that of 'Romance' bred by Lionel Richardson, and that of 'Magician'
from Grant Mitsch. Although they have 'Rose Caprice' as an important common factor, they show two different strands in breeding.

PEDIGREE OF 'ROMANCE'

**1st
generation**
1 'Romance'

**2nd
generation**
2 'Rose Caprice'   ×   3 'Infatuation'

**3rd
generation**
4 'Templemore' × 5 'Green Island'   6 'Glenshane' × 7 'Waterville'

**4th
generation**

| 8 'White Sentinel' × 9 open pollen | 10 'Gracious' × 11 'Seraglio' | 12 'Mitylene' × 13 'Rinsey | 14 'White Sentinel' × 15 'Seraglio' |

**5th
generation**

16 'Beacon'   24 'Beacon'   28 'Beacon'
× 17 seedling   × 25 seedling   × 29 seedling

                  22 'Mozart'   26 'Silver Coin'   30 'Mozart'
                  × 23 'Gallipoli'   × 27 ?   × 31 'Gallipoli'

**6th
generation**

32 'Princess   44 'Princess   48 'Princess   56 'Princess
Mary'   Mary'   Mary'   Mary'
× 33 *poeticus*   × 45 ?   × 49 *poeticus*   × 57 *poeticus*

                    46 'Will Scarlett' 52 *poeticus*   60 'Princess
                    × 47 'Bernardino'   *hellenicus*   Mary'
                                                           × 61 ?

                                                           62 'Will Scarlett'
                                                           × 63 'Bernardino'

**7th
generation**

                    92 *abscissus*   124 *abscissus*
                    × 93 *p. poetarum*   × 125 *p. poetarum*

                    94 'Duchess of Brabant'   126 'Duchess of
                    × 95 'Lulworth'   Brabant'
                                                           × 127 'Lulworth'

PEDIGREE OF MAGICIAN

1st generation

1 'Magician'

2nd generation

2 seedling   ×   3 'Cool Flame'

3rd generation

4 'Accent' × 5 'Rose Caprice'   6 'Precedent' × 7 'Accent'

4th generation

| 8 'Interim' | 10 'Templemore' | 12 'Mabel Taylor' | 14 'Interim' |
| × 9 'Interlude' | × 11 'Green Island' | × 13 'Green Island' | × 15 'Interlude' |

5th generation

16 'Cushlake'	20 'White Sentinel'	24 'Mrs Backhouse'	28 'Cushlake'
× 17 ?	× 21 'White Sentinel'	× 25 ?	× 29 ?
18 'Tunis'	22 'Gracious'	26 'Gracious'	30 'Tunis'
× 19 'Shadeen'	× 23 'Seraglio'	× 27 'Seraglio'	× 31 'Shadeen'

6th generation

32 'Dactyl'	40 'Beacon'
× 33 ?	× 41 seedling
	42 'Beacon'
	× 43 seedling

The breeding of doubles

Today's new doubles are very often fertile, as not all the stamens and stigmas are used up to make extra petaloides. 'Falaise' is the king-maker, the founder of a dynasty, a seedling from 'Mary Copeland'. Breeders will use the 'Falaise' seedling, 'Gay Time', as a seed parent, or one of the other 'Falaise' or 'Gay Time' seedlings.

'Gay Challenger's' pedigree, in common with the majority of modern doubles, has only one double parent.

PEDIGREE OF 'GAY CHALLENGER'

1st
generation
1 'Gay Challenger'

2nd
generation
2 'Gay Time'   ×   3 'Arbar'

3rd
generation
4 'Falaise' × 5 'Limerick'   6 'Monaco' × 7 'Forfar'

4th
generation

8 'Mary Copeland' × 9 'Mary Copeland'	10 'Folly' × 11 'Hades'	12 ? × 13 ?	14 seedling × 15 'Sunstar'

5th
generation

16 *poeticus* × 17	20 'Beacon' × 21 ? 22 'Will Scarlett' × 23 ?		28 'Beacon' × 29 'Fortune' 30 *poeticus recurvus* ? × 31 2 W–R ?

The breeding of the changing-coloured cultivars

The most important parents of these interesting 'toned' flowers are 'Aircastle', 'Old Satin', and 'Irish Coffee' with flowers opening with white petals but becoming coloured after a few days. However to this palette are added some of the pinky and orange-petalled flowers such as 'Altruist'. We may be only at the beginning of the road with these. At present there are only short and long-cupped ones, and if long-cupped they are likely to only just make the necessary proportions. This new characteristic is still to be introduced in the trumpets and the main long-cupped kinds except in the reversed bicolour forms. These were the first to change dress in the middle of the party, and they make obvious partners to join with such as the following.

PEDIGREE OF 'EARTHLIGHT', 'JOHNNIE WALKER', 'SUAVE', 'WEDDING BAND', WHITE TIE'

**1st
generation**
1 'Earthlight' etc

**2nd
generation**
2 'Aircastle'   ×   3 'Irish Coffee'

**3rd
generation**
4 'Green Island' × 5 'Chinese White' 6 'Green Island' × 7 'Chinese White'

**4th
generation**
(common parentage, therefore one set only listed.)
8 'Gracious × 9 'Seraglio'   10 'Silver Plane' × 11 'Rinsey'

**5th
generation**
16 'Mme de Graaff' 18 'Mozart'   20 ?   22 'Silver Coin'
× 17 ?   × 19 'Gallipoli' × 21 ?   × 23 ?

**6th
generation**
32 'Empress'   36 'Princess Mary' 44 ?
× 33 *albescens*   × 37 ?   × 45 *poeticus
                                        hellenicus*

**7th
generation**
                   76 'Duchess of Brabant'
                   × 77 'Lulworth'
                   78 *abscissus*
                   × 79 *poeticus poetarum*

**8th
generation**
                   152 'Minnie Hume'
                   × 153 ?

**9th
generation**
                   304 *albescens*
                   × 305 *poeticus radiiflorus*

20

Pests and diseases

To dwell at inordinate length on these troubles would be to overemphasize their importance – the persistence and generally robust healthiness of daffodils is all around to be seen. However it seems that everything in creation is prey to its own particular misfortunes.

Most important of all daffodil troubles is the microscopic eelworm which can attack and destroy a bulb and a plantation quickly. Other problems are altogether of a lesser kind.

Diseases

Viruses

There is a bunch of different viruses that attack daffodils. They cause pale streaks in leaves, and growers use descriptive names to label them: yellow stripe, silver leaf, white streak, and mosaic. The effect of a virus may be different in different cultivars. Deleterious results may not be all that noticeable in the garden and may take a long time to affect the performance of bulbs badly. However all viruses are debilitating and, where more than one virus is present, the damage may be considerably compounded.

There is no cure for virus. Either one lives with it, or a regime of seek out-and-destroy is adopted. It should be mentioned that, whilst there is no garden cure, an infected bulb which is very imporant can have the tiny meristem growing point removed and, by careful manipulation under an electron microscope, this tissue cleared of virus can then be used to repropagate the bulb under laboratory conditions.

The classic case is that of 'Soleil d'Or'. Grown as an important flower crop in the Isles of Scilly, it was of considerable economic importance, especially in pre-tourist days. Over the years the stocks became prey to a cocktail of viruses, and the number and size of the flowers was greatly reduced. By meristem culture clean clones were built up and propagated, and new stock was kept clear of infected bulbs. Comparison of the flowers before and after treatment would put some body-building adverts in the shade. The cleaned version was successfully launched on the market and looks set to regain and enlarge its share of sales. The stems, foliage and bulbs, as well as the flowers, are all astonishingly better.

The best advice is to destroy all bulbs with disease symptoms. If you feel bulbs of an infected kind must be kept, these should be segregated as far away as possible. Viruses are spread in at least three ways. First by ever-present but non-malignant eelworms in the soil; secondly, by insects such as aphids that innoculate leaves as they are drawing nourishment from them; and thirdly by human agency when a cutting tool used when gathering flowers passes from infected to clean plants. Insects like aphids are more active in the warmer weather towards the end of the daffodil season. Some partial check on virus spread by this means is made by early lifting of the bulbs, or by cutting foliage away six or seven weeks after flowering has finished.

Some lemon flowers show virus infection clearly – flowers of attacked bulbs have something of the zebra about them. The striped effect is an absolute disaster to my eye, but people have quite often told me they thought them very pretty! Eventually the virus will cause completely anaemic blooms, ghosts of their former selves.

The symptoms of virus are, very briefly:

Yellow stripe   The most obvious and familiar. Golden-yellow stripes disfigure the leaves longitudinally. It is sufficiently unsightly to persuade most people to destroy blighted bulbs.

Mosaic   Light striping or pale mottling of the foliage may be noticed if viewed against strong light. This is much less obvious, resulting in a consequent temptation to overlook it. Debilitating effects may be slow but are present, and the disease is no respecter of the monetary value of the bulbs – some pessimistic growers fancy pests and diseases have a natural predilection for the high priced.

Chocolate spot   Some cultivars are more susceptible to this. It manifests itself in dark brown spots on the foliage. If they appear for more than one year it is likely to be virus. Some fungus diseases also cause brown spots, but are usually less dark.

White streak, silver leaf Relatively rare, and noticed when plants are in full growth as white stripes that give an overall silvery look. Attacked plants will have their foliage brought low earlier at the season's end than that of clean bulbs.

Fungus diseases

Basal rot (Fusarium bulbigenum) Some kinds are more prone to this than others. Important commercial plants like 'Golden Harvest' can be attacked, and trumpets and some long cups like 'Carlton' seem more prone. Usually it is a greater worry to the commercial grower than the amateur, since huge losses are possible whilst bulbs are in store. The worst inroads of the disease are made in periods of warm damp weather in the weeks prior to lifting and whilst bulbs are being lifted.

Areas of reddish-brown and greyish-brown around the basal plate may confirm suspicions, and discoloration will strike up into the interior of the bulb. Biscuity-coloured powder over the infected areas will be the fungus spores.

Basal rot is worst in ill-drained soils. Plants having an uneven stunted look may be suspected. If Basal rot is likely to be a problem it is wise to avoid susceptible cultivars. It is also sensible to plant new stock in clean ground. Bulbs should be planted their correct depth. Damage whilst cultivating or lifting helps the fungus. Bulbs ought to be rapidly dried in a cool airy place – do not leave in the heat on the soil surface when lifting, and storage temperatures should not be more than 17°C. There are good possibilities that recent research will provide controls to this disease in the not-too-distant future.

Pests

Much may be done to reduce the effect of pests in borders by clean cultivation. Hoeing, keeping weeds down, and top dressing with peat or shredded bark all help. Slugs can be a nuisance but are kept at bay by hygienic growing, and both large and small daffodil flies are similary discouraged.

Eelworm All other troubles fade into insignificance compared with this dread affliction of the daffodil world. The microscopic organism,

Ditylenchus dipsaci, nearly wiped out commercial daffodil production 60 to 70 years ago. Single eelworms penetrating a bulb build up populations of millions quickly and, living on the tissue, reduce bulbs to pulpy waste. These then rot away in the ground leaving no trace and the eelworms migrate in the soil-water to nearby bulbs. In the absence of bulbs they can transform themselves into a dormant form, a cyst that can remain alive in the soil for three or four years, an invisible time bomb.

Some other bulbs and plants can act as hosts to daffodil eelworms: onions and plantains are two. There being no safe way of eliminating eelworm in growing plants, attacked bulbs are best dug up together with a generous amount of the surrounding soil, placed in plastic bags, and incinerated or dumped in the dustbin. Extreme care should be taken not to distribute soil from the affected area by cultivation, on tools, or on footwear. It may be easiest to grass over an attacked site, or to install semi-permanent plants like heathers or shrubs. Minimum quarantine periods of four years timed from the removal of the last bulb must elapse before there is a chance of allowing bulbs back.

The first symptoms of eelworm may be small raised semi-transparent pimples on foliage or stems. More advanced attacks distort foliage and sometimes cause flower stems to be ridiculously short, the flowers appearing to be scarcely above the soil surface. When unsure of a diagnosis, a bulb may be lifted and cut transversely to show the rings of scales. Eelworm attacks show up as brown rings, the decaying tissue caused as the pests make their way round the scales.

Eelworm was found to be vulnerable to heat treatment. The problem was to establish the level that would kill the pest without dispatching the patient – there was only a narrow temperature band that worked the saving miracle.

Bulbs immersed for a period of at least three hours at 44° to 46°C were cleared of eelworm. Only a degree or two higher would have killed the bulbs. Only first-class equipment and careful attention achieve the necessary control. It is more a job for a professional than an amateur, but it may be possible to get a commercial grower to treat amateur bulbs.

Hot water treatment for the control of eelworm   The main benefits of the treatment are the elimination of:

Stem eelworm
Bulb scale mite

Large daffodil fly
Small narcissus fly

With chemical additives the following fungus troubles can be considerably reduced and checked:

Basal Rot
Smoulder
Leaf Scorch

Apart from the benefits of release from the above lists of plagues, growers agree that bulbs appear to respond to the treatment as if to a tonic. Not infrequently some minor hot-water damage may occur, and in the spring the leaves may be marked with paler spots or mottling, especially towards the tips, but such trivial damage is a small price to pay to know that all bulbs are free of eelworm. Late-treated bulbs may produce spoilt blooms, but this will right itself the following season.

After a long history of trials the treatment recommended by the British Ministry of Agriculture is as follows, and differs very little from Dutch and American practice:

1   Dry bulbs kept in store at 30°C for one week before HWT. The best treatment period will be from mid July to mid August.

2   If eelworm is known to be present in dried form, making them impervious to heat, bulbs are left in cold water with formalin and a wetting agent overnight, or for at least three hours before HWT. (Note, if bulbs are presoaked the higher HWT temperature is used, 45°C.)

3   Three hours in HWT at 46°C. To the water is added a non-ionic wetting agent at .03%, and formalin as supplied commercially at .5% (The Dutch use formalin at double this strength).

4   Treated bulbs must only touch cleaned areas after treatment, i.e. floors, trays, containers, trucks.

Where bulbs cannot be stored for the preheating week at 30°C the treatment is not to presoak the bulbs but to give them treatment in the tank for three hours at 44.4°C.

Obviously, on entry the bulbs reduce the temperature of the tank water and so the timing of the three-hour period must begin from the moment the correct temperature is regained.

After treatment bulbs must be cooled quickly and not allowed to contact eelworm on dirty floors, containers, etc.

Scale mite (tarsonemus laticeps)   This spoils the appearance of bulbs but is not a major worry. It can be more troublesome in forced bulbs when populations increase rapidly in ideal warm conditions. Heat and chemical treatment by commercial growers has kept this pest under control and it is unlikely to cause much bother. Tiny mites increase within the bulb, especially in wet warmth. They enjoy finding cavities and open areas in bulbs where they multiply quickly. Cut bulbs will show populations as brown marks between scales. They take their daily nourishment by puncturing the scales alongside.

The large narcissus fly (Lampetia equestris)   *The Merodon fly.* Looking like a small bee, this energetic fly usually awaits warmer weather to get out and about. Landing close to the daffodils it approaches as close as possible to the bulb. Dying foliage is likely to provide it with a ready-made tunnel to its destination. The fly lays its eggs close to the bulb and then moves to the next port of call. It is a mistake to underestimate the damage that this pest can accomplish where cultivation is haphazard. The eggs hatch and one small grub enters a bulb, usually through the base. The small larva eats its way to the centre, becoming noticeably less small on the way. It ends up as a fat, dirty cream, tough, but squashable item about 10 millimetres long. A grub can destroy a small bulb. Larger bulbs may be badly damaged but survive by producing sideshoots.

   Populations of this fly can be resident in bluebell woods, but they will also be present in old-established daffodil plantations, though normally without threatening their existence.

   Hot Water Treatment kills the fly larva. In the garden clean cultivation and moving the soil around the base of the bulb foliage can thwart the fly.

The small narcissus fly (Eumerus tuberculatus + E. strigatus)   This is a secondary pest, and it only attacks damaged bulbs. Large clutches of eggs hatch into a mass of much smaller larvae than those of the large narcissus fly. These grubs are scavengers living off damaged tissue rather than being instigators of wholesale destruction. When fully grown these larvae measure only up to 25mm. Whilst not causing catastrophic damage, they can accelerate the rotting of damaged tissue. Larvae complete a full feeding programme quickly, and enter into a six-week pupation period before emerging as a fly all too ready to act as parent to a fresh generation of eggs and so continue the horrible cycle. Second-generation larvae are likely to stay put in the bulbs throughout the winter.

Bibliography

Below are listed some of the more important publications dealing with daffodils botanically and as garden plants.

American Daffodil Society/RHS. 1980. *Daffodils to Show and Grow. An Abridged Classified List of Daffodil Names.*

Baker, J. G. 1875. *Review of the genus Narcissus* in Burbridge, F. W., *The Narcissus; its history and culture.*

1888. *Handbook of the Amaryllideae.*

Barnes, D. 1988. *Daffodils for Home, Garden and Show* David & Charles.

Barr, P. 1884. *Ye Narcissus of Daffodil Flower, and hys Roots.*

Blanchard, J. 1990. *Narcissus. A Guide to Wild Daffodils* Alpine Gardening Society.

Bourne, S. E. 1903. *The Book of the Daffodil* John Lane: The Bodley Head.

Bowles, E. A. 1934. *A Handbook of Narcissus* Martin Hopkinson Ltd.

Calvert, A. F. 1929. *Daffodil Growing for Pleasure and Profit.*

Fernandes, A. 1953. *Sobre a distribicao geografica de N. cyclamineus DC e N. calcicola Mendonca* Bol. Soc. Brot.

1959 *On the origin of N. romieuxii Br-Bl + Maire* Bol. Soc. Brot.

1959 *Sur l'origine du N. romieuxii Br-Bl + Maire* Compt. Rendus. Acad. Sc.

1959 *On the origin of N. cantabricus DC* Bol. Soc. Brot.

1963 *Sobre a evolucao no subgenero Corbularia do genero Narcissus L* Mem. Acad. Cien. Lisboa.

1964 *Contribution à la connaissance de la genetique de l'heterostylie chez le genre Narcissu L l. Resultats de quelques croisements* Bol. Soc. Brot.

1965 *II. L'heterostylie chez quelques populations de N. triandrus var cernuus et N. t. var concolor* Genet. Iberica.

1966 *Nouvelles études caryologiques sur la section Jonquilla DC du genre Narcissus* Bol. Soc. Brot.

1966 *Le problème du N. triandrus L., II* Bol. Soc. Brot.

1967 *Contribution à la connaissance de la biosystematique de quelques especes du genre Narcissus L* Port. Act. Biol.

1968 *Keys to the identification of native and naturalised taxa of the genus Narcissus L* Daff. & Tulip Yearbook, RHS.

1968 *Sur la caryologie du N. serotinus L.* Collectanea Bot.

1969 *Contribution to the knowledge of the biosystematics of some species of genus Narcissus L* Simposio de Flora Europea

Fernandes & Almeida M. T. de 1968. *La meiose chez Narcissus bulbocodium × N. concolor Rozeira* Port. Acta. Biol.

1971 *Sur les nombes chromosomique de quelques formas horticoles du genre Narcissus L.I* Bol. Soc. Brot.

Fernandes & Franca, F. 1970 *Sur la meiose d'un descendant du croisement de formes triploides de N. bulbocodium L* Bol. Soc. Brot.

1971 *Sur la meiose d'une plante de N. bulbocodium L à 40 chromosomes* Bol. Soc. Brot.

Sobre a descendencia do cruzamento de triploides em Narcissus bulbocodium An. Estacion Exper. de Aula Dei.

Fernandes & Queiros, M. 1970. *Sur quelques particularities d'use population triploide de N. gaditanus Bois & Reut* Bol. Soc. Brot.

Flora Europaea 1980 Vol. 5.

Gray, A. 1955. *Miniature Daffodils* W. H. & L. Collingridge Ltd.

Hartland, W. B. 1884–1912. *Little Book of Daffodils* (catalogues).

Haworth, A. H. 1831. *Narcissearum Monographia.*

Henriques, J. A. 1887. *Amaryllideas de Portugal* Bol. Soc. Broteriana. 1st series.

Herbert, W. 1836 *Amaryllidacea.*

Jacob, J. 1910. *Daffodils* (Present-day Gardening series) J. C. & E. C. Jack.

Jefferson-Brown, M. 1951. *The Daffodil* Faber and Faber.

1952. *Daffodils for Amateurs* Faber and Faber.

1969. *Daffodils and Narcissi* Faber and Faber.

Kirby, A. M. 1907. *Daffodils, Narcissus and how to grow them.*

Ministry of Agriculture. 1951 *Narcissus Flies* Leaflet 183 HMSO.

1951 *Narcissus Culture* Bulletin No 44 HMSO.

1970 *Narcissus Pests* Bulletin No 51 HMSO.

1981 *Basal Rot in Narcissus* Leaflet 783 HMSO.

1983 *Stem Nematode on Narcissus* Leaflet 460 HMSO.

Pugsley, H. W. 1915. 'Narcissus Poeticus and its allies' *Journal of Botany.* LIII.

1933. 'A Monograph of Narcissus, subgenus Ajax' *Journal of Botany.* LVIII.

Quinn, C. E. 1959. *Daffodils, Outdoor and In* Hearthside Press Inc. New York.

Royal Horticultural Society, 1913–1915, 1933–1971 *Daffodil Year Books.*

R.H.S. 1972-continuing. *Daffodils.*

R.H.S. 1989. *The International Daffodil Checklist.*

R.H.S./Cassell. *Daffodils* (Wisley Handbook series).

Wells, J. S. 1989. *Modern Miniature Daffodils: Species and Hybrids* Timber Press Inc. Portland, Or. USA and Batsford (London).

Organizations and societies

Royal Horticultural Society
Vincent Square
London SW1P 2PE

International authority for the registration of all cultivar names.

American Daffodil Society
Executive Director
Miss Leslie E. Anderson
Rt 3. 2302 Byhalia road
Hernando
MS 38632
USA

The thriving American membership is augmented by other enthusiasts from all parts of the world where daffodils are grown.

The Daffodil Society
c/o D. Barnes
32 Montgomery Avenue
Sheffield
S7 1NZ

List of
colour illustrations

General index

Index of species and cultivars